# Secrets of
# RSS

## Steven Holzner

Peachpit
Press

# Secrets of RSS

Steven Holzner

**Peachpit Press**
1249 Eighth Street
Berkeley, CA 94710
510/524-2178
800/283-9444
510/524-2221 (fax)
Find us on the World Wide Web at: www.peachpit.com

To report errors, please send a note to errata@peachpit.com

Peachpit Press is a division of Pearson Education

Copyright © 2006 by Steven Holzner

Editor: Carol Person
Production Coordinator: Simmy Cover
Copyeditor: Jacqueline Aaron
Compositor: Maureen Forys, Happenstance Type-O-Rama
Indexer: Patti Schiendelman
Cover design: Charlene Charles Will
Interior design: Kim Scott, with Maureen Forys

## Notice of Rights

## Notice of Liability

The information in this book is distributed on an "As Is" basis, without warranty. While every precaution has been taken in the preparation of the book, neither the author nor Peachpit Press shall have any liability to any person or entity with respect to any loss or damage caused or alleged to be caused directly or indirectly by the instructions contained in this book or by the computer software and hardware products described in it.

## Trademarks

Many of the designations used by manufacturers and sellers to distinguish their products are claimed as trademarks. Where those designations appear in this book, and Peachpit was aware of a trademark claim, the designations appear as requested by the owner of the trademark. All other product names and services identified throughout this book are used in editorial fashion only and for the benefit of such companies with no intention of infringement of the trademark. No such use, or the use of any trade name, is intended to convey endorsement or other affiliation with this book.

ISBN 0-321-42622-3

9 8 7 6 5 4 3 2 1

Printed and bound in the United States of America

*To Nancy, always and forever!*

# Table of Contents

## Chapter 8  Publicizing Your Feeds    231

## Chapter 9  Converting RSS Feeds to a Web Site    261

## **Chapter 10**  Doing It Right: RSS Best Practices       293

# Introduction

Have you noticed those small RSS icons while you're online reading your favorite newspaper or looking at the results of a search? RSS, an acronym for Really Simple Syndication, is essentially a way for Web sites to syndicate new items.

RSS lets you select the source of your information. The idea is that instead of being inundated by email or millions of matches in Google searches, you can select the RSS feeds you want to read, filter them, and get only the information you want. You find an RSS feed, subscribe to it, and read the feed using an RSS reader installed on your computer.

The popularity of RSS has exploded since it first arrived on the scene, and today there are millions of RSS feeds. Just about any kind of information is available in an RSS feed—local news, political activism, pet news, international news, blogs, and more.

To use RSS, find an item you're interested in reading that has an RSS button or an XML button (as you'll learn in Chapter 1, "Gotta Get My RSS"), and click the button to connect the RSS feed to the RSS reader on your computer. When you do that, you are subscribing to that RSS feed.

After you subscribe to the feed you want, the new items will be sent to your RSS reader. Those new items are displayed as headlines in your RSS reader. All you have to do is scan the titles, double-click a headline, and the RSS reader downloads and displays the full text of the article. When your RSS reader is active, it automatically downloads new items.

RSS is the next step in the information revolution, and this book is your guided tour of all aspects of RSS.

## Who Should Read This Book?

There are two types of individuals involved with RSS—readers and publishers—and this book is designed for both.

For those who are interested in learning about RSS and reading RSS feeds, I'll describe many of the RSS readers available today, and how to use them. You'll learn not only how to subscribe to RSS feeds using RSS readers, but also how to work with those feeds inside RSS readers. You'll learn how to download new RSS items, how to view lists of new items' titles, how to read the text of items that interest you, how to access the item online for more information, and more. You'll see how to locate RSS feeds on the Internet—not only by using those RSS and XML buttons, but also by searching huge directories of RSS feeds for the ones that interest you.

If you want to be an RSS publisher, this book is for you as well. I'll guide you through the seemingly endless options for getting your information out to a large number of eagerly waiting readers. I'll show you how to create your own RSS feeds both from scratch and by using RSS feed creation tools (some free, some not). You'll see how to publish your feed online, as well as how to publicize your feed and get listed in the RSS directories. In no time, you'll end up with readers from all over, and getting the word out is going to prove easier than you imagined.

# What's in This Book?

This book covers the history of RSS and RSS feeds today, both for people who want to read RSS feeds, and for those who want to publish and publicize feeds. Here are the topics we'll explore:

- Subscribing to RSS feeds

- Grabbing RSS with readers

- Creating RSS feeds

- Creating feeds from scratch

- Blogging and RSS

- Automating creation of RSS feeds

- Podcasting: adding multimedia to your feeds

- Spreading the word about your RSS feed

- Converting RSS feeds to Web sites

- RSS best practices

RSS is fantastic for dealing with the information glut by getting just the news you want, and you're going to get the full scoop here—including the secrets behind successful RSS.

# What Will You Need?

This book is designed to give you all the information you need to handle RSS, from finding and reading feeds, all the way to creating your own feeds and even merging feeds and creating Web pages from them.

This book is self-contained. A working knowledge of HTML and XML would be helpful, although not necessary; I provide a XML primer.

You will need a computer with an Internet connection to follow along, and if you want to upload and publish your own RSS feeds, you'll need a way of hosting files on the Internet. Nothing special is required, just an ISP. In general, if you can host Web pages, you can host the XML-based documents that make up RSS feeds.

To publish an RSS feed, all you really need is a way to upload files, just as you upload Web pages. You can use an FTP program, available from some ISPs.

If you only want to read RSS feeds, you will need to be able to download files—in particular, RSS feeds themselves, as well as the many free software packages that let you read and handle those RSS feeds.

Later in the book, I describe how you can automatically read and convert RSS feeds into HTML and display them on your Web pages (Chapter 9, "Converting RSS Feeds to a Web Site").

And that's it—we're ready to start the grand tour of RSS. For an overview of the RSS world today, and what you'll find in it, turn to Chapter 1.

# Gotta Get My RSS

It's morning and you're checking your email. Your in-box is stuffed, with both real email and spam. Your stomach tightens. How are you ever going to wade through all that mail before the morning meeting?

Now it's afternoon, and it's time to do some research on the Internet. You're supposed to be keeping track of the latest developments in your field, and the task has proven far harder than you thought. When you search the Internet for the latest news, you get 17 million pages, some dating back years. How can you possibly sort through all those pages to get just this month's news?

Let's face it, it's great that the Internet has made finding information simpler and quicker than ever. But it's also a problem: People are drowning in piles of information to work through. By some estimates, it takes a worker two hours a day just to respond to emails.

Much of the trouble is that until recently it has been difficult to choose where your information comes from. When you use a search engine to find information, you're searching more than 3 billion World Wide Web resources at once. When you open your email program, anyone (and sometimes it feels like everyone) is dumping email on you.

That's where RSS comes in. And this book is your guided tour to all the secrets of RSS.

# What Is RSS?

The great advantage of RSS is that you can select your sources of information if you're the reader, and you can publicize selected information if you're the publisher. RSS is the next step in the information revolution and it's transforming the Internet and the world.

*RSS* is an acronym for at least three different phrases, but the most common one is *Really Simple Syndication. Syndication* has to do with syndicating your information flow—in other words, you can *subscribe* to the information feeds you want. And when you subscribe, you automatically get the news you want. If you don't subscribe, you don't get the news you don't want. That's a breath of fresh air, but who publishes this news flow? Are there many feeds out there?

RSS feeds are a good idea in theory, but according to www.pubsub.com, which specializes in RSS feeds, the site now tracks feeds from 21,201,699 sources, 13,489,779 of which are currently active. Many of these feeds come from Web logs, or blogs, and are automatically converted into RSS feeds by the Web site that hosts that blog. So, there's an immense number of feeds you can choose from. (Are there too many? That's a different question!)

You can find feeds on just about every aspect of modern life, from commercial to professional to personal. You'll find medical RSS feeds, news RSS feeds (for example, from almost all the major national newspapers), feeds on new software, on hobbies, finances, press releases, new products, shopping hints, human resources, fiction writing, and just about everything else you can think of.

So the information is out there, and if you're interested in a certain type of information, you can subscribe to the appropriate feed. But how does RSS work? And how do you handle a feed?

You start with the software.

# How RSS Works

As you may know—and if you don't, you'll learn all about it in this book—RSS is based on XML. (XML stands for Extensible Markup Language, in case you've not heard of it—but don't panic, RSS is easy to master.) A typical RSS feed is actually an XML file that contains one or more news items. (You can read all about XML in Chapter 4, "Creating RSS Feeds from Scratch.")

An RSS feed is an XML file that resides on a Web server and is accessible by URL. How do you know if there's an XML file just waiting as an RSS feed? When you see a button on a Web page (**Figure 1.1**), with the icon *XML* or *RSS* (there are other possible icons as well, as you'll see in Chapter 2, "Grabbing RSS with Readers"), you know there's an RSS feed available. Figure 1.1 shows some of the RSS feeds on CNN.com—just about all CNN's stories are available in RSS now.

**Figure 1.1**
RSS feed buttons are plentiful on www.cnn.com.

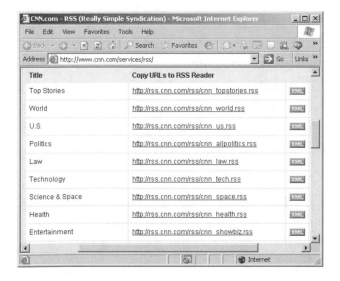

In fact, there are scores of RSS feeds out there, and your first step is to find the ones you want. To that end, you can search dozens of RSS feed directories using keywords. Here's a starter list of online RSS feed directories, each of which lists many RSS feeds you can subscribe to:

- www.syndic8.com/feedlist.php

- www.blogstreet.com

- www.search4rss.com

- http://feedfinder.feedster.com/

- www.completerss.com

- www.newsgator.com/ngs/default.aspx

- www.blogsearchengine.com (add *rss* after your search term)

- www.2rss.com/index.php

- www.rss-network.com/

- www.rssfeeds.com/

- www.shas3.com/RSS.html

You'll learn how to work with RSS feed directories in the next chapter, but here's the idea: You just navigate to a directory site in your browser and use an RSS feed directory such as Feedster (**Figure 1.2**), then enter the relevant term.

After you click the Find Feeds button, you'll get a list of feeds (**Figure 1.3**).

How do you read the feeds you've found? The idea is you subscribe to the feeds you want using an RSS reader. Essentially, XML buttons link to the URL for the RSS feed, and you simply paste that URL into your RSS reader.

**Figure 1.2**

Enter a term in the Feedster RSS directory, then click the Find Feeds button.

**Figure 1.3**

Click the Find Feeds button to get your list of RSS feeds from Feedster.

With the RSS reader program SharpReader, the feed is listed in the left-hand pane. Each feed consists of a number of news items. When you click a subscribed feed, the news items from that feed appear in the top right pane of the RSS reader (**Figure 1.4**).

**Figure 1.4**

Get news items from
RSS feeds in
SharpReader.

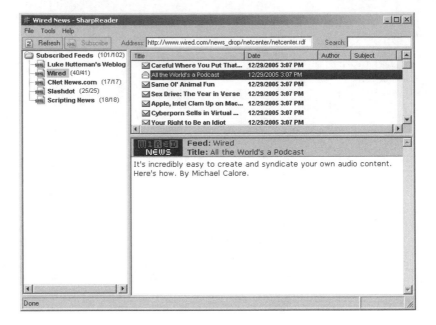

Those news items are also listed by title. After you click an item's title,
the text for that item appears in the bottom right pane, as you see in
the SharpReader figure. Often there's a hyperlink that appears with the
item's text that you can click to get more information.

That's how you handle RSS feeds—using software to collect the
data from feeds (RSS readers are also called *aggregators*) and then
seeing that data displayed in an easily read format. Of course, this is
just an overview of the process. The full details—including how to
subscribe to an RSS feed, what RSS readers are available, and how to
use online RSS readers—are covered in Chapter 2, "Grabbing RSS
with Readers."

# Good for Readers

So you can see that by using an RSS reader program, you can corral the
information you want in one place, and read it much more easily. RSS
readers typically check subscribed feeds approximately once an hour,

so when an RSS feed is updated, your RSS reader notifies you. All you have to do is to let the highly filtered information come in.

RSS feeds are also called *channels*, like in broadcasting. So when you subscribe to an RSS feed, you're subscribing to a channel. And in the same way that you can select what channel to watch on television, you can select what channel to read using your RSS reader software.

 **You can republish RSS feeds if you want, as described in Chapter 9, "Converting RSS Feeds to Web Sites." Got a special topic you're very interested in? Health care? Industry statistics? Movie reviews? Hamsters? You can merge a number of feeds and automatically create your own Web page. Your Web page can display the items, and because your page is viewable in a browser, you can republish the feeds and make them available to anyone who browses your site. (Of course, you'll have to get permission first.)**

# Good for Publishers

If you're interested in publishing your own information, RSS is good for you too. Want to get the word out on your favorite topics? That series of French language classes you're thinking of starting, your grassroots campaign to set aside space for a farmer's market, updates for the software you write, or just tips on pet care—anything is fair game when it comes to RSS.

The word *simple* in *Really Simple Syndication* was aptly chosen—RSS really *is* simple. To create your own RSS feeds, all you need is a Web site where you can store your feeds. You can create an RSS feed using an easy program (see Chapter 3, "Creating RSS Feeds"), or you can create a feed from scratch (see Chapter 4, "Creating RSS Feeds from Scratch"). Some RSS editors even upload your feed to your Web site for you; it's all automatic—just fill out the form fields with the title and text you want to add to your feed and click a button. The program takes it from there.

Now that more and more people are interested in RSS, getting folks to read your feed has become easier too. Check out Chapter 8, "Publicizing Your Feeds," which covers ways you can popularize your feed.

RSS is also a good alternative for people who want to spread the word about their product or line of products without inadvertently resorting to spam. Because people must subscribe to your RSS feed to read it, you don't have to worry that you might be pushing email on anyone. Besides, laws are finally being enacted to crack down on spam email.

Another benefit of RSS, from the publisher's point of view, is that you can have each RSS item include a link back to your site. That's great, because you bring more traffic to your site and you have a chance to involve your subscribers more fully in your interests.

## RSS and Blogging

RSS also has a special relationship with Web logs—*blogs,* that is. Blogs are those online journals that have become very popular recently, and usually include commentary on just about anything.

Most blogging sites now automatically convert blog entries into RSS items. That means you don't have to go to a blog's site to check for new entries—you can have those new entries sent directly to your RSS reader.

To learn more about creating blogs and converting them into RSS feeds, see Chapter 5, "Blogging with RSS."

How do you subscribe to a blog as an RSS feed? As at most blog sites, you'll find a link or a button connected to the blog's RSS feed. For example, the "Subscribe to this blog's feed" link on the left links to the blog's automatically created RSS feed (**Figure 1.5**). You use the URL pointed to by that link to subscribe to the feed in your RSS reader.

Blogging and RSS are a natural combination: If the blog author adds entries to his blog from time to time, why wouldn't he convert those entries into RSS feed items? That way, the blog entries can come to you. What could be more convenient?

**Figure 1.5**
A blog site at
typepad.com
provides a link to
the blog's RSS feed.

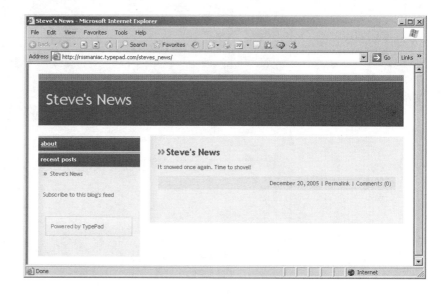

# Podcasting Too

RSS also plays a part in podcasting. The term *podcasting* originally came from a combination of Apple's *iPod* and *broadcasting*, but it has since come into its own, no iPod needed. *Podcasts* are recorded MP3 audio files usually disseminated over the Internet, and can be played on your computer or downloaded into an MP3 player.

Podcasts are based on RSS, and starting with RSS version 0.92, RSS can include *enclosures*. An enclosure for a podcast is simply the URL of a resource on the Internet. That resource doesn't have to be text—it can be an audio recording or a video recording, for example.

That's how podcasts work—an RSS file includes an enclosure, which points to an audio file or a video file. Both the RSS file and the audio/video podcast file must be online. To read podcasts, you can use special podcast software, like the Juice podcast receiver (**Figure 1.6**).

Podcast software reads the RSS feed file and determines from the enclosure where the podcast is located. Some podcast receiver programs automatically download a podcast, some wait until you request the download, and some let you choose when and how the download will occur.

**Figure 1.6**

The Juice podcast receiver lets you read podcasts.

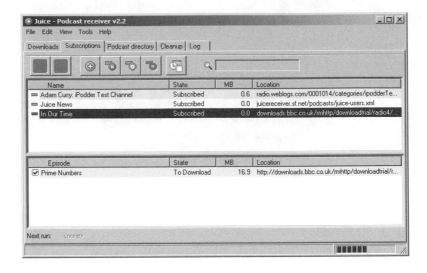

In fact, more and more standard RSS readers support podcasts. In some RSS readers, for example, you'll see a small link to an enclosure at the end of an RSS item's text. Clicking that link will play the podcast. And a new development is the online podcast receiver, which lets you play podcasts as if you had downloaded podcast software to your computer.

For a look at how to create your own podcasts and then listen to them in podcast programs, turn to Chapter 7, "Podcasting: Adding Multimedia to Your Feeds."

## A Brief History of RSS

Where did RSS come from? How long has it been around? RSS has had quite a history, some of which is shrouded in folklore, so I can't guarantee that my understanding of RSS history is 100 percent flawless. In fact, even what RSS stands for has changed over the years! There are three meanings for RSS and the version in which they were introduced:

- Rich Site Summary (RSS 0.91)

- RDF Site Summary (RSS 0.90 and 1.0)

- Really Simple Syndication (RSS 2.0)

Today, the most common meaning is Really Simple Syndication.

So where did the idea of syndication—subscribing to a site's content—come from? Long before RSS, there were various other formats (you couldn't quite call them languages) that supported syndications. You might recall Microsoft's Channel Definition Format (CDF), which worked with the Active Channel feature of Microsoft's Internet Explorer. Using CDF, you could subscribe to various online publication sites. Internet Explorer would check those publishers regularly and download new data as it became available. CDF was introduced in 1997, and in the same year, a developer at Userland.com, Dave Winer, introduced his own XML-based format for syndication in his Scripting News Web log. Userland.com, which first appeared in 1997, specializes in Web publishing software, and figures heavily in the history of RSS.

The first true version of RSS was created by Dan Libby of Netscape. Created in March 1999, it became known as version 0.90 (and was designed to be used with the My Netscape portal). In July 1999, version 0.90 was modified, and version 0.91, the first popular version, appeared. At that time, RSS stood for Rich Site Summary. Version 0.91 adopted parts of Dave Winer's Scripting News format and has become one of the major versions of RSS.

However, Netscape abandoned RSS not long after that, so although RSS was in some use, no one was in charge of it. Chaos resulted, as you might expect. Here's what happened: A mailing list named RSS-DEV appeared and became popular. At the same time, Dave Winer created a modified version of RSS 0.91, which was already being used in Userland's software.

Eventually, the approaches to RSS from the RSS-DEV group and Dave Winer diverged, creating what became known as the RSS fork. The RSS-DEV group created RSS 1.0 in December 2000. This version of RSS was quite a departure from the earlier versions, and was strongly based on the XML-based language Resource Description Format, or RDF (www.w3.org/TR/rdf-primer/), especially the RDF extension Dublin Core (http://dublincore.org/). Thus RSS 1.0 was named RDF Site Summary.

Only about three weeks after RSS 1.0 was announced, Dave Winer released RSS version 0.92. RSS 1.0 was also a major RSS version, but its syntax is so different from that of the other RSS fork people were used to, that many found it hard to use.

Then things got a little turbulent. In April 2001, Dave Winer came out with RSS 0.93, which was similar to version 0.92. A draft of version 0.94 appeared in August 2001, which removed the changes made in version 0.93 and made a few minor changes.

Finally, in September 2002, Dave Winer released a successor to version 0.92, which he called version 2.0, because the *version 1.0* name was already taken. At this time, RSS started being known as Really Simple Syndication. (In fact, things were pretty turbulent then too, because a few versions of RSS 2.0 appeared; but things have now settled down.) RSS 2.0 extended RSS 0.92, adding ways for people to extend RSS on their own. RSS 2.0 has since become a major version—*the* major version—of RSS.

In July 2003, Dave Winer passed ownership of RSS 2.0 to Harvard Law School's Berkman Center for Internet & Society (http://cyber.law.harvard. edu/home/), where he was working at the time. That move calmed things down quite a bit, and RSS 2.0 has been stable ever since.

Things are still happening with RSS. In January 2005, Sean B. Palmer and Christopher Schmidt released a draft of RSS 1.1, which simplifies the language somewhat. However, as of this writing, RSS 1.1 has not taken off. In November 2005, Microsoft proposed some extensions to RSS, informally named Real Simple Synchronization.

About five years ago, a number of developers, including Sam Ruby, offered a new format named Atom (first called Echo, then Pie, and then Atom) as a replacement for RSS. Atom is based on XML, but is quite a bit more difficult to learn and is more complex than RSS. Atom improves RSS by adding internationalization, standardizing the syntax, and allowing people to add their own features. Atom has yet to catch on in a really big way, however, compared with RSS.

So as you can see, RSS development is still going on, but the situation has stabilized. Today, versions 0.91, 1.0, and 2.0, as well as Atom, are in widespread use. These are the formats you'll see in this book.

# RSS Resources

Now that RSS is everywhere, there are RSS resources everywhere as well, and sometimes it's hard to wade through everything you find with a Web search.

Where do you begin? With RSS tutorials online. Here's a starter list of good tutorials you might want to check out:

- **www.w3schools.com/rss/default.asp**  A useful multipage RSS 2.0 tutorial (**Figure 1.7**).

- **www.eevl.ac.uk/rss_primer**  A thorough primer, easy to use and understand.

- **www.mnot.net/rss/tutorial**  A helpful primer and overview. It shows you how to work with the different versions of RSS, and includes tips as well as links to RSS tools.

- **www.rss-specifications.com/create-rss-feed.htm**  Good tutorial text on creating RSS.

- **http://rssgov.com/rssworkshop.html**  Part of the Government Information Locator Service site. As the site boasts, "In this workshop you'll learn how to create, validate, parse, publish, and syndicate your own RSS news channel."

**Figure 1.7**
Here's the start of w3schools' RSS tutorial.

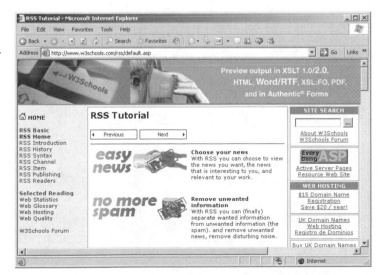

Here's a list of the official RSS and Atom specifications and where to find them online. If a feed you've created doesn't work in your RSS reader, take a look at the rules for the version of RSS or Atom you're working with (as discussed in Chapter 3, "Creating RSS Feeds," you can also check your feeds online—just go to http://feedvalidator.org/):

- **RSS 0.90**  www.purplepages.ie/RSS/netscape/rss0.90.html

- **RSS 0.91**  http://backend.userland.com/rss091 and also see http://my.netscape.com/publish/formats/rss-spec-0.91.html

- **RSS 0.92**  http://backend.userland.com/rss092

- **RSS 0.93**  http://backend.userland.com/rss093

- **RSS 1.0**  http://web.resource.org/rss/1.0/spec

- **RSS 1.1**  http://inamidst.com/rss1.1/

- **RSS 2.0**  http://blogs.law.harvard.edu/tech/rss (**Figure 1.8**)

- **Atom**  http://xml.coverpages.org/draft-ietf-atompub-format-11.txt

You can also find information on the RSS specifications at www.rss-specifications.com/rss-specifications.htm.

**Figure 1.8**

The RSS 2.0 specification page at Harvard Law.

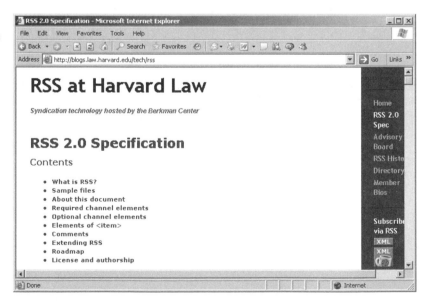

Additionally, there are tons of articles on RSS online, some on very interesting topics. For example, here are a few articles that review and compare RSS readers:

- **www.pcworld.com/resource/printable/article/0,aid,116018,00.asp** Good article on RSS and a review of 18 different RSS readers (**Figure 1.9**).

- **www.mediathink.com/rss/whitepaper.asp** Compares 12 RSS readers.

**Figure 1.9**

A *PC World* article compares 18 RSS readers.

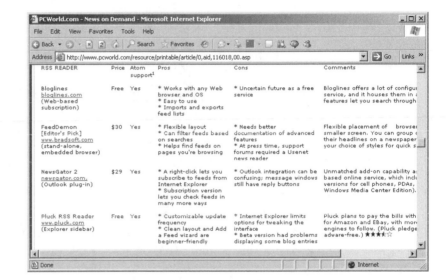

Some Yahoo Groups provide discussion and support:

- **http://groups.yahoo.com/group/rss-dev/** RSS 1.0 discussion group.

- **http://groups.yahoo.com/group/RSS2-Support** RSS 2.0 support (**Figure 1.10**).

Here are some articles on the best ways to write and use RSS:

- **www.ariadne.ac.uk/issue35/miller/** Lists best practices.

- **http://webservices.xml.com/pub/a/ws/2002/11/19/ rssfeedquality.html** Lists more best practices.

**Figure 1.10**

Ask questions and enter short discussions at the Yahoo Groups RSS 2.0 support page.

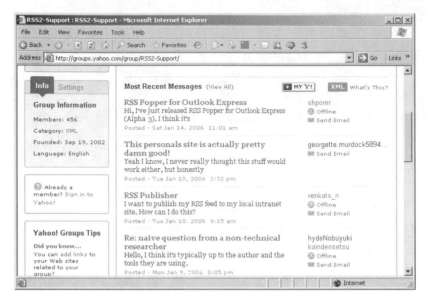

Here's an article on how advertisers are moving into RSS feeds (unfortunately!):

- www.wired.com/news/ebiz/0,1272,65745,00.html

At Syndic8 you'll find a page on RSS statistics (**Figure 1.11**) such as the number of feeds Syndic8 tracks, what fraction of people use version 0.92 versus 2.0, and so on:

- www.syndic8.com/stats.php

For more information on RSS, such as the percentage of people who use what version, click the RSS link at the top.

In fact, there are even RSS feeds on RSS, which makes sense if you think about it. What better way to spread the word on what's new in the RSS world than with RSS feeds? Here's a starter list of RSS feeds on what's happening in the RSS world:

- **Dave Winer's site RSS feed**   www.scripting.com/rss.xml
  (Web site: www.scripting.com)

- **RSS and Atom tips RSS feed**   www.lockergnome.com/rss/rss.php
  (Web site: http://channels.lockergnome.com/rss)

**Figure 1.11**

You will find various RSS statistics on Syndic8.

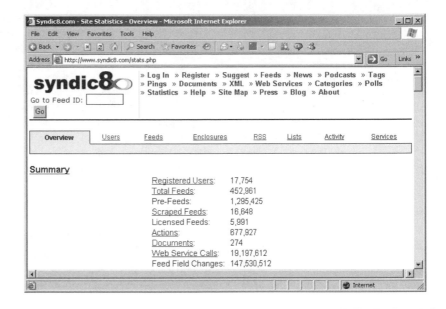

- **Robin Good's Independent Publishing News RSS feed**
  www.masternewmedia.org/index-independent_publishing.rdf
  (Web site: www.masternewmedia.org/independent_
  publishing.htm)

Here's a good starter list of interesting sites that have RSS feeds:

- **CNN** www.cnn.com/services/rss/

- *USAToday* http://asp.usatoday.com/marketing/rss/index.aspx

- *The New York Times* www.nytimes.com/services/xml/rss
  (**Figure 1.12**)

- *The Christian Science Monitor* www.csmonitor.com/rss

- **The Motley Fool** (for financial advice) www.fool.com/about/
  headlines/headlines_rss.htm

- **Moreover.com** http://w.moreover.com/categories/category_list_
  rss.html (more than 300 feeds listed)

- **National Weather Service** www.weather.gov/data/current_obs

- **CBS MarketWatch** www.marketwatch.com/rss/default.asp

**Figure 1.12**

As you can see on the RSS feed page for *The New York Times*, there's a feed for just about every part of the paper.

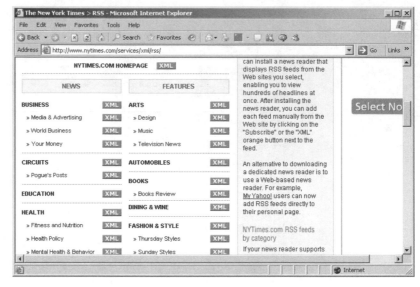

To select the RSS feeds that are right for you, check the list of RSS directories earlier in the chapter. The Syndic8 searchable feed directory (www.syndic8.com/feedlist.php), for example, lists 103,396 RSS feeds.

Also, there are RSS tools available for download (I'll provide many more RSS tools in the book):

- **Atom2RSS (www.2rss.com/software.php?page=atom2rss)** Converts Atom feeds to RSS feeds.

- **NewsAloud (www.nextup.com/NewsAloud/)** Reads RSS feeds aloud.

- **WebNews.TV (www.webnews.tv/)** Reads RSS feeds and other news sources aloud—using an animated penguin!

- **Take-Off (www.take-off.as/index.htm)** Converts RSS feeds to database format and displays them in other formats, such as PowerPoint.

You can also find a list of RSS tools at www.socialtext.net/rss-winterfest/index.cgi?great_rss_tools. For a list of Atom tools, you can go to www.atomenabled.org/everyone/atomenabled/.

And that's it—now you're ready to get started reading RSS feeds, so just turn to Chapter 2.

# 2

# Grabbing RSS with Readers

So now you know there are many thousands of RSS feeds you can subscribe to and read. So what if you want to start reading? Say you want to read specific feeds from *The New York Times*, or *The Wall Street Journal*, or *The Washington Post*—or from any of the thousands upon thousands of other feeds. This chapter is all about subscribing to and reading those feeds.

RSS readers are sometimes called aggregators because they aggregate items, or gather data from various RSS feeds. But whether you call them RSS readers or aggregators, they're your primary RSS tools. They grab news items for you and display those items in a format that's easy to handle. This chapter gives you an overview of readers so you can select the one that's right for you.

# Using an RSS Reader

There are hundreds of RSS readers these days, and they all have different features. Most of them, including the highly popular RSS-Reader (**Figure 2.1**), share the same basic way of handling RSS feeds.

But first you need to subscribe to an RSS feed, and the next section describes how that works.

**Figure 2.1**
Using a reader of some kind is the basis of reading any RSS feed.

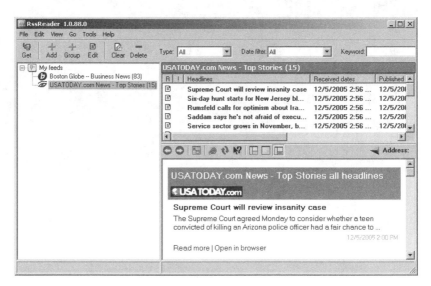

# Subscribing to a feed

Start by targeting an RSS site you want to subscribe to. A site with RSS content usually displays blue or orange icon buttons (**Figure 2.2**).

**Figure 2.2**
Sites with RSS feeds display one of these buttons.

Why three different buttons? The RSS button is clearly for subscribing to an RSS feed. The XML button—for subscribing to XML feeds—is becoming more prevalent on RSS sites, probably because RSS is an XML format. (See Chapter 4,"Creating RSS Feeds from Scratch," for a discussion of XML.)

Most people looking for an RSS feed expect to find an RSS button, not an XML button. But XML buttons are starting to take over some sites with RSS feeds, such as USAToday.com (**Figure 2.3**).

**Figure 2.3**

USAToday.com provides RSS feeds for almost every section of the paper.

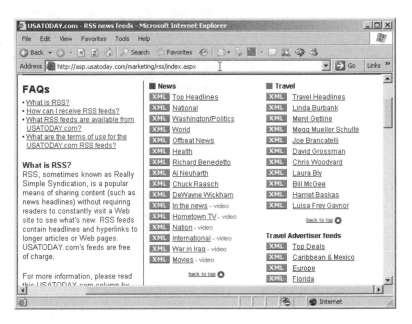

 Atom feeds, discussed in more depth in Chapter 3, "Creating RSS Feeds," and Chapter 4 are marked with Atom buttons (Figure 2.2) and indicate an Atom version 0.3 feed.

 How do you find feeds you're interested in? Take a look at the section "Finding RSS Feeds" near the end of this chapter. You can use your RSS reader to search, look at RSS directories, browse the Internet, and so on.

After you've found a feed you want to read, how do you tell an RSS reader that you want to subscribe to the feed? There are a number of ways.

## Click the XML button

One way to subscribe to an RSS feed is simply to click the XML button on the feed's site in your browser. That's not usually the most helpful approach, however, since doing so usually displays the raw XML code that makes up the RSS feed (**Figure 2.4**).

**Figure 2.4**

Viewing RSS data from a browser will usually display XML code.

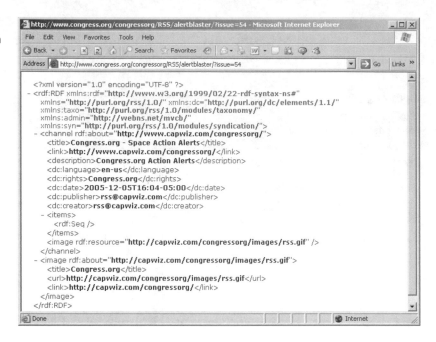

So how do you convert the mess of XML code into an RSS feed you can read? Just select the URL displayed in your browser and copy it to the clipboard, where your RSS reader will find the feed.

After you've captured the URL for the RSS feed, you can add the feed to your RSS reader. Different readers let you do this in various ways; for example, in RSSReader, clicking the Add button in the toolbar (the button with a plus sign, as shown near the top in Figure 2.1) opens a dialog to add a new feed. RSSReader then copies the RSS feed's URL automatically and displays it.

To give the feed a title, click the Next button. In this case, RSSReader automatically enters and displays the feed's title, "Congress.org - Space Action Alerts," from the feed's XML (**Figure 2.5**). Click the Next button again.

**Figure 2.5**

Displaying the feed's title is automatic with RSSReader.

RSSReader then asks you where you want to add the new feed, and has the default group, My Feeds, automatically selected. In RSS readers like RSSReader, you can group feeds into various categories; in this case, just click the OK button, and the new feed is added to the My Feeds group (**Figure 2.6**).

**Figure 2.6**

Not much going on in the Space Action Alerts feed today.

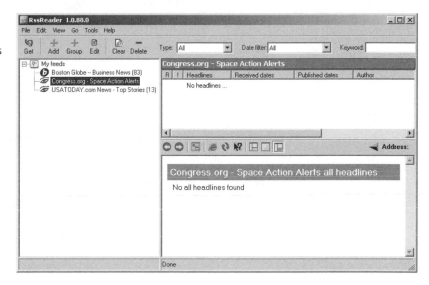

Other RSS readers accept the URL of an RSS feed in other ways. Say, for example, you want to subscribe to the top news stories in the world from *USA Today*. In SharpReader, you would enter the URL of *USA Today*'s feed by selecting the File > Open RSS Feed menu item, thus opening the dialog that lets you subscribe to the feed (**Figure 2.7**).

**Figure 2.7**

Subscribing to a feed is easy in SharpReader.

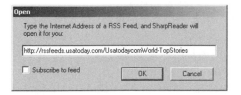

In the Feed Demon RSS reader, you select File > New > New Channel. Leave the "I will enter the URL of the feed" radio button selected, click Next, and then enter the URL of the feed (**Figure 2.8**).

**Figure 2.8**

Subscribing to a feed in Feed Demon takes just a few steps.

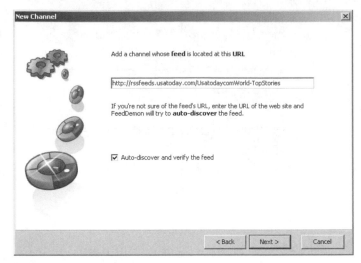

Although entering the URL varies from reader to reader, most readers are easy to figure out. What's important is getting the URL of the feed in the first place. Clicking the XML button is one way to get the URL, but an even easier way is to right-click (Control-click on the Mac) the XML button instead.

## Right-click the XML button

Clicking an XML button usually displays the RSS feed's XML data, but the whole point of using an RSS reader is to avoid reading XML directly (usually an unedifying experience). It's a better idea to right-click the XML button: Instead of XML code, a menu appears in your browser. In this example, I'm subscribing to a feed from the British BBC (**Figure 2.9**).

To copy the URL for the RSS feed, choose Copy Shortcut in Microsoft Internet Explorer, or choose Copy Link Location in Mozilla Firefox. After you've captured the URL (which is stored in the clipboard in Windows), you can add it to your RSS reader in the usual way. Some RSS readers can read the URL directly from the clipboard and display that URL when you open the dialog to add an RSS feed. With other RSS readers, you have to paste the URL into the appropriate dialog.

**Figure 2.9**

Right-click to access the shortcut menu to subscribe to a feed.

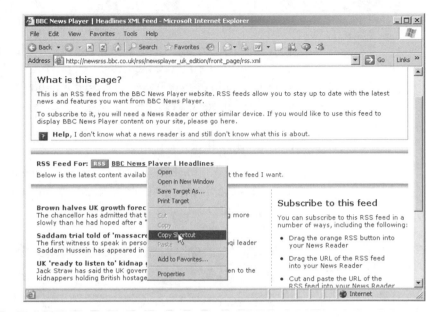

## Type in the URL

Some RSS readers, such as SharpReader, display an Address box for you to enter the URL of a feed, just like the kind you see in standard Web browsers (**Figure 2.10**).

**Figure 2.10**

Enter a URL in the Address box to subscribe to a feed.

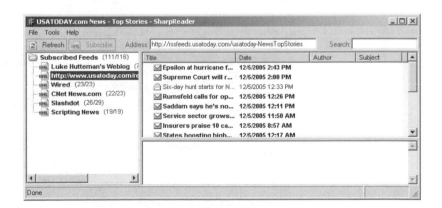

After you enter the URL in the Address box, just press Enter to read that feed.

## Drag and drop

Some RSS readers, such as SharpReader, let you drag and drop an RSS feed to subscribe. All you have to do is drag the XML button into the RSS reader and drop it. Drag and drop is a handy technique, and you can expect more RSS readers to support it in the future.

## Use feed:// links

Another way to subscribe to RSS feeds in RSS readers is to use *feed://* links. This is a relatively new prefix for RSS feed URLs, much as a standard URL starts with *http://* (**Figure 2.11**).

**Figure 2.11**

To subscribe to a feed using a *feed://* link, all you have to do is click a button.

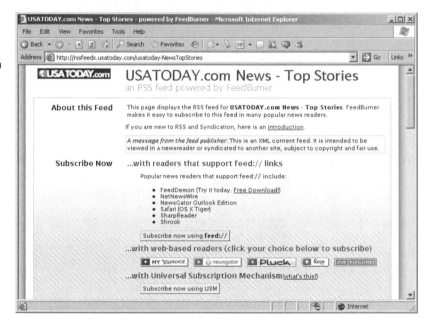

When you find a feed that can be added to your RSS reader using a *feed://* link, you usually see a button to click that says something like "Subscribe now using feed://." Only a few RSS readers support *feed://*, however, including the following:

- FeedDemon

- NetNewsWire

- NewsGator Outlook Edition

- SharpReader

- Shrook

- Safari (OS X Tiger)

## Use the Universal Subscription Mechanism

There's yet another way to subscribe to RSS feeds: the Universal Subscription Mechanism, or USM. For example, go to *USA Today*'s feeds page at http://asp.usatoday.com/marketing/rss/index.aspx and open an RSS feed, such as the Health feed (http://rssfeeds.usatoday.com/ UsatodaycomHealth-TopStories). You can subscribe to this feed by clicking the button marked "Subscribe now using USM."

Clicking the USM button opens the RSS feed in your RSS reader, if it supports USM. Using Juice, after you click the USM button on a Web site, Juice opens the feed (**Figure 2.12**).

**Figure 2.12**

Opening an RSS feed using USM in Juice.

However, at this point in time, very few RSS readers support USM. Most people just grab the URL of the feed they want and enter it into their RSS reader.

 **The next version of Windows, code-named Longhorn, will have built-in support for RSS. Although Longhorn isn't available yet, Microsoft claims that Windows will have special features that will let users discover and create RSS feeds and be able to read RSS feeds directly in Internet Explorer.**

# Reading feeds in your RSS reader

So, how do RSS readers work and how do they let you read RSS feeds? To start, take a look at RSSReader (**Figure 2.13**).

**Figure 2.13**
RSSReader, like most readers, has three main windows.

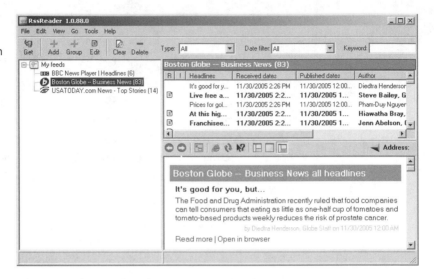

Let's take a look at RSSReader's three main windows.

## The feeds window

The feeds window, on the left side of the opening screen of RSSReader, lists the feeds you've subscribed to (again see Figure 2.13). You'll see a vertical list of clickable RSS feeds, usually preceded by an icon. By default, the icon displayed for a feed in RSSReader is a small eye-shaped image, but a feed can also have its own icon, which RSSReader displays (see the icons for the *Boston Globe* and BBC feeds in Figure 2.13).

With RSS readers that refer to an RSS feed as a *channel*, this window is called the channel window.

When you select an RSS feed, that feed's current items appear in the titles window, located on the right in RSSReader (again see Figure 2.13). When you right-click a feed in the feeds window, the RSS reader presents you with a menu of options, which vary depending on the reader. Most RSS readers offer a Properties item in this menu. The Feed Properties dialog tells you about the feed you've selected. RSSReader's Feed Properties dialog shows the RSS feed's URL, the last update time, whether the feed is active, and more (**Figure 2.14**).

**Figure 2.14**

Use the Feed Properties dialog to get information about the feed.

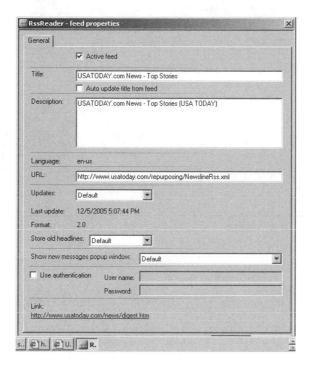

By default, most RSS readers automatically check an RSS feed hourly while the RSS reader is running. You can usually see the most recent items in a feed by right-clicking (Control-clicking on the Mac) the feed's name in the feeds window and selecting the menu option that checks for new items to read. That menu item is often named Refresh, Update Channel, or (in RSSReader) Get New Feed Headlines.

Although RSS readers usually grab new items from RSS feeds hourly by default, you can change the amount of time the reader waits before it fetches more news from a particular feed (**Figure 2.15**). You can usually set a time interval by selecting Tools > Options (or Tools > Preferences) to open an options dialog.

**Figure 2.15**

Most RSS readers let you set the refresh rate of a feed.

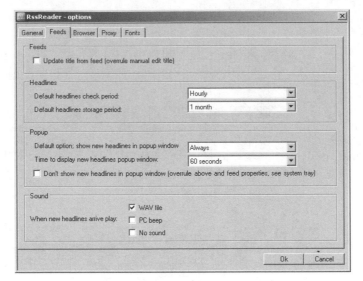

You can also set the amount of time the RSS reader stores item titles—also called headlines in some readers—from the feed. In Figure 2.15, that time is set to one month, which means that RSSReader will store headlines for a month.

That's how it works: The RSS feeds you've subscribed to appear in the feeds window, and your reader automatically fetches new items periodically. If you want to check the new items from a feed, just select that feed in the feeds window. To configure that feed—such as reading new items immediately—right-click the feed name in the feeds window and select from the items in the menu that appears.

**How do you unsubscribe from a feed? See the topic "Unsubscribing from a feed" later in this chapter.**

The feeds window shows the RSS feeds you've subscribed to, but what about handling the actual items that your reader fetches from those feeds? That's coming up next.

## The titles window

The window in the upper-right part of the opening screen in RSSReader is the titles window, which displays the titles of new items, or headlines, fetched from an RSS feed (again see Figure 2.13). When you check an RSS feed, all the titles of the new items in that feed are added to the titles window.

So when you want to check the new headlines from an RSS feed, you select that feed in the feeds window, and the RSS reader displays the current headlines from the feed.

**RSS 0.91 has a limit of 15 new items per refresh when you check an RSS feed. That limit was removed in subsequent versions.**

You can scroll the feed's new headlines to look for item titles that interest you. When an item title piques your interest, just click the title in the titles window to see the item's content which appears in the description window.

To indicate previously read items, most RSS readers change the appearance of the item title. Unread titles are usually displayed in bold in the titles window, and titles that have been read change to plain text. You can see examples of both in Figure 2.13.

**Most RSS readers let you mark multiple item titles as already read. In RSSReader, for example, you can choose titles in the titles window and select Edit > Mark as read menu item to indicate the selected titles have been read. Converting titles to plain text is a good way to mark the titles you're not really interested in so you don't have to bother with them.**

The whole process is a little like working with newspapers: You select the newspaper you want to read in the feeds window, scan the headlines in the titles window, and then read the stories in the description window.

## The description window

Say you've just checked your favorite RSS feed from Fish-R-Us, and you notice an enticing item title, "New Bali Flying Fish Are In!" No one can resist that, you think, so you immediately click that title. The content of this interesting item appears in the description window, at the lower right part of the RSSReader screen (Figure 2.13).

The description for a particular item will vary by RSS feed. Most feeds don't display the whole story in the description window. Instead, you typically see some text introducing the item, and two links below the text: Read More and Open in Browser. Some feeds, however, display the entire article in the description window. Others might show only a title from an RSS feed, although that's rare.

If the text in the description window makes you want to read more, click the Read More link to open the full item in the description window (**Figure 2.16**). In this example, the description window's content only describes an article on the *Boston Globe* Web site; clicking the Read More link opens the full article from the *Boston Globe* Web site, for you to read in RSSReader.

**Figure 2.16**

Clicking the Read More link opens the item in the description window.

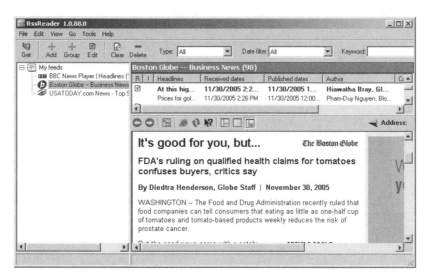

Another way to get the full *Boston Globe* article is by clicking the Open in Browser link. As you would expect, the article opens in your browser.

You can navigate forward and backward in an RSS reader, just as you can in a browser: Just click the back and forward buttons that appear in the toolbar above the description window. If you are looking at a full article and want to go back to the item's description, just click the back button.

## Getting alerts

Many RSS readers display a pop-up alert when a new item appears in the feed it's reading. In Windows, the pop-ups appear from the system tray (the bar at the bottom of the screen).

Depending on how you feel about your screen being cluttered with alerts periodically, you can leave the alerts on or turn them off. Personally, my system tray shows too many alerts as computer manufacturers and Windows itself are now adding more and more unwanted popups, so I like to turn off the alerts.

You can turn off the periodic alerts usually by selecting Tools > Options in an RSS reader to open the Options dialog. To turn off alerts, change the setting for "Default option; show new headlines in pop-up window" from *Always* to *Never*.

## Sending an item through email

See a particularly juicy item that you just know a friend would appreciate? Many RSS readers let you email items. In RSSReader, you simply select the Tools > Email to Friend menu item, and the current item is passed to your email program. The title of the item appears in the email's Subject line, and the description appears as the body of the email.

## Grouping feeds together

Some RSS readers let you create your own *groups* of feeds to better organize your incoming news. To create a new group of feeds in RSSReader, you click the Group button in the toolbar to open the Add New Feed Group dialog, which asks you to name the new feed group (**Figure 2.17**). The new group appears in the RSS Feeds window.

**Figure 2.17**
In this example, the new feed group *Newspapers* is being created.

To put a feed into a new group, all you have to do is to drag it into the feeds window. In this example, I've dragged the feed from the *Boston Globe* into the Newspapers group (**Figure 2.18**).

**Figure 2.18**
The Newspaper feed group now appears in the titles window on the right.

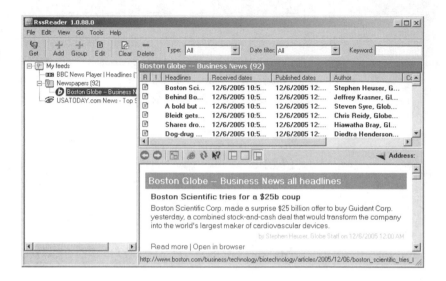

After you've used RSS readers for a long time and you've built a dozen feeds or more, organizing the feeds into groups can be very useful, especially if you have a set of specialty feeds that you check infrequently (such as holiday sales).

## Unsubscribing from a feed

Are you sick of a feed? Or has a feed gone dead? It's time to unsubscribe. As usual, how you do that varies by RSS reader. In most readers, you right-click a feed in the feeds window and select the menu item that will unsubscribe the feed. That menu item can be called Unsubscribe, Delete Feed, or Delete Channel, depending on the RSS reader. In any case, the item name is usually recognizable.

Want to *re*subscribe to a feed you've unsubscribed from? Just grab its URL and subscribe to it again, as usual.

## Getting RSS on your PDA or phone

After you get truly addicted to RSS, you might never want to be out of touch. And now, if you have a Web-enabled PDA or cell phone, you can stay in touch. For example, here are a few RSS readers for the Pocket PC:

- A4News

- PocketRSS

- Egress

- Mobile News

Want to see RSS feeds on your PDA? Try www.mobilerss.net, which converts RSS feeds into HTML that you can view on your PDA. How about an RSS reader on your cell phone? Take a look at www.dace.fi for a reader that you can download to some cell phones and use to read RSS.

 **For more RSS readers designed for PDAs and cell phones, take a look at http://directory.google.com/Top/Reference/Libraries/Library_and_ Information_Science/Technical_Services/Cataloguing/Metadata/RDF/ Applications/RSS/News_Readers/Handhelds/.**

# What Kind of Reader Do You Want?

There are plenty of RSS readers, but which one is right for you? Currently there are two main types of readers—online (browser-based) and desktop (software that resides on your computer).

The following resources list hundreds of available RSS readers, most of which are free:

- http://directory.google.com/Top/Reference/Libraries/Library_ and_Information_Science/Technical_Services/Cataloguing/ Metadata/RDF/Applications/RSS/News_Readers/

- www.rssreaders.net/

- www.tucows.com/ (Enter "RSS reader" in the Search box, select your operating system, and click Go.)

You can even find a list of email-based RSS readers at http://directory. google.com/Top/Reference/Libraries/Library_and_Information_Science/ Technical_Services/Cataloguing/Metadata/RDF/Applications/RSS/ News_Readers/E-mail_Based/.

As of this writing, the Google site lists six RSS readers for Linux, 14 for Mac OS, 51 online RSS readers, and 88 for Windows—quite a selection. How do you choose? Starting with online RSS readers, the next section covers the most popular RSS readers and gives you a taste of each of them.

# Online RSS Readers

Online RSS readers have some advantages over the ones you run on your computer. For one thing, online RSS readers are free for the most part. For another, they're often easier to use.

To use an online RSS reader, you typically need to register with the site that hosts the reader and select a username and password. Beware, however: It might ask for your email address, which can leave you open for spam emails.

## Easy RSS reading with CompleteRSS

CompleteRSS is an easy-to-use online RSS reader that you can find at www.completerss.com. You just enter some search terms for the feed you're looking for, such as an eWeek Technology News feed (**Figure 2.19**), and click the Go button. (Or you can browse through the RSS Feed Sampler you see in the middle of the page.)

CompleteRSS displays a list of matches to the terms you've entered. You select the one you want (eWeek Technology News in this example), and the current items for that feed are displayed (**Figure 2.20**).

**Figure 2.19**

You can use CompleteRSS to search eWeek Technology News for a feed.

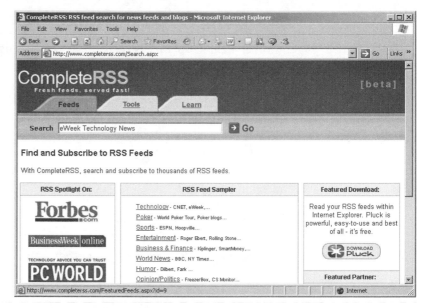

**Figure 2.20**

CompleteRSS displays the latest feed items from eWeek Technology News.

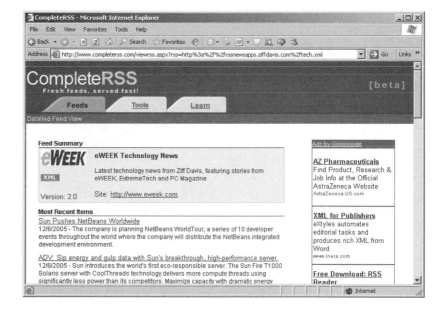

## Searching for feeds with Feedster

Another great RSS source is Feedster, at www.feedster.com. Much like CompleteRSS, Feedster searches for feeds that match your search terms and displays those items.

Feedster, however, is much more aggressive about searching the Internet for RSS feeds. In fact, it claims to search the largest index of RSS feeds. As of this writing, Feedster claims to search more than 18 million RSS feeds. (How many of those feeds are active is an open question, however.)

This is a nice, easy way of handling RSS feeds, but it's a little too lightweight for many people: Every time you want to read a feed, you have to search for it again. But there is another way.

## Reading RSS with Bloglines

Bloglines, another online reader (www.bloglines.com), keeps track of all the RSS feeds you've subscribed to. First you have to register as a new user: Click the Registration link to go to the registration page, and Bloglines will send you an email. Clicking the link in the email completes your registration and lets you choose which feeds you want to subscribe to (**Figure 2.21**).

Bloglines stores the feeds you're subscribed to, and you can see them when you return to the Bloglines page and click the My Feeds tab (**Figure 2.22**).

## Using NewsIsFree

NewsIsFree is purported to be the oldest online RSS reader, and you can sign up to use it at www.newsisfree.com (**Figure 2.23**). You go through the usual registration process by providing a username and email address. NewsIsFree then sends you an email containing a link, which you click to set up your custom page.

**Figure 2.21**

Bloglines lists staff selections as well as the most popular subscriptions.

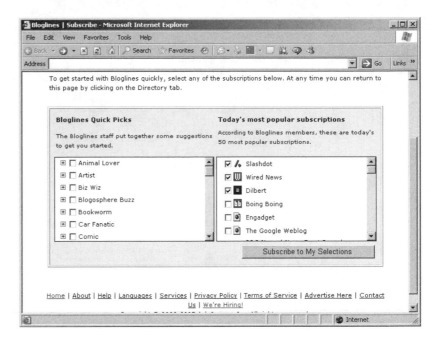

**Figure 2.22**

Your Bloglines selections are stored in the My Feeds tab.

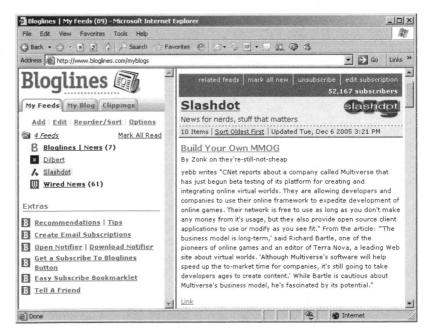

**Figure 2.23**
NewsIsFree lets you browse by category or date.

## Whooping it up with My Yahoo

Another online champ is My Yahoo, which has tons of major RSS feeds for you to choose from (**Figure 2.24**). First sign up on the My Yahoo site at http://myyahoo.com (see Tip below). This reader is especially popular because it's easy to use, and you can add many RSS feeds to your My Yahoo page with a few clicks. Many people use My Yahoo as their home page, and the ability to customize the feeds you see each morning is great.

Several people have noted a problem with the My Yahoo registration process. The directions say you will receive an email so you can complete the sign-up process, but the email never arrived. In fact, it didn't in my case either. However this omission doesn't seem to affect signing into the site. If you don't receive the email, just wait a few hours and try signing on with the username and password you've selected.

**Figure 2.24**

It's easy to read RSS feeds using My Yahoo.

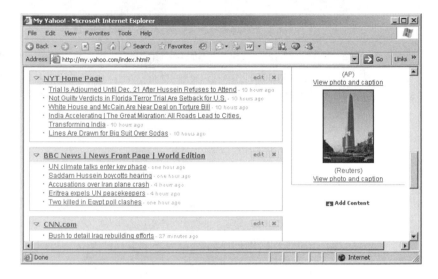

## Grabbing RSS feeds with NewsGator

With NewsGator, another popular online RSS reader (**Figure 2.25**), you can create a specialized feed based on the URL of a Web site, so that, for example, whenever someone mentions your Web site in their feed, you'll know about it. You can also synchronize NewsGator to work with Microsoft Outlook. Sign up at www.newsgator.com/home.aspx.

**Figure 2.25**

NewsGator can track different sites on one page that you create.

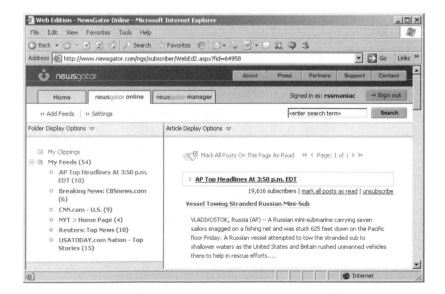

# Desktop RSS Readers

Most RSS readers are designed to run on your computer. These desktop readers often come packed with all kinds of features, such as importing and exporting lists of RSS feeds, marking items as read or not, filtering item titles by keyword, grouping feeds, configuring looks, integrating with online RSS feed directories that let you browse for RSS feeds, and more.

 **How do the desktop RSS readers stack up? There aren't many recent comparisons available, but here is one: Mediathink.com compares the capabilities of 12 readers and can be found at www.mediathink.com/ rss/mediathink_rss_white_paper.pdf.**

Want to see the various RSS readers rated? Go to www.tucows.com, a popular software repository site, and search for *RSS readers*. More than 100 RSS readers for just about every operating system are available for download, all rated and listed by popularity. The next section examines some of the most popular desktop RSS readers.

## A good choice: RSSReader

You've already seen RSSReader, available at www.rssreader.com/, at work in the beginning of this chapter (see Figure 2.1). It has a good balance of features and power—not overwhelming—but enough to make it easy to use. And it's free.

RSSReader is the reader I personally use most often, and while it doesn't have all the features some of the most powerful readers sport, its ease of use and well-designed interface makes it a good one. RSSReader works with any RSS or Atom feed. And another great feature—using the File > Add feeds from directory menu—lets you see a large directory of feeds that you can choose from (not all RSS readers tie into directories of RSS feeds this way).

## Getting sharp with SharpReader

SharpReader, available at www.sharpreader.com and mentioned toward the beginning of this chapter (see Figure 2.8), is also free. To use this reader, you need the .NET Framework, version 1.1 SP1 (which you probably have if you're running Windows XP—and if not, the SharpReader site tells you how to get it).

Like RSSReader, SharpReader works with any RSS or Atom feed. This reader is a lot like RSSReader, but the absence of navigation buttons such as forward or back buttons makes it harder to use.

## Crawling for news with NewzCrawler

NewzCrawler is a full-featured RSS reader that lets you read news posts from usenet and browser Web pages like a Web browser (**Figure 2.26**). It's not free—it costs $24.95 as of this writing—but you can use it for a free 14-day evaluation trial period.

NewzCrawler works with any RSS or Atom feed. It's packed with features, but test it out using the free trial period to see if it's for you (www.newzcrawler.com).

**Figure 2.26**

Unread items are displayed in bold in NewzCrawler's channel tree.

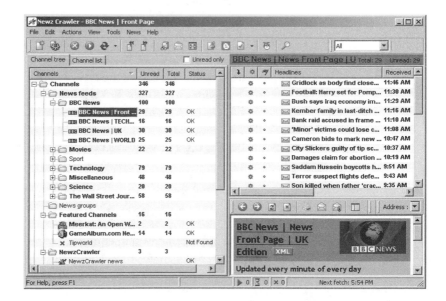

## Accelerating with AmphetaDesk

The AmphetaDesk RSS reader is a hybrid reader: It installs a mini Web server on your computer and lets you browse RSS feeds using your browser (**Figure 2.27**). It's free at www.disobey.com/amphetadesk. A hybrid reader is a clever idea, but the interface is very basic and lacks most of the functionality of dedicated desktop RSS readers.

**Figure 2.27**

AmphetaDesk is cross platform and has versions for Windows, Mac OS X, and Linux.

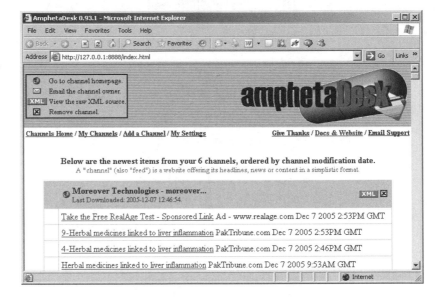

AmphetaDesk is an older RSS reader, and as of this writing it doesn't support Atom feeds. It is one of the few cross-platform RSS readers, supporting versions for Windows, Mac, and Linux.

## Getting your news with FeedDemon

FeedDemon is a full-featured RSS reader that costs $29.95 as of this writing. You can download this reader at www.feeddemon.com and use it for a 20-day trial period for free.

FeedDemon supports a newspaper display of feeds, special "watches" that let you gather RSS news from keyword searches, a news bin to store news for later reading, a podcast receiver, and more (**Figure 2.28**).

**Figure 2.28**
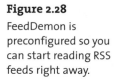
FeedDemon is preconfigured so you can start reading RSS feeds right away.

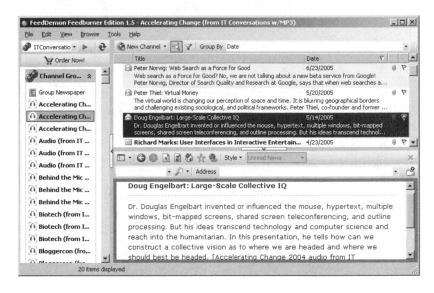

FeedDemon can handle RSS and Atom. It comes preconfigured with dozens of popular feeds, and you can schedule your RSS downloads to happen overnight.

## Getting plucky with Pluck

The Pluck RSS reader is free at www.pluck.com and has three editions: an online version, a plug-in for Internet Explorer, and a plug-in for Firefox. You need Internet Explorer or Firefox installed to run this reader on your desktop.

Like other readers that use browsers for their interface, some users might not like the basic nature of the interface, and the toolbars full of buttons. Pluck also inserts ads in the display.

## Other desktop readers

There are dozens and dozens more desktop RSS readers to choose from. For a good selection, take a look at www.tucows.com for readers for all operating systems; here are some favorites:

- **Optimal Desktop** www.tucows.com/preview/231866

- **FleetNews** www.tucows.com/preview/400274

- **My RSS Toolbar** www.tucows.com/preview/405414

- **Feed Scout** www.tucows.com/preview/405416

- **RSSPoint** www.tucows.com/preview/405867

- **Active Web Reader** www.tucows.com/preview/352545

- **Omea Reader** www.tucows.com/preview/373485

You can find other good listings of RSS readers at www.rssreaders.net
and http://directory.google.com/Top/Reference/Libraries/Library_and_
Information_Science/Technical_Services/Cataloguing/Metadata/RDF/
Applications/RSS/News_Readers/.

# Finding RSS Feeds

OK, you've chosen your RSS reader and you're ready to go—except
for one thing. Just where are you going to search for RSS feeds that
interest you? The usual way is to browse the Web looking for those
blue and orange XML, RSS, or Atom buttons. The Firefox browser helps
out by displaying an RSS icon (a small orange square) in its status bar,
at the bottom right of the screen, when you come across a site with an
RSS feed (**Figure 2.29**).

**Figure 2.29**

The RSS feed icon (at
lower right) for Firefox
is the small (orange)
square in the wndow's
status bar.

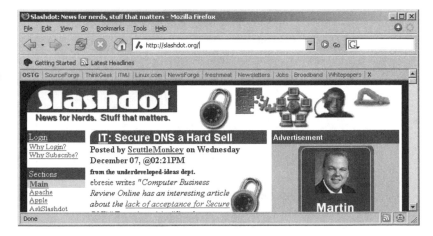

You can also use some RSS readers, such as Feed Demon, as browsers, which display similar icons when you find sites with RSS feeds.

But there's an even simpler way: You can use some RSS readers to find feeds for you automatically.

## Using RSS readers

Some RSS readers—RSSReader, Feedster, Pluck, and others—conveniently give you access to lists of RSS feeds, If you want to see what feeds you might be interested in, all you do is select feeds from the list your RSS reader presents you.

For example, in RSSReader, when you select File > Add feeds from a directory menu, a dialog gives you a list of feeds to choose from (**Figure 2.30**). You can select the feeds you want and add them to the feeds window by clicking the Add button.

 Many RSS readers include lists of feeds already installed. This feature is probably less useful than the creators of these readers think, because everyone wants to look at different feeds. Most users delete the default feeds that come with these readers and add the feeds they're interested in.

**Figure 2.30**
Clicking the Add button adds feeds in RSSReader.

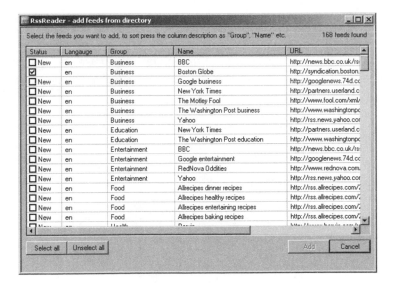

## Using feed directories

Still another way to find feeds is by turning to online directories of RSS feeds. Some are massive lists, and some let you enter search terms. Want to track down the feeds that are right for you? Take a look at these online directories—you're sure to find some appealing feeds.

- www.syndic8.com/feedlist.php

- www.blogstreet.com

- www.search4rss.com

- www.feedster.com

- www.completerss.com

- www.newsgator.com/ngs/default.aspx

- www.blogsearchengine.com (add *rss* after your search term)

- www.2rss.com/index.php

- www.rss-network.com

- www.rssfeeds.com

- www.shas3.com/RSS.html

## Using searches

Another way of finding feeds is to use an RSS feed's search engine. Here are a few sites that let you find RSS feeds based on keyword searches of the items in those feeds:

- www.blogdigger.com

- www.daypop.com

- http://feedfinder.feedster.com

- www.moreover.com

- www.newsgator.com

- www.newsisfree.com

For example, you can find the RSS reader Feedster at http://feedfinder. feedster.com (**Figure 2.31**).

**Figure 2.31**

Feedster lets you search for RSS feeds by keyword or a combination of two or more words.

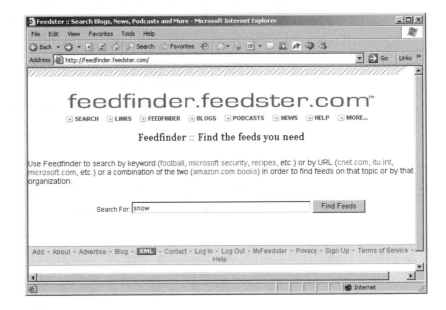

Then you enter a keyword and click the Find Feeds button. Feedster give you a list of articles that contain the keyword *snow* (**Figure 2.32**).

**Figure 2.32**

Using the keyword *snow* in a Feedster search brings up a list of articles.

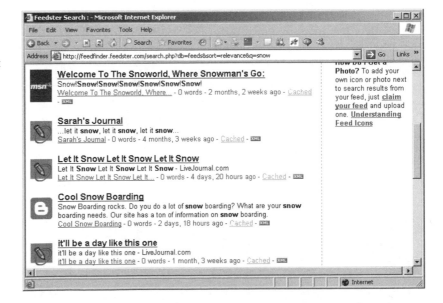

# Importing and Exporting RSS Feeds

Upgrading to a new RSS reader? There's an easy way to group the feeds you've subscribed to, export them to a single file, and use that file to subscribe to all the feeds at once.

RSS readers most often let you export your current list of feeds to a file written in OPML (Outline Processor Markup Language) format. For example, all you have to do in the SharpReader RSS reader is select File > Export Subscriptions to save and name your current list of RSS feeds in an OPML file.

In your new RSS reader, you just open that OPML file—in SharpReader, for example, you select File > Import Subscriptions, and your previous subscriptions are added to your new RSS reader. Very convenient.

# 3

# Creating RSS Feeds

This chapter is all about creating your own RSS feeds by using RSS creation applications. With RSS creators like NewzAlert Composer, for example, all you have to do is enter the data for your new feed and you're set. When you're finished creating your feed, you can also publish it automatically, again with an RSS creator. And once you've published your new feed, you can read it in any RSS reader. In the next chapter, you'll see how to create your own feeds from scratch.

# Picking an RSS Format

Congratulations, you've decided to publish your own RSS feed! The first step is to decide which version of RSS you will use. You'll learn more about the inner workings of RSS and its various versions in the next chapter, but this overview of versions will help you start the RSS publishing process on the right foot.

There are three main versions of RSS as of this writing: 0.91, 1.0, and 2.0. According to www.syndic8.com—the huge RSS site that keeps all kinds of statistics on RSS and the many feeds out there—this is the percentage breakdown of RSS usage worldwide by version:

- RSS 0.91: 13 percent

- RSS 1.0: 17 percent

- RSS 2.0: 67 percent

- Less popular RSS versions: 3 percent

Besides RSS, there's Atom to consider, although it's currently less in use than RSS. How do you decide which version to work with? The next section examines the differences between these versions to help you choose.

## RSS 0.91

RSS 0.91 is the simplest version. It's the easiest to work with, but it's also the most limited. Officially, it's been replaced by version 2.0, but it's still in widespread usage. It's easy to upgrade RSS 0.91 to version 2.0, and generally speaking, all RSS readers should be able to read version 0.91 (although that might not be true in the future).

This version has some restrictions; for example, you're limited to 15 news items per feed.

## RSS 1.0

This version of RSS, which differs significantly from versions 0.91 and 2.0, is a bit of an offshoot: Based on the Resource Description Framework (RDF) language (which you can find out more about at www.w3.org/RDF), it's useful if you want to connect to RDF-based software. But in many ways, RSS 1.0 represents a branch of the main RSS tree.

## RSS 2.0

The most common RSS version by far, RSS 2.0 may be your best choice as of this writing, if you want the most widespread audience. This version is an extension of version 0.92 (which was the successor to version 0.91). Versions 0.92 and 2.0 add power—notably, the ability to use *enclosures*, which is what makes podcasting possible. As you can see from the www.syndic8.com data above, RSS 2.0 is more widely used than versions 0.92 and 1.0 combined.

 **You'll see more on the new features of RSS 2.0 in Chapter 4, "Creating RSS Feeds from Scratch."**

## Atom

One of the attractions of Atom is that it makes it easy to work with the data stored in the feed. The content of your feed is also easily filtered and organized.

# Understanding an RSS Document

Let's begin by taking a look at an RSS 2.0 document. To create your own RSS document, you need to know the names of the various parts of such a document.

Start composing your RSS document by opening an RSS creator program such as NewzAlert Composer and giving your RSS feed a name—"Steve's News" in the example shown here (**Figure 3.1**). This is the RSS feed name that appears in the RSS reader (**Figure 3.2**).

**Figure 3.1**

NewzAlert Composer provides property information about your feed.

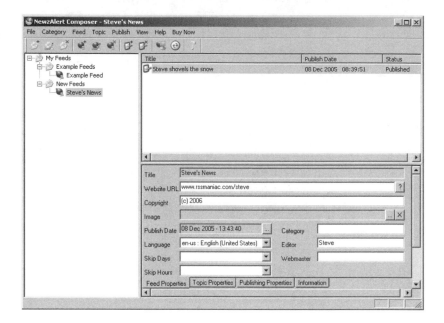

**Figure 3.2**

Here's the NewzAlert feed displayed in RSSReader.

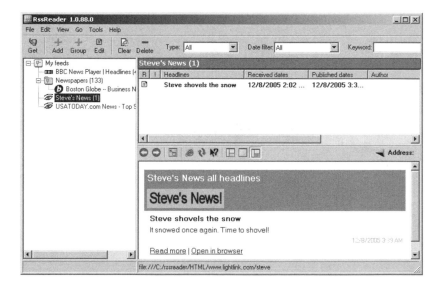

The name of the actual RSS document is news.xml, and like all XML documents, this one starts with an XML declaration:

```
<?xml version="1.0" encoding="ISO-8859-1"?>
        .
        .
        .
```

The next line of code in the RSS document is called the *document element* because it contains all other elements in the document. Thus, it is here that the document specifies that its version is RSS 2.0.

```
<?xml version="1.0" encoding="ISO-8859-1"?>
<rss version="2.0">
      .
      .
      .
</rss>
```

As you can see, the <rss> element looks much like the HTML elements you're already familiar with. (For more about how XML elements work, see Chapter 4.)

Inside the <rss> element is a <channel> element. A channel element, referred to as the *channel* in an RSS document, provides details about the feed you're creating.

```
<?xml version="1.0" encoding="ISO-8859-1"?>
<rss version="2.0">
  <channel>
       .
       .
       .
  </channel>
</rss>
```

You'll see many different elements inside an RSS <channel> element. When you're creating your own RSS feeds using a tool like NewzAlert Composer, these are the elements you need to know about:

- The <title> element contains the title of the feed. This is the name that will appear in the feeds window.

- The <link> element contains a link for your feed. Usually this is a link to your home page for anyone reading your feed who wants more information.

- The <description> element explains what your feed is all about.

- The <language> element indicates the language the feed is in. For example, *en-us* means U.S. English (see Chapter 4).

- The <image> element holds the URL of an image for your feed (see Figure 3.2).

- The <copyright> element provides copyright information, if you want to add it.

- The <managingEditor> element holds the name and/or email of the person responsible for the feed.

Here's what these elements for our news.xml code look like as stored by NewzAlert Composer:

```xml
<?xml version="1.0" encoding="ISO-8859-1"?>
<rss version="2.0">
 <channel>
  <generator>NewzAlert Composer v1.70.6, Copyright (c) 2004-2005
   Castle Software Ltd, http://www.NewzAlert.com</generator>
  <lastBuildDate>Thu, 08 Dec 2005 14:01:27 -0500</lastBuildDate>
  <pubDate>Thu, 08 Dec 2005 14:01:34 -0500</pubDate>
  <title>Steve's News</title>
  <description><![CDATA[This feed contains news from
   Steve!]]></description>
  <link>http://www.rssmaniac.com/steve</link>
  <language>en-us</language>
  <copyright>(c) 2006</copyright>
  <managingEditor>Steve</managingEditor>
  <image>
   <title>Steve's News</title>
   <url>http://www.rssmaniac.com/steve/Image.jpg</url>
   <link>http://www.rssmaniac.com/steve</link>
   <description>Steve's News</description>
   <width>144</width>
   <height>36</height>
```

```
    </image>
        .
        .
        .
    </channel>
</rss>
```

 **NewzAlert Composer uses the XML `<!CDATA ]]>` element to store text data. Elements tell the software, such as RSS readers, that is checking your RSS documents not to check their content. In other words, the content of `<!CDATA ]]>` elements is considered simple text data. Although many RSS creator programs surround text with `<!CDATA and ]]>`, you can safely omit this markup when writing your own RSS document, because RSS readers are smart enough not to need it.**

Each of the items in the feed is stored in an `<item>` element. An `<item>` element contains these elements:

- The `<title>` element is the text that will appear in the titles window of an RSS reader.

- The `<description>` element will appear in an RSS reader's description window when the user clicks the item's title in the title window.

- The `<pubDate>` element holds the date the item was published.

- The `<link>` element holds the URL to get more information about the item.

Here's what these elements look like in the single `<item>` element:

```
<?xml version="1.0" encoding="ISO-8859-1"?>
<rss version="2.0">
 <channel>
  <generator>NewzAlert Composer v1.70.6, Copyright (c) 2004-2005
   Castle Software Ltd, http://www.NewzAlert.com</generator>
  <lastBuildDate>Thu, 08 Dec 2005 14:01:27 -0500</lastBuildDate>
  <pubDate>Thu, 08 Dec 2005 14:01:34 -0500</pubDate>
  <title>Steve's News</title>
  <description><![CDATA[This feed contains news from
```

*(code continues on next page)*

```
   Steve!]]></description>
   <link>http://www.rssmaniac.com/steve</link>
   <language>en-us</language>
   <copyright>(c) 2006</copyright>
   <managingEditor>Steve</managingEditor>
   <image>
    <title>Steve's News</title>
    <url>http://www.rssmaniac.com/steve/Image.jpg</url>
    <link>http://www.rssmaniac.com/steve</link>
    <description>Steve's News</description>
    <width>144</width>
    <height>36</height>
   </image>
     <item>
      <title>Steve shovels the snow</title>
      <description><![CDATA[It snowed once again.
      Time to shovel!]]></description>
      <pubDate>Thu, 08 Dec 2005 08:39:51 -0500</pubDate>
      <link>http://www.rssmaniac.com/steve</link>
     </item>
   </channel>
  </rss>
```

Now that you have an overview of how an RSS 2.0 document works, it's time to start creating an RSS feed.

# Creating RSS Feeds Online

There are many online tools you can use to create RSS feeds; this section examines some of the more popular ones. They all have the advantage of being free, and that's hard to beat!

## UKOLN

One of the most venerable tools for creating feeds is UK's Office for Library Networking, usually called UKOLN RSS-xpress (**Figure 3.3**). This RSS channel editor, which you can find at http://rssxpress.ukoln.ac.uk, creates RSS 1.0 feeds.

**Figure 3.3**

Use UKOLN's RSS-xpress channel editor to create, modify, and register your RSS feeds.

To create a new RSS feed, just click the New button to open the new page (**Figure 3.4**).

**Figure 3.4**

Entering channel information in the RSS-xpress channel editor is just a matter of filling in the blanks.

Here's what to enter in the blanks provided in UKOLN's RSS-xpress editor (see Figure 3.4):

- **Channel Title:** The name of your channel, which will appear in the titles window an RSS reader.

- **Channel Link:** A URL for people to get more information on your channel—for example, your home page.

- **Description:** A description of your RSS feed, as you want it to appear in the Feed Properties window in an RSS reader.

- **Copyright:** The copyright date you want to add to your feed.

- **Webmaster:** The name and/or email address of the person who maintains the feed.

- **Language:** The language of your RSS feed.

- **Image Title:** Text that will be displayed if the image for your channel can't be displayed.

- **Image URL:** The image file URL, where the RSS reader goes to fetch the image.

- **Image Link:** A URL you want users to navigate to if they click the image for your channel.

 **When you enter a URL in an RSS editor or document, include *http://* as part of the URL to create valid RSS. If you don't include this information, the RSS reader might not be able to follow your links.**

After you've set up your new channel's information, scroll down to the section labeled Item 1 in RSS-xpress (**Figure 3.5**).

You can enter text for the various items in your feed. When you're using RSS 1.0, as in this case, you're only allowed 15 items. Here's what to enter for each item:

- **Title:** The title of the current item you want to appear in the titles window in an RSS reader.

- **Link:** The URL that the RSS reader should open if the user requests more information on the item.

**Figure 3.5**

Fill out the title, link, and description for each item after you set up your new channel.

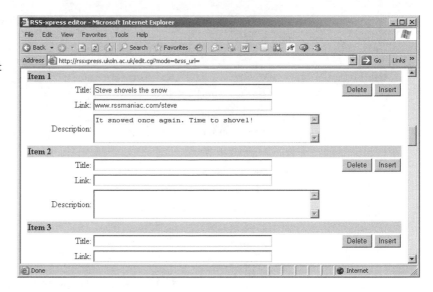

- Description: The text for the item that you want to appear in an RSS reader's description window when the user clicks the item's title in the titles window.

You can keep adding more items, up to 15, as you please. Then go back to the top of the page and click the Save button. The browser opens a dialog box where you download and save the XML document, which is stored as an RSS file named rss.xml.

This document is based on RSS version 1.0 and is derived from the XML RDF language (for more on RSS version 1.0, see Chapter 4). Here's what the document looks like:

```
<?xml version="1.0" encoding="UTF-8"?>

<rdf:RDF
 xmlns:rdf="http://www.w3.org/1999/02/22-rdf-syntax-ns#"
 xmlns="http://purl.org/rss/1.0/"
 xmlns:dc="http://purl.org/dc/elements/1.1/"
 xmlns:syn="http://purl.org/rss/1.0/modules/syndication/"
 xmlns:admin="http://webns.net/mvcb/"
```

*(code continues on next page)*

```
  xmlns:taxo="http://purl.org/rss/1.0/modules/taxonomy/"
>

<channel rdf:about="www.rssmaniac.com">
<title>Steve's News</title>
<link>http://www.rssmaniac.com</link>
<description>This feed contains news from Steve!&#13;
</description>
<dc:language>en-us</dc:language>
<dc:rights>(c) 2006</dc:rights>
<dc:date>2005-12-08</dc:date>
<dc:creator>Steve</dc:creator>
<items>
 <rdf:Seq>
  <rdf:li rdf:resource="www.rssmaniac.com/steve" />
  <rdf:li rdf:resource="" />
  <rdf:li rdf:resource="" />
  <rdf:li rdf:resource="" />
  <rdf:li rdf:resource="" />
  <rdf:li rdf:resource="" />
  <rdf:li rdf:resource="" />
  <rdf:li rdf:resource="" />
  <rdf:li rdf:resource="" />
  <rdf:li rdf:resource="" />
  <rdf:li rdf:resource="" />
  <rdf:li rdf:resource="" />
  <rdf:li rdf:resource="" />
  <rdf:li rdf:resource="" />
  <rdf:li rdf:resource="" />
 </rdf:Seq>
</items>
<image rdf:resource="http://www.rssmaniac.com/steve/Image.jpg" />
</channel>

<image rdf:about="http://www.rssmaniac.com/steve/Image.jpg">
<title>Steve's News</title>
<url>http://www.rssmaniac.com/steve/Image.jpg</url>
```

```
<link>http://www.rssmaniac.com</link>
</image>

<item rdf:about="www.rssmaniac.com/steve">
<title>Steve shovels the snow</title>
<link>www.rssmaniac.com/steve</link>
<description>It snowed once again. Time to shovel!&#13;
</description>
</item>

</rdf:RDF>
```

Now that you've seen how to create feeds based on RSS 2.0 and 1.0, how about some RSS 0.91, the simplest of the three versions? Coming up next, we look at more online RSS editors.

# WebReference

WebReference (www.webreference.com/cgi-bin/perl/rssedit.pl) is an online RSS editor that you can use to create RSS 0.91 documents. You already know what these elements mean, so all you have to do to set up your new feed is fill in the blanks on the Channel Summary page (**Figure 3.6**).

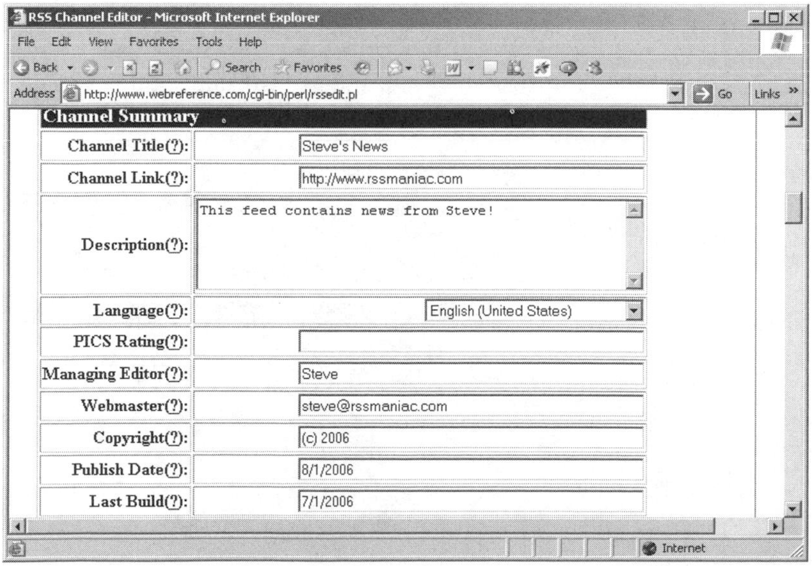

**Figure 3.6**

Use WebReference to create RSS 0.91 feeds.

**tip**

What's the PICS Rating element in WebReference (see Figure 3.6)? The idea of PICS ratings is to restrict access to content by minors. In practice, however, this rating isn't used very often. PICS, or Platform for Internet Content Selection, filtering is supported by the World Wide Web Consortium (www.w3.org), the folks who brought you HTML and XML in the first place.

In WebReference's Channel Image section, you can also add an image to your RSS feed (**Figure 3.7**). You fill in the usual suspects: the image's title, URL, link, width and height, and description.

**Figure 3.7**

It's easy to add an image to your RSS feed in WebReference.

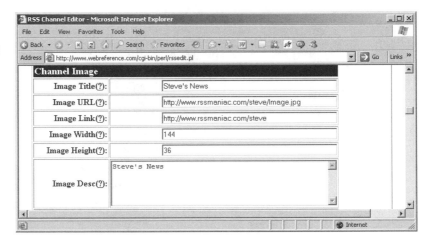

WebReference has space for up to 15 news items, so you scroll down the items page and add the news items you want in your feed (**Figure 3.8**).

**Figure 3.8**

After you've added the information for your news item, click the Build RSS button.

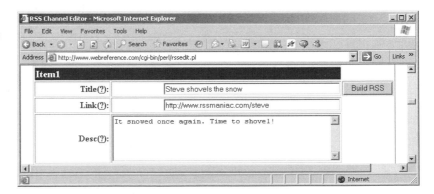

When you're finished with each item, click the Build RSS button next to your final news item, and WebReference will build your RSS 0.91 file—and display it in the browser (**Figure 3.9**).

**Figure 3.9**
Here's the RSS 0.91 created by WebReference for the news item.

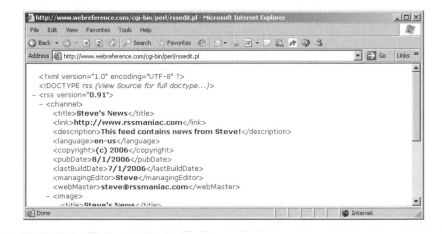

You can copy the XML displayed in the browser and paste it into your new XML file.

If you're using Microsoft Internet Explorer, be careful. Internet Explorer displays plus (+) and minus (–) signs next to XML elements that contain other XML elements. Make sure you edit those plus and minus signs out of your XML before saving the file. When you collapse and expand XML elements in Internet Explorer, all its child elements disappear, so be careful.

Here's the RSS 0.91 file generated by WebReference (see Figure 3.9):

```
<?xml version="1.0" encoding="UTF-8" ?>
<!DOCTYPE rss (View Source for full doctype...)>
<rss version="0.91">
<channel>
  <title>Steve's News</title>
  <link>http://www.rssmaniac.com</link>
  <description>This feed contains news from Steve!</description>
  <language>en-us</language>
  <copyright>(c) 2006</copyright>
  <pubDate>8/1/2006</pubDate>
```

*(code continues on next page)*

```
<lastBuildDate>7/1/2006</lastBuildDate>
<managingEditor>Steve</managingEditor>
<webMaster>steve@rssmaniac.com</webMaster>
<image>
<title>Steve's News</title>
<url>http://www.rssmaniac.com/steve/Image.jpg</url>
<link>http://www.rssmaniac.com/steve</link>
<description>Steve's News</description>
</image>
<item>
<title>Steve shovels the snow</title>
<link>http://www.rssmaniac.com/steve</link>
<description>It snowed once again. Time to shovel!</description>
</item>
</channel>
</rss>
```

# RSS Headliner

Another RSS 0.91 online RSS generator is RSS Headliner from WebDevTips (www.webdevtips.com/webdevtips/codegen/rss.shtml). So far, you've seen two methods of generating an RSS feed in XML—as a downloaded XML file and as raw XML displayed in the browser. RSS Headliner uses a third way: It displays the generated XML in an HTML text area control (which is like a multiline HTML text field control), and then you can simply copy it.

First, you have to indicate how many items you want in your feed (for some reason, RSS Headliner restricts you to 10), using the drop-down select control (**Figure 3.10**). When you select a number from 1 to 10, the controls you see in the figure appear (that is, the text fields, text areas, and drop-down list control).

All you do next is enter your data, select the Make the Code button and your RSS (version 0.91) will appear in a text area control (**Figure 3.11**). Then, just select the generated code, and copy and paste it into a new document to save your new RSS feed.

**Figure 3.10**

RSS Headliner restricts you to 10 items.

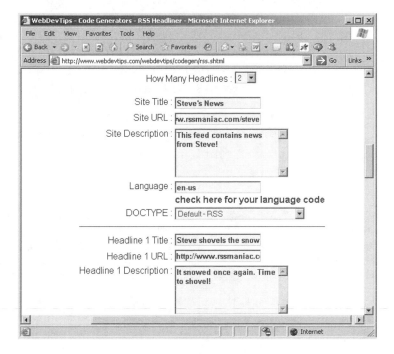

**Figure 3.11**

Copy and paste the code to a new document to save your RSS feed.

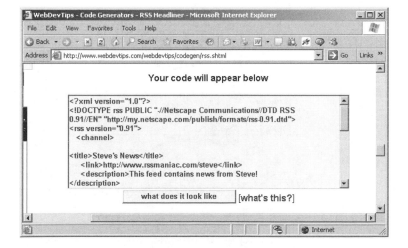

# IceRocket

The online RSS editors you've seen so far create XML for you, and it's up to you to host that XML on your Web site. IceRocket is different: It lets you host your RSS 2.0 feed on its Web site (http://rss.icerocket.com).

To register to use the IceRocket site, click the Register link in the toolbar, then provide your email address and a password. After registering, click the Sign In button in the toolbar on the main page (**Figure 3.12**).

**Figure 3.12**

There are three clearly defined steps in IceRocket to create a channel.

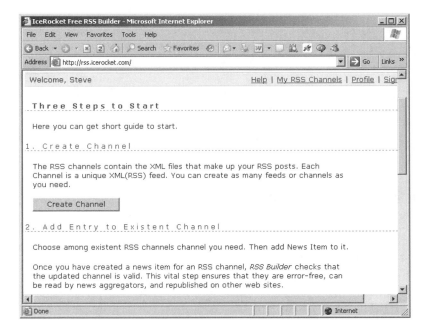

To create a new feed that will be hosted on the IceRocket site, click the Create Channel button to access the Edit Channel Configuration page (**Figure 3.13**).

You enter the information for your new channel, or feed, which is automatically hosted on the IceRocket site. After you save the data for your new channel (feed), you'll see a page that keeps track of the feeds you've created (**Figure 3.14**).

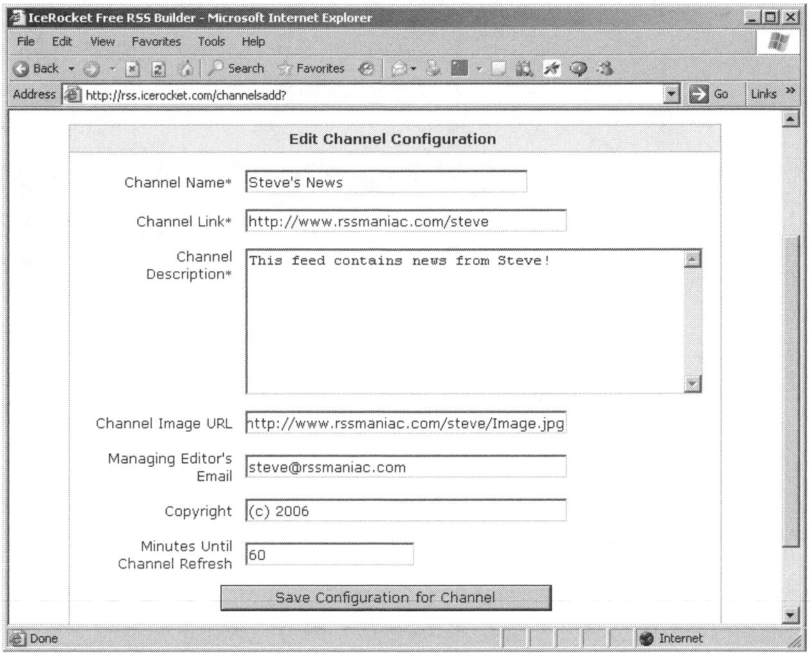

**Figure 3.13**

After you create your new channel, IceRocket hosts your feed.

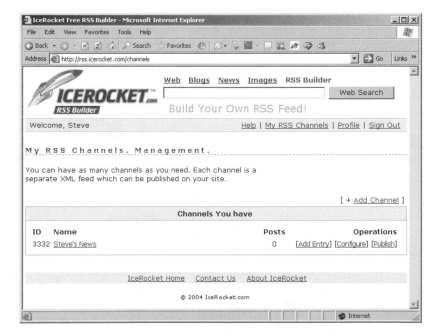

**Figure 3.14**

You can have as many channels as you need in IceRocket.

It's easy to add a news item—usually called an entry in IceRocket to your new feed. Click the Add Entry link to open a new page where you can create a new item for your feed (**Figure 3.15**).

**Figure 3.15**

IceRocket makes it easy to create a new item.

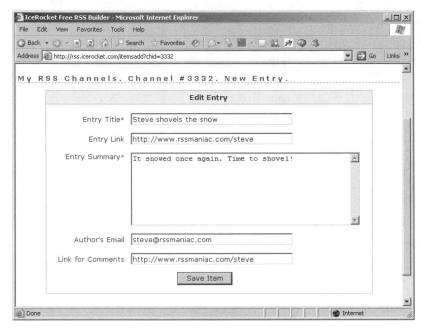

You add the item's title, link, and description (called a summary in IceRocket) using the Edit Entry page. You can also add the author's email address and a link for comments.

After you save your channel, IceRocket displays the new item in your feed (**Figure 3.16**).

How do you actually publish your new RSS feed so that it's accessible? Just click the Publish link (see Figure 3.16) to publish your new RSS feed and display the page (**Figure 3.17**).

**Figure 3.16**

The new item has been added to your RSS feed.

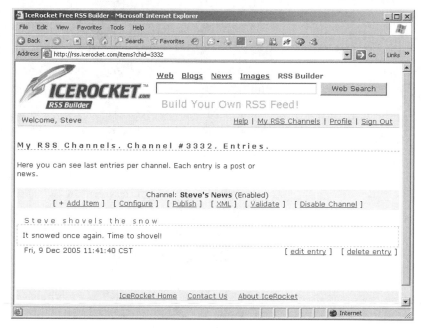

**Figure 3.17**

IceRocket provides customized HTML code to use on your Web page to publicize your feed.

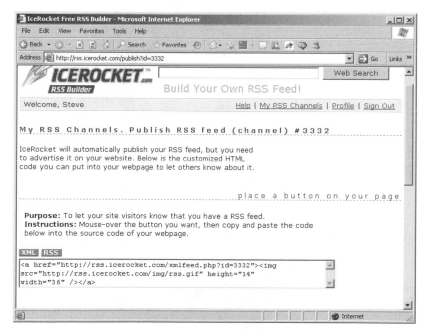

IceRocket hosts your RSS feed, but asks you to paste an XML or RSS button into your home page, to indicate that you have an RSS feed. IceRocket provides the actual HTML code to paste into your home page. Here's what the HTML that will display an RSS button on your home page looks like:

```
<a href="http://rss.icerocket.com/xmlfeed.php?id=3332"><img
src="http://rss.icerocket.com/img/rss.gif" height="14" width="36"
/></a>
```

Note the URL of your new RSS feed: http://rss.icerocket.com/xmlfeed.php?id=3332. If someone wants to read your RSS, all they have to do is subscribe to that URL. The following is the actual XML generated by IceRocket for our sample feed.

```
<?xml version="1.0" encoding="UTF 8" ?>
  <rss version="2.0">
  <channel>
  <title>
  <![CDATA[ Steve's News
  ]]>
  </title>
  <link>
  <![CDATA[ http://www.rssmaniac.com/steve
  ]]>
  </link>
  <description>
  <![CDATA[ This feed contains news from Steve!

  ]]>
  </description>
  <ttl>
  <![CDATA[ 60
  ]]>
  </ttl>
  <language>en us</language>
  <copyright>
  <![CDATA[ (c) 2006
  ]]>
```

```
</copyright>
<managingEditor>
<![CDATA[ steve@rssmaniac.com
]]>
</managingEditor>
<generator>IceRocket RSS Builder 1.0</generator>
<item>
<title>
<![CDATA[ Steve shovels the snow
]]>
</title>
<link>
<![CDATA[ http://www.rssmaniac.com/steve
]]>
</link>
<description>
<![CDATA[ It snowed once again. Time to shovel!

]]>
</description>
<author>
<![CDATA[ steve@rssmaniac.com
]]>
</author>
<comments>
<![CDATA[ http://www.rssmaniac.com/steve
]]>
</comments>
<pubDate>
<![CDATA[ Fri, 9 Dec 2005 11:41:40 CST
]]>
</pubDate>
</item>
</channel>
</rss>
```

## Shared RSS

You can host your own feeds using Shared RSS (www.sharedrss.com). It's available for free for people who infrequently add new material or for a fee for people who want their feed on their own Web site. It also has various RSS editors that let you create your own RSS 2.0 files.

## My RSS Creator

My RSS Creator is an online RSS 2.0 creator that lets you host your RSS feeds on its site (www.myrsscreator.com). After the 14-day free trial, the fee is $19.95 per month.

This is the only online service I know that supports enclosures, which means you can do podcasting from this site (for more on podcasting, see Chapter 7, "Podcasting: Adding Multimedia to Your Feeds").

## Internet search

An easy way to create your own RSS feed is from the results of a keyword search on the Web. This is a cool technique, because your feed can be based on the most current information from your search of news and blogs. You can convert the results into an RSS feed and make your own custom feed based on many sources.

You can even list these RSS feeds on your home Web site and allow others to subscribe to them as well. In this way, it's easy to create customized RSS feeds crammed full of information that people may otherwise not see.

Here's a list of sites that let you create your own custom RSS feeds, based on keyword searches:

- www.blogdigger.com
- www.daypop.com
- www.feedster.com
- www.findarticles.com

- www.googlealert.com

- www.justinpfister.com

- www.moreover.com

- www.newsgator.com

- www.newsisfree.com

For example, take a look at Blogdigger, a search engine for online blogs. Say, for example, you start a search of the blogs that Blogdigger tracks using the keyword *snow* (**Figure 3.18**).

**Figure 3.18**

You can sort your search by date or relevance at Blogdigger.

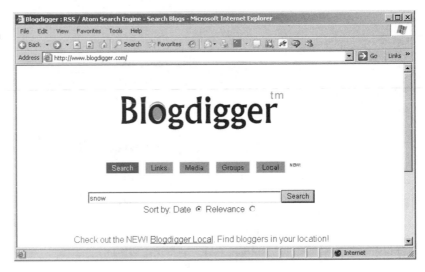

As a result of that keyword search, Blogdigger displays a number of relevant blog entries. Note in particular the Subscribe to This Search section in the results page on the right (**Figure 3.19**). You can use the XML and Atom buttons to subscribe to this search as you can any RSS feed.

If you can narrow down what you're searching for with a few well-chosen keywords, Blogdigger lets you watch what's going on in the many blogs with those keywords, all from the convenience of your RSS reader.

**Figure 3.19**
Blogdigger found
89,928 blogs for the
keyword *snow*.

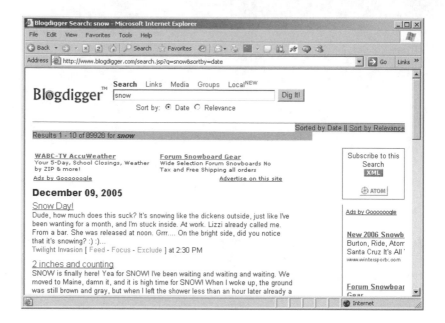

**Figure 3.19**
Blogdigger found
89,928 blogs for the
keyword *snow*.

# Creating RSS on Your Computer

There are plenty of RSS creator applications online, but there are also many that work on your computer. If you're serious about publishing your own feeds, you should consider an RSS creator for the desktop (or laptop). Some of these let you not only create your own feed but also upload it to your Web site with a click.

The tucows.com software-repository site lists many desktop RSS creator applications, some free and some not. Here's a sampling of some of the most popular ones:

- **RSS Publisher**  www.tucows.com/preview/406993

- **RSS Wizard**  www.tucows.com/preview/414998

- **Super Simple RSS**  www.tucows.com/preview/336311

- **AggPub**  www.tucows.com/preview/406651

- **Feed Editor**  www.tucows.com/preview/410070

- **NewzAlert Composer**  www.tucows.com/preview/367467

# NewzAlert Composer

NewzAlert Composer is a powerful RSS creator application that costs $19.95 (as of this writing), but before you buy, check out the 15-day free trial version (www.castlesoftware.biz/NewzAlertComposer.htm). You can create feeds with enclosures (which means you can do podcasting), and upload your RSS files to your Web site with just a click. Choosing File > New Feed Wizard opens the New Feed Wizard where you create a new feed. First you enter the name of the new feed (**Figure 3.20**).

**Figure 3.20**

NewzAlert Composer uses a wizard to help you create an RSS feed.

You then select a feed category to store the new feed. In this example, I selected the New Feeds category (**Figure 3.21**).

**Figure 3.21**

Your new feed is saved in the Feed Category you select.

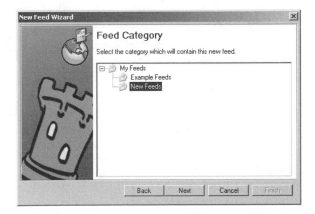

Use the Feed Details dialog to specify more details about the feed, such as its Web site URL and description (**Figure 3.22**).

**Figure 3.22**

NewzAlert Composer lets you choose the language for your RSS feed in addition to its Web site URL and description.

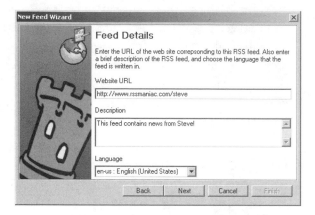

You also use the Feed Details dialog to enter the feed's managing editor and copyright (**Figure 3.23**).

**Figure 3.23**

You enter the managing editor and copyright date in NewzAlert Composer's Feed Details dialog.

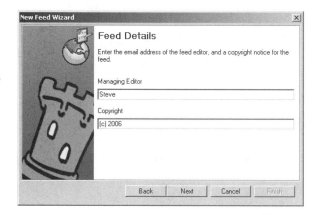

Enter the title, link, and description of your new item in the First Topic dialog (**Figure 3.24**). NewzAlert Composer calls a feed a *topic*.

**Figure 3.24**

The New Feed wizard asks you for the title, link, and description of your RSS feed.

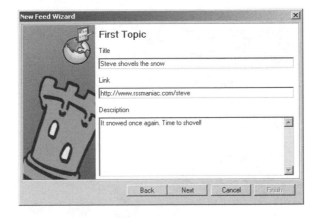

The next dialog asks for publishing information. For example, if you want to upload your RSS feed to a Web site using the File Transfer Protocol (FTP), you enter the FTP server information along with your user name and password (**Figure 3.25**; more on uploading RSS files at the end of this chapter).

**Figure 3.25**

You can publish your feed from an FTP site or use the NewzAlert Composer server.

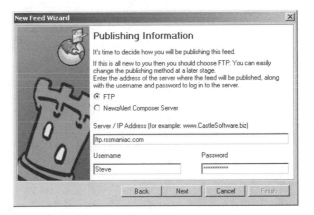

You can store your RSS file in a particular directory on the server, and name the file that will be created (**Figure 3.26**). After you enter this data, if any, click the Finish button to create your new RSS feed.

**Figure 3.26**
When you publish from an FTP server, enter the path and file where the RSS will be published.

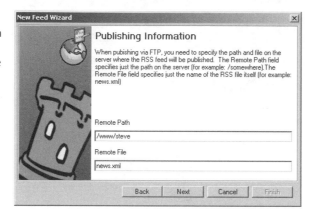

Your new RSS feed and the new item are ready to go (**Figure 3.27**). You can now publish your new RSS feed to your Web site just by selecting a menu item or by clicking a button.

**Figure 3.27**
NewzAlert provides property information on the new feed.

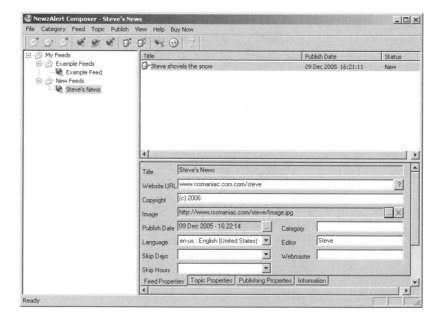

To publish your RSS file—which means uploading the feed's RSS file to the directory you've specified on your Web site—just choose Publish > Publish Feed. Alternatively, you can click the Publish button in the toolbar to have your new RSS file uploaded to your Web site automatically. No problem at all.

To create a new item in your feed, simply use the Add Topic button (also in the toolbar) to create a new topic.

As you can see, NewzAlert Composer is a very convenient way of creating your own RSS feed.

# FeedForAll

FeedForAll is a powerful RSS editor that you can download (www.feed-forall.com). It's packed with features and costs $39.95 as of this writing, but you can check out a 30-day free trial version first.

After you start FeedForAll, you'll get a dialog box asking if you want to use the Feed Creation wizard to create a new feed. Click Yes, then click the Next button in the Introduction dialog that appears.

You are then asked for the title of your new feed; enter the title and click Next (**Figure 3.28**).

**Figure 3.28**
FeedForAll also uses a wizard to help you get started.

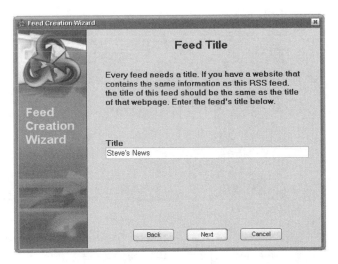

Then enter the new feed's description and click Next (**Figure 3.29**).

**Figure 3.29**
The Feed Creation wizard describes the information you need to enter for your feed.

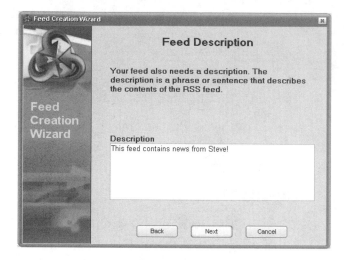

After you enter your new feed's link, the wizard explains that each new feed should have at least one item; click Next and then enter the new item's title (**Figure 3.30**).

**Figure 3.30**
FeedForAll's wizard is easy to use and provides all the information you need to complete each page.

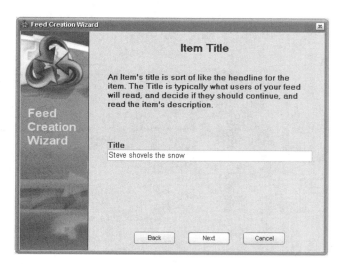

The next two dialogs ask for the new item's description and link, and are followed by a Finalize page and the Finish button. The FeedForAll wizard asks you to save your feed in an XML file.

The new feed then opens in the FeedForAll editor (**Figure 3.31**). As with other RSS editors, you can edit and update your feed using the editor.

**Figure 3.31**

Edit and update your feed using FeedForAll's editor.

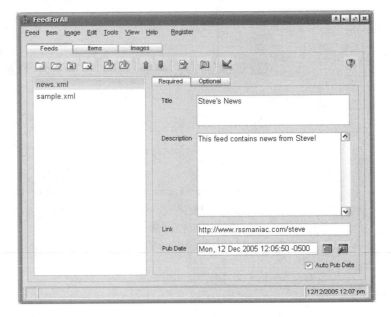

What about uploading your new feed? As with NewzAlert Composer, you can upload without leaving the program. In FeedForAll, just choose Feed > Upload to open the FTP Upload dialog (**Figure 3.32**). To upload your new feed, fill out the fields in this dialog and click the Upload button.

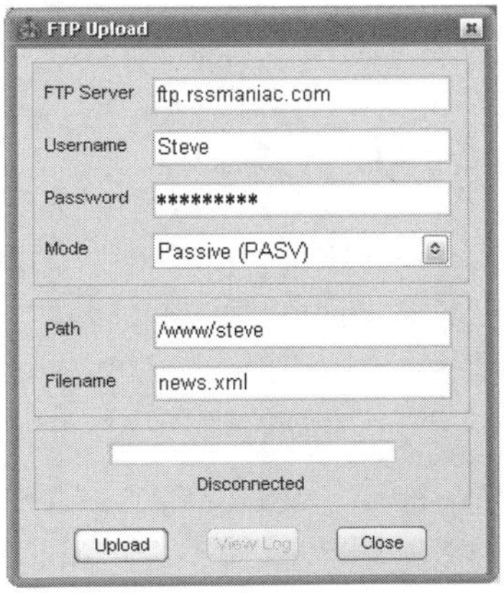

**Figure 3.32**

After you've provided all the information for your new feed, click the Upload button.

FeedForAll comes with some nice features, such as automatic publication dates and default field values, that make it easy to keep your feeds up-to-date. Is it worth the price? That depends on what you're looking for; use FeedForAll's 30-day free trial and decide for yourself.

# Uploading Your RSS Feed

Now that you've created your new feed, you can make it available to the rest of the world. Start by uploading your RSS feed's XML file to a Web server.

 **Some sites specialize in hosting RSS feeds and give you online tools to create those feeds. For example, Global Syndication (www.globalsyndi-cation.com/rss-hosting) offers a service that starts at $3.95 per month or $39.95 per year as of this writing. There are other sites that even let you host for free, such as IceRocket.**

There are as many ways to upload XML files as there are to upload HTML files to Web servers. The two most common ways of uploading files are using FTP and HTML interfaces.

 **When you upload XML files to a Web server, you may have to set a *protection level* so that the files can be accessed but not modified by others. For example, if your Web server is Unix-based, you could set the protection level to 644, which lets you read and write the file, and allows others only to read them. To determine if you need to set the protection level of your RSS files, check with your Web server's technical team.**

## Using an FTP interface

You may already have an FTP application, and if not, it's easy to find one. Take a look at the software-distribution site www.tucows.com, for example, which lists more than 100 FTP programs (just search for *FTP*). Most of these applications are shareware or freeware.

FTP applications have been getting easier and easier to use. One of the most popular programs is CuteFTP. To upload files using CuteFTP, just drag the file from the window on the left, which shows files on your computer, to the window on the right, which shows files on your Web server (**Figure 3.33**).

**Figure 3.33**

CuteFTP is an easy-to-use file transfer application.

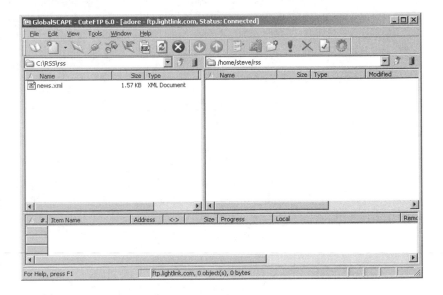

When you upload an RSS XML file, store it in the appropriate directory on your Web server, just as you would an HTML file. Your XML file must be accessible using a URL for users to read it, just as they would need a URL to read an HTML file.

Besides using a dedicated FTP application to upload RSS files, you can let your RSS editor do this for you. After all, you created your RSS feeds in your RSS editor—what could be more convenient than letting it upload and install your feed on the server? That's particularly useful when you want to use previous items as a template, and make the modifications you need to create new items from the old ones.

Most people who frequently edit and change their RSS feeds use a dedicated desktop or laptop RSS editor that lets them not only create new items, but also look at and modify old ones. And to upload, it's just a click of a button.

As you've seen, both NewzAlert Composer and FeedForAll RSS let you create, edit, and upload feeds easily. But desktop RSS editors usually cost somewhere in the $20 to $40 range.

There's only one RSS editor that will upload your RSS feeds and is free: RSS Publisher from Extra Laboratories, which you can find at www.extralabs.net/products.htm. If you're interested, better snap it up quick, because it looks like the company might be phasing it out— Extra Laboratories now has a similar for-pay product, and RSS Publisher is no longer listed on its Web site's home page.

## Using an HTML interface

Another way to upload RSS XML files is to use an HTML interface. These are Web pages that you navigate to and let you upload files.

There are no generic HTML uploaders—they're all ISP-specific. Your ISP must have one set up before you can use it. HTML uploaders are set up by ISPs to let their users upload HTML files easily, but they can also upload XML files for you.

# Adding the XML Button

OK, so you've uploaded your RSS file onto your Web server. How do you let your eager public subscribe to your new feed? Answer: Display an RSS, XML, or Atom button on your Web page. You can download those buttons from the Internet (**Figure 3.34**). You can even capture RSS buttons from other RSS feeds; just make sure you have permission first.

You can also find RSS buttons using an image search on Google. Just click the Image link above the search box instead of selecting the default Web link.

**Figure 3.34**
You can download XML, RSS, or Atom buttons from the Internet.

**Want to create your own XML/RSS button? Take a look at www. feedforall.com/public/rss-graphic-tool.htm.**

How do you actually display an XML button and make it active in a Web page? First, put together the Web page in which you want to display your XML button, something like this:

```
<html>
  <head>
    <title>Subscribe to my feed</title>
  </head>

  <body>
    <h1>Subscribe to my feed</h1>
    Want to hear more of Steve's news? Subscribe to my feed!
    <br>
        .
        .
        .
  </body>
</html>
```

Then add the XML button. It's set up as a hyperlink to your XML file like this:

```
<html>
  <head>
    <title>Subscribe to my feed</title>
  </head>

  <body>
    <h1>Subscribe to my feed</h1>
    Want to hear more of Steve's news? Subscribe to my feed!
    <br>
    <a href="http://www.rssmaniac.com/steve/news.xml">
        .
        .
        .
    </a>
  </body>
</html>
```

Next, add the image for the RSS button. Assuming the name of the RSS button's image file is rss.jpg and it's in the same directory as the Web page where you want to display that button, the code might look like the following (the `border="0"` below removes the hyperlink border that would appear around the button—XML buttons don't usually show that border).

If your button's image is in another directory, make sure you add the right path to the image file's name—you can even use a URL that points to the image file on another server.

```
<html>
  <head>
    <title>Subscribe to my feed</title>
  </head>

  <body>
    <h1>Subscribe to my feed</h1>
    Want to hear more of Steve's news? Subscribe to my feed!
    <br>
    <a href="http://www.rssmaniac.com/steve/news.xml">
      <img src="rss.jpg" border="0">
    </a>
  </body>
</html>
```

This code gives you the Web page in which the XML button appears (see Figure 3.34). Very nice—now you've made your feed publicly available.

There's another way to add your RSS feed to a Web page. You can use the *autodetect* method, and browsers (like Firefox) or RSS readers that support this feature display an icon in the status bar (or use another technique) that allow users to automatically subscribe to your feed.

To set up autodetect, add a `<link>` element to a Web page's `<head>` section. For example, here's how you can set up autodetect to a news feed at http://rssmaniac.com/steve/news.xml using a `<link>` element:

```
<html>
  <head>
```

```
    <title>Subscribe to my feed</title>
    <link rel="alternate" type="application/rss+xml" title="RSS 2.0"
      href="http://rssmaniac.com/steve/news.xml" />
  </head>

  <body>
    <h1>Subscribe to my feed</h1>
    Want to hear more of Steve's news? Subscribe to my feed!
    <br>
    <a href="http://www.rssmaniac.com/steve/news.xml">
      <img src="rss.jpg" border="0">
    </a>
  </body>
</html>
```

# Validating Your RSS Feed

Is your RSS feed actually correct RSS? As you'll see in the next chapter, there are rules for writing correct RSS, and even using RSS tools to create your feed is no guarantee that your RSS will obey the rules. For example, the URLs you enter in an RSS document should be a full URL starting with *http://* (such as http://www.rssmaniac.com/steve/news.xml, not www.rssmaniac.com/steve/news.xml), and your RSS editor might not tell you that.

If your RSS isn't valid, the RSS reader might have problems reading your feed or working with it. To check an RSS feed's validity, you can use an RSS validator, such as the one at http://feedvalidator.org/. To validate your RSS feed, all you have to do is enter the URL of your feed into the text field (**Figure 3.35**) and click the Validate button. If your feed validates, as in this case, you'll see a congratulatory message (**Figure 3.36**).

If, on the other hand, your RSS feed has errors, the validator will tell you in detail what the errors are—and how to fix them. Very handy.

**Figure 3.35**

Always use a feed validator before publishing an RSS feed.

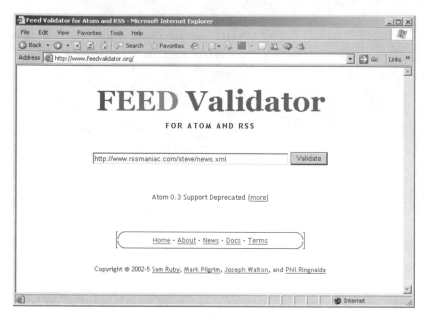

**Figure 3.36**

If your feed is valid, you receive confirmation from the validator.

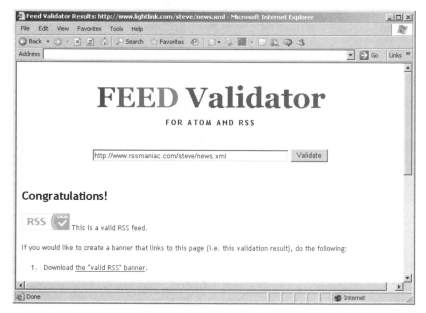

# Creating RSS Feeds
# from Scratch

There are plenty of RSS editors that let you create an RSS feed and upload
it to a Web site. But as you get more sophisticated with handling RSS,
there will be times you'll want to do the work yourself. You may need to
do some things your editor can't do, for example, or you might just want
to set up a template for your RSS feed and periodically edit the items
yourself.

Working with RSS directly gives you all the power this rich set of
languages has to offer. But now the question is, which version of RSS
do you want to use?

To make sure you know how to work with a particular version of RSS,
you have to read the specification for that version. The specification
tells you how to write the actual XML for that version of RSS. You can

find the specifications for the various RSS versions and Atom at the following sites:

- **RSS 0.90**  www.purplepages.ie/RSS/netscape/rss0.90.html

- **RSS 0.91**  http://backend.userland.com/rss091 and also see http://my.netscape.com/publish/formats/rss-spec-0.91.html

- **RSS 0.92**  http://backend.userland.com/rss092

- **RSS 0.93**  http://backend.userland.com/rss093

- **RSS 1.0**  http://web.resource.org/rss/1.0/spec

- **RSS 1.1**  http://inamidst.com/rss1.1/

- **RSS 2.0**  http://blogs.law.harvard.edu/tech/rss

- **Atom**  http://xml.coverpages.org/draft-ietf-atompub-format-11.txt

I can't include all the specifications in this chapter, but I'll cover the version that started the whole RSS explosion—version 0.91, still in widespread use. I will also include RSS 2.0, the most popular version and by far the one in most common use today.

What about RSS version 1.0? Although in common use as well, RSS 1.0 is a different language and not a part of the original RSS tree. Based mainly on Resource Description Framework (RDF), RSS 1.0 is a departure from the rest of the RSS versions. (RSS 2.0 is more a descendent of RSS 0.91 than RSS 1.0 is.) I'm going to give an overview of RSS 1.0; if you want more details, take a look at the RSS 1.0 specification at the URL listed earlier. (Also see Chapter 1, "Gotta Get My RSS," for a brief history of RSS.)

I will also touch on Atom. It differs from the RSS specifications mainly because it was developed by a true standards body, the Internet Engineering Task Force (IETF). However, Atom is a complex language and has yet to be widely adopted. A Web survey shows that Atom is still in relatively small use compared with RSS.

My feeling is that while there will always be a place for Atom, it's too complex for the majority of RSS writers. Few have the patience or time to work through a 50-plus-page formal specification before starting to write. The charm of RSS has always been that it's easy to work with, and Atom's complex specifications have a much tougher time winning converts. People had the same problems when the World Wide Web Consortium (W3C) introduced XHTML (Extensible Hypertext Markup Language) as the successor to HTML, and XHTML was so complex that it never took off. Atom might still take off, of course, and certainly if you use RSS editors that write Atom files the whole process becomes easy. Atom has quite a way to go, but it's an important specification, so an overview of Atom will be given in this chapter.

RSS and Atom are XML-based languages, and RSS and Atom files are really XML files. To write RSS and Atom from scratch, then, you have to know some of the rules of XML, and that's where we begin—with an XML primer.

# An XML Primer

XML stands for Extensible Markup Language, and the key word here is *extensible*. The idea is that you can write and extend your own language from scratch, as long as you follow the XML rules. XML is like HTML in that it's based on enclosing text inside elements. But with XML, you are the one who creates the elements (unlike with HTML, which has predefined elements).

 **XML was created and is maintained by the W3C. You can find the formal specification for the most recent version, XML 1.1, at www.w3.org/TR/ xml11/, and the specification for XML 1.0, the version used to create RSS and Atom documents, at www.w3.org/TR/REC-xml.**

## Starting with the XML declaration

Creating XML documents is best understood by example. Say you have a group of employees and you want to keep track of the projects they're working on. You could do this in an XML document, and, as with any other XML document (including RSS and Atom documents), you have to start with an XML declaration.

```
<?xml version = "1.0" encoding = "UTF-8"?>
         .

         .

         .
```

That's the way all RSS and Atom documents must start, with the declaration that says it is an XML document and gives the version. This declaration has a special form, starting with <?xml and ending with ?>. Like HTML elements, this declaration can support attributes—that is, items such as version and encoding that you see in this case.

**A version attribute is required in the XML declaration, and the encoding attribute is not.**

The version attribute sets the XML version used to create the document, and is always 1.0 for RSS and Atom. The encoding attribute sets the *character encoding*—that is, the character set used in the document. UTF-8 (8-bit Unicode Transformation Format) is a good choice for an encoding attribute, and in fact is the default encoding for XML documents. A subset of Unicode, UTF-8 matches the ASCII character set used by Microsoft WordPad in Windows and most other text editors in English-speaking countries. If you want to write your RSS feed in languages with other character sets, such as Japanese, you'd use different encoding.

Note especially that each attribute is assigned a quoted text string; in our example this is version = "1.0". In XML, and so in RSS and Atom, you always assign quoted text strings to attributes. In HTML you don't need the quotes, and some attributes don't need to be assigned values; in XML, if you use an attribute, it must have an assigned value.

## Creating the document element

Now that you've started with the XML declaration, you can add the elements that make up the body of an XML document. Just as in HTML, you store text data in XML elements. Unlike in HTML, you make up the elements you want to use in XML. For example, if you want to create an XML element to store an address, you might come up with a new XML element, the <address> element. Just as in HTML, XML elements have an opening tag and a closing tag, so here's how you might store someone's address:

```
<address>
   14 Picklewood Avenue
</address>
```

There are some rules for XML element names: They can't contain any spaces, they can't start with a number, and they can't start with a punctuation mark. Here are some invalid XML elements:

```
<phone number>890-5555</phone number>
<5feettall>John</5feettall>
```

The text inside the element is referred to as the element's content, and if an element has content, it needs an opening *and* a closing tag in XML. Unlike HTML, where some elements don't need a closing tag (such as the `<img>` or `<input>` elements), XML requires a closing tag for elements that have content.

Elements that don't have content are referred to as *empty elements* in XML. An empty element doesn't have any text content between the opening and closing tags, but it can have attributes. Elements in XML do not need a closing tag, but you can use the XML markup `/>` to end an empty element if you want.

```
<data language = "English" />
```

 **The data for empty elements is stored in attributes, not as content between an opening and closing tag.**

The first element in every XML document is the *document element*. This element *contains* all the other elements in the document (just as in HTML, one element can contain others), for example:

```
<name>
    <lastname>Connery</lastname>
    <firstname>Sean</firstname>
</name>
```

I'll call the document element `<document>` in our example, just to make it clear it's the document element, but you can use any valid XML element name (in an RSS document, for example, you use `<rss>` as the document element):

```
<?xml version = "1.0" encoding = "UTF-8"?>
<document>
        .
        .
        .
</document>
```

Now it's time to start adding to our document the elements that will contain the document's data.

## Creating XML elements

Let's say you want to store some data about your two employees. You could create two `<employee>` elements and add the elements to your new document:

```
<?xml version = "1.0" encoding = "UTF-8"?>
<document>
    <employee>
        .
        .
        .
    </employee>
    <employee>
        .
        .
        .
    </employee>
</document>
```

You now have two new XML elements in your document. So far, so good.

## Creating XML attributes

As with HTML, in XML you can add attributes to an element, starting with the opening tag. For example, you might add a status attribute to the `<employee>` element that indicates the employee's status (active or retired):

```
<?xml version = "1.0" encoding = "UTF-8"?>
<document>
    <employee status="retired">
        .
        .
        .
    </employee>
    <employee status="active">
```

```
          .
          .
          .
      </employee>
    </document>
```

## Nesting XML elements

Terrific, now you're set. In XML, elements can contain either text data or other elements, so you can add all the data you want about your employees, such as a <name> element that contains nested <lastname> and <firstname> elements:

```
<?xml version = "1.0" encoding = "UTF-8"?>
<document>
    <employee status="retired">
        <name>
            <lastname>Connery</lastname>
            <firstname>Sean</firstname>
        </name>
            .

            .

            .
    </employee>
    <employee status="active">
        <name>
            <lastname>Hepburn</lastname>
            <firstname>Audrey</firstname>
        </name>
            .

            .

            .
    </employee>
</document>
```

You can add more information about each employee, such as the date they were hired and the projects they're working on:

```
<?xml version = "1.0" encoding = "UTF-8"?>
<document>
```

*(code continues on next page)*

```
<employee status="retired">
    <name>
        <lastname>Connery</lastname>
        <firstname>Sean</firstname>
    </name>
    <hiredate>October 15, 2006</hiredate>
    <projects>
        <project>
            <product>Printer</product>
            <id>111</id>
            <price>$111.00</price>
        </project>
        <project>
            <product>Laptop</product>
            <id>222</id>
            <price>$989.00</price>
        </project>
    </projects>
</employee>
<employee status="active">
    <name>
        <lastname>Hepburn</lastname>
        <firstname>Audrey</firstname>
    </name>
    <hiredate>October 20, 2006</hiredate>
    <projects>
        <project>
            <product>Desktop</product>
            <id>333</id>
            <price>$2995.00</price>
        </project>
        <project>
            <product>Scanner</product>
            <id>444</id>
            <price>$200.00</price>
        </project>
    </projects>
</employee>
</document>
```

That's a complete XML document. To create your file, you can use any plain-text editor you have, such as WordPad in Windows (**Figure 4.1**). Make sure you save your document as a plain-text file, however. When you save it in WordPad, choose Text Document as the document's type, not Rich Text Format (RTF), which includes all kinds of formatting codes and will make your XML document invalid.

**Figure 4.1**

This XML document was created in Microsoft WordPad.

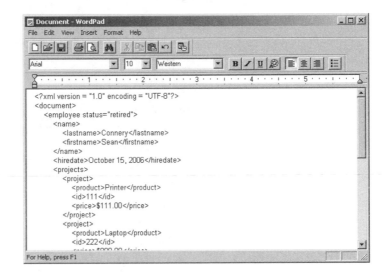

## Well-formed and valid XML documents

There are two more criteria: XML documents must be *well formed* and *valid*. There are various rules you need to follow to make an XML document well formed, and you can find them in the XML specifications. The most important rule says that each XML document must have only *one* document element, and that element must contain all the other elements in the document. You must also avoid any nesting errors. Take a look at the following XML, in which everything is nested properly.

```
<projects>
    <project>
        <product>Desktop</product>
        <id>333</id>
        <price>$2995.00</price>
```

*(code continues on next page)*

```
        </project>
        <project>
            <product>Scanner</product>
            <id>444</id>
            <price>$200.00</price>
        </project>
    </projects>
```

The following XML is not well formed because the first `<project>`
element doesn't end before the next one starts, thus creating a nesting
error. In other words, the two `<project>` elements are mixed up:

```
    <projects>
        <project>
            <product>Desktop</product>
            <id>333</id>
            <price>$2995.00</price>
        <project>
        </project>
            <product>Scanner</product>
            <id>444</id>
            <price>$200.00</price>
        </project>
    </projects>
```

What makes an XML document valid? When you create an XML
document, you can specify its grammar or syntax. For example, what
attributes can the `<employee>` element have? What elements must the
`<project>` element contain? And so on. There are two ways of specifying the grammar for XML documents these days: You can use a
Document Type Definition (DTD) or an XML schema. You can use both
DTDs and XML schema to check whether an RSS or Atom document
adheres to the correct RSS or Atom syntax—all you have to do is use
an XML validator (such as www.stg.brown.edu/service/xmlvalid/) and
check your document against the standard RSS or Atom DTD or XML
schema. Since you can find RSS validators online (such as www.feed-
validator.org), there's no need to go into great detail about the DTDs or
XML schema here, but I highly recommend you always validate your
RSS or Atom feeds.

This introduction to XML gives you the foundation you'll need to write RSS and Atom documents. I haven't covered all the XML rules, of course—there are entire books on the topic if you want more information. Or, take a look at the XML specifications online if you have the stomach for it (they're very slow reading).

XML itself isn't really a language, despite the name Extensible Markup Language. It's really a set of rules you use to write your own language. That's how RSS and Atom came to be: Their authors created a set of elements, such as the <rss> element, that adhered to the XML rules. In other words, they used the XML rules to create new languages—RSS and Atom—with their own built-in elements.

Now it's time to take a look at RSS, starting with version 0.91.

# Writing RSS 0.91 Documents

In Chapter 3, "Creating RSS Feeds," you got a good start with RSS 0.91 documents, but only simple ones. Here's a more complete RSS 0.91 document, which will be referred to throughout this section:

```
<?xml version="1.0"?>
<!DOCTYPE rss SYSTEM
  "http://my.netscape.com/publish/formats/rss-0.91.dtd">
<rss version="0.91">
  <channel>
    <copyright>Copyright 2005.</copyright>
    <pubDate>Wed, 14 Dec 2005 07:00:00 GMT</pubDate>
    <lastBuildDate>Mon, 12 Dec 2005 07:00:00 GMT</lastBuildDate>
    <docs>http://www.rssmaniac.com/steve/info.html</docs>
    <description>This feed contains news from Steve!</description>
    <link>http://www.rssmaniac.com/steve</link>
    <title>Steve's News!</title>
    <language>en-us</language>
    <image>
      <title>Steve's News</title>
      <url>http://www.rssmaniac.com/steve/Image.jpg</url>
      <link>http://www.rssmaniac.com/steve</link>
```

*(code continues on next page)*

```
        <description>Steve's News</description>
        <width>144</width>
        <height>36</height>
      </image>
      <managingEditor>steve@rssmaniac.com (Steve)</managingEditor>
      <webMaster>steve@rssmaniac.com (Steve)</webMaster>
      <skipHours>
        <hour>8</hour>
        <hour>9</hour>
        <hour>10</hour>
      </skipHours>
      <skipDays>
        <day>Sunday</day>
      </skipDays>
      <item>
        <title>Steve shovels the snow</title>
        <description>It snowed once again.
          Time to shovel!>
        </description>
        <link>http://www.rssmaniac.com/steve</link>
      </item>
      <textinput>
        <title>Search for other items</title>
        <description>What do you want to find?</description>
        <name>search</name>
        <link>http://www.rssmaniac.com/find.php</link>
      </textinput>
    </channel>
  </rss>
```

Let's take this document apart, piece by piece.

## The XML declaration and DTD

As all RSS documents should, this one starts with an XML declaration. This XML declaration includes only the required version attribute, which must be set to "1.0" in RSS 0.91. Note also the <!DOCTYPE> element.

```
<?xml version="1.0"?>
```

```
<!DOCTYPE rss SYSTEM
  "http://my.netscape.com/publish/formats/rss-0.91.dtd">
      .
      .
      .
```

The `<!DOCTYPE>` element specifies the RSS 0.91 DTD (which can be found at http://my.netscape.com/publish/formats/rss-0.91.dtd), so that your RSS reader can check your document for correct syntax if it wants to. Although the `<!DOCTYPE>` element as written here is officially required in RSS 0.91, many people omit it, and many RSS validators don't insist on it.

Here's some technical stuff. The XML declaration has an optional attribute, encoding, which lets you specify the character set you want to use in your feed. For example, if you want to use Japanese, you specify an encoding that supports Japanese characters. You can find the legal character encodings for RSS 0.91 in **Table 4.1**. The default is UTF-8, which is a condensed version of Unicode and includes all the standard ASCII characters that most text editors use.

## Table 4.1: Valid Character-Set Encodings

| Character Set | Encoding |
| --- | --- |
| Any IANA standard name MIME name | ISO_8859-1:1987 ISO-8859-1 |
| ISO_8859-2:1987 ISO-8859-2 | ISO_8859-5:1988 ISO-8859-5 |
| ISO_8859-7:1987 ISO-8859-7 | ISO_8859-9:1989 ISO-8859-9 |
| Shift_JIS | Extended_UNIX_Code_Packed_Format_for_Japanese EUC-JP |
| GB2312 | EUC-KR |
| Big5 | Windows-1250 |
| Windows-1251 | UTF-8 |
| x-mac-roman | ANSI_X3.4-1968 US-ASCII |

# The <rss> element

The <rss> element is the document element, and starts the data-storage part of an RSS 0.91 document.

```
<?xml version="1.0"?>
<!DOCTYPE rss SYSTEM
  "http://my.netscape.com/publish/formats/rss-0.91.dtd">
<rss version="0.91">

        .

        .

        .

</rss>
```

Remember, because this is the document element, it contains all the other elements in the document (the XML declaration and the <!DOCTYPE> element are not part of the document element). The version attribute is required and must be set to "0.91" for an RSS 0.91 document.

There is one child element of the <rss> element—the <channel> element—and it is required.

# The <channel> element

The <channel> element contains all the information needed to set up a particular channel. Each <rss> element must contain only one <channel> element. The <channel> element has no attributes.

```
<?xml version="1.0"?>
<!DOCTYPE rss SYSTEM
  "http://my.netscape.com/publish/formats/rss-0.91.dtd">
<rss version="0.91">
  <channel>

        .

        .

        .

  </channel>
</rss>
```

The <channel> element has a number of child elements, some required, some optional. The required child elements are the following:

- <description>
- <language>
- <link>
- <title>

Here are the optional child elements inside a <channel> element:

- <copyright>
- <docs>
- <image>
- <item> (maximum of 15 <item> elements allowed)
- <lastBuildDate>
- <managingEditor>
- <pubDate>
- <rating>
- <skipDays>
- <skipHours>
- <textinput>
- <webMaster>

## The <copyright> element

The <copyright> element is an optional element inside the channel element that contains copyright information for the feed.

```
<?xml version="1.0"?>
<!DOCTYPE rss SYSTEM
    "http://my.netscape.com/publish/formats/rss-0.91.dtd">
```

*(code continues on next page)*

```
<rss version="0.91">
  <channel>
    <copyright>Copyright 2005.</copyright>
       .
       .
       .
```

This element has no attributes, and allows no child elements.

## The <pubDate> element

The <pubDate> element, an optional child element of the <channel> element, contains the date at which the channel was published:

```
<?xml version="1.0"?>
<!DOCTYPE rss SYSTEM
  "http://my.netscape.com/publish/formats/rss-0.91.dtd">
<rss version="0.91">
  <channel>
    <copyright>Copyright 2005.</copyright>
    <pubDate>Wed, 14 Dec 2005 07:00:00 GMT</pubDate>
       .
       .
       .
```

There's no special format for the date and time; that's up to you. The <pubDate> element has no child elements and no attributes.

## The <lastBuildDate> element

As you can tell from its name, the <lastBuildDate> element contains the last time this document was written and published.

```
<?xml version="1.0"?>
<!DOCTYPE rss SYSTEM
  "http://my.netscape.com/publish/formats/rss-0.91.dtd">
<rss version="0.91">
  <channel>
    <copyright>Copyright 2005.</copyright>
```

```
<pubDate>Wed, 14 Dec 2005 07:00:00 GMT</pubDate>
<lastBuildDate>Mon, 12 Dec 2005 07:00:00 GMT</lastBuildDate>
   .
   .
   .
```

The `<lastBuildDate>` element is an optional child element of the `<channel>` element. It has no child elements and no attributes, so it's nice and simple. And there's no special format for recording the date.

The last build date can be useful: Among other things, it tells your readers how often you update your feed (so if you don't update your feeds often, you might want to omit this element!).

## The `<docs>` element

The `<docs>` element contains the URL for more information and a description of the channel.

```
<?xml version="1.0"?>
<!DOCTYPE rss SYSTEM
   "http://my.netscape.com/publish/formats/rss-0.91.dtd">
<rss version="0.91">
  <channel>
    <copyright>Copyright 2005.</copyright>
    <pubDate>Wed, 14 Dec 2005 07:00:00 GMT</pubDate>
    <lastBuildDate>Mon, 12 Dec 2005 07:00:00 GMT</lastBuildDate>
    <docs>http://www.rssmaniac.com/steve/info.html</docs>
       .
       .
       .
```

This element, another optional child element of the `<channel>` element, has no child elements and no attributes. All it contains is a URL that contains documentation (hence the name, `<docs>`) for this channel. This is where you can give your readers more information about your channel, such as help files on a Web site, so make the most of it.

Note that URLs must begin with either *http://* or *ftp://*—not *www*.

# The <description> element

Like an HTML field, in which you enter text, the <description> element holds a text description of a channel, an item, or a text-input control. It's a required child element of the <channel> element; each <channel> element must have one <description> child element. The <description> element is also a required child element of the <item> and <textinput> elements. In our example, it describes our new channel.

```
<?xml version="1.0"?>
<!DOCTYPE rss SYSTEM
  "http://my.netscape.com/publish/formats/rss-0.91.dtd">
<rss version="0.91">
  <channel>
    <copyright>Copyright 2005.</copyright>
    <pubDate>Wed, 14 Dec 2005 07:00:00 GMT</pubDate>
    <lastBuildDate>Mon, 12 Dec 2005 07:00:00 GMT</lastBuildDate>
    <docs>http://www.rssmaniac.com/steve/info.html</docs>
    <description>This feed contains news from Steve!</description>
      .
      .
      .
```

The <description> element doesn't have any child elements or attributes. It's an important element, so make sure you add appropriate text to it. This is the text that will be displayed in the RSS reader when the user asks for the properties of your feed.

# The <link> element

The <link> element is a required child element of the <channel>, <image>, <item>, and <textinput> elements, and represents the URL the user can click. When used as a child element of the <channel> element, it usually holds the home page of the channel's creator or organization, for example. When used as a child element of an <item> element, it's a link to the full item on a Web site. It is used to define a link for the new channel in our RSS 0.91 document:

```
<?xml version="1.0"?>
<!DOCTYPE rss SYSTEM
  "http://my.netscape.com/publish/formats/rss-0.91.dtd">
```

```
<rss version="0.91">
  <channel>
    <copyright>Copyright 2005.</copyright>
    <pubDate>Wed, 14 Dec 2005 07:00:00 GMT</pubDate>
    <lastBuildDate>Mon, 12 Dec 2005 07:00:00 GMT</lastBuildDate>
    <docs>http://www.rssmaniac.com/steve/info.html</docs>
    <description>This feed contains news from Steve!</description>
    <link>http://www.rssmaniac.com/steve</link>
            .
            .
            .
```

Note that URLs must begin with either *http://* or *ftp://*, not *www*.

## The <title> element

The <title> element is a required element in the <channel>, <image>, <item>, and <textinput> elements, and, as you know, holds a title for that channel, item, or text-input control. The <title> element is used to give a title to the new channel.

```
<?xml version="1.0"?>
<!DOCTYPE rss SYSTEM
  "http://my.netscape.com/publish/formats/rss-0.91.dtd">
<rss version="0.91">
  <channel>
    <copyright>Copyright 2005.</copyright>
    <pubDate>Wed, 14 Dec 2005 07:00:00 GMT</pubDate>
    <lastBuildDate>Mon, 12 Dec 2005 07:00:00 GMT</lastBuildDate>
    <docs>http://www.rssmaniac.com/steve/info.html</docs>
    <description>This feed contains news from Steve!</description>
    <link>http://www.rssmaniac.com/steve</link>
    <title>Steve's News!</title>
            .
            .
            .
```

The title for a channel appears in an RSS reader's feeds window; the title for an item appears in the titles window; and the title for a text-input control is used to label that control.

# The <language> element

The <language> element, a required child element in the <channel> element, specifies the language for the channel. Our example specifies U.S. English.

```
<?xml version="1.0"?>
<!DOCTYPE rss SYSTEM
  "http://my.netscape.com/publish/formats/rss-0.91.dtd">
<rss version="0.91">
  <channel>
    <copyright>Copyright 2005.</copyright>
    <pubDate>Wed, 14 Dec 2005 07:00:00 GMT</pubDate>
    <lastBuildDate>Mon, 12 Dec 2005 07:00:00 GMT</lastBuildDate>
    <docs>http://www.rssmaniac.com/steve/info.html</docs>
    <description>This feed contains news from Steve!</description>
    <link>http://www.rssmaniac.com/steve</link>
    <title>Steve's News!</title>
    <language>en-us</language>
       .
       .
       .
```

The <language> element has no attributes and no child elements. The content of this element, such as en-us, is called a language code. A large number of language codes are allowed for RSS 0.91 (**Table 4.2**).

## Table 4.2: Valid Language Codes

| Language Code | Language | Language Code | Language |
| --- | --- | --- | --- |
| af | Afrikaans | be | Belarusian |
| bg | Bulgarian | ca | Catalan |
| cs | Czech | da | Danish |
| de | German | de-at | German (Austria) |
| de-ch | German (Switzerland) | de-de | German (Germany) |

## Table 4.2: Valid Language Codes (continued)

| Language Code | Language | Language Code | Language |
|---|---|---|---|
| de-li | German (Liechtenstein) | de-lu | German (Luxembourg) |
| el | Greek | en | English |
| en-au | English (Australia) | en-bz | English (Belize) |
| en-ca | English (Canada) | en-gb | English (United Kingdom) |
| en-ie | English (Ireland) | en-jm | English (Jamaica) |
| en-nz | English (New Zealand) | en-ph | English (Philippines) |
| en-tt | English (Trinidad) | en-us | English (United States) |
| en-za | English (South Africa) | en-zw | English (Zimbabwe) |
| es | Spanish | es-ar | Spanish (Argentina) |
| es-bo | Spanish (Bolivia) | es-cl | Spanish (Chile) |
| es-co | Spanish (Colombia) | es-cr | Spanish (Costa Rica) |
| es-do | Spanish (Dominican Republic) | es-ec | Spanish (Ecuador) |
| es-es | Spanish (Spain) | es-gt | Spanish (Guatemala) |
| es-hn | Spanish (Honduras) | es-mx | Spanish (Mexico) |
| es-ni | Spanish (Nicaragua) | es-pa | Spanish (Panama) |
| es-pe | Spanish (Peru) | es-pr | Spanish (Puerto Rico) |
| es-py | Spanish (Paraguay) | es-sv | Spanish (El Salvador) |
| es-uy | Spanish (Uruguay) | es-ve | Spanish (Venezuela) |
| eu | Basque | fi | Finnish |
| fo | Faeroese | fr | French |
| fr-be | French (Belgium) | fr-ca | French (Canada) |
| fr-ch | French (Switzerland) | fr-fr | French (France) |
| fr-lu | French (Luxembourg) | fr-mc | French (Monaco) |
| ga | Irish | gd | Gaelic |
| gl | Galician | hr | Croatian |
| hu | Hungarian | id | Indonesian |

*continues on next page*

## Table 4.2: Valid Language Codes *(continued)*

| Language Code | Language | Language Code | Language |
|---|---|---|---|
| is | Icelandic | it | Italian |
| it-ch | Italian (Switzerland) | it-it | Italian (Italy) |
| ja | Japanese | ko | Korean |
| mk | Macedonian | nl | Dutch |
| nl-be | Dutch (Belgium) | nl-nl | Dutch (Netherlands) |
| no | Norwegian | pl | Polish |
| pt | Portuguese | pt-br | Portuguese (Brazil) |
| pt-pt | Portuguese (Portugal) | ro | Romanian |
| ro-mo | Romanian (Moldova) | ro-ro | Romanian (Romania) |
| ru | Russian | ru-mo | Russian (Moldova) |
| ru-ru | Russian (Russia) | sk | Slovak |
| sl | Slovenian | sq | Albanian |
| sr | Serbian | sv | Swedish |
| sv-fi | Swedish (Finland) | sv-se | Swedish (Sweden) |
| tr | Turkish | uk | Ukranian |
| zh-cn | Chinese (Simplified) | zh-tw | Chinese (Traditional) |

 RSS readers use language codes to determine the language your feed uses, but to select a character set for that language, don't forget to set the XML declaration's encoding attribute.

## The <image> element

As you know, the <image> element is used to connect an image to the channel, and the RSS reader displays the image.

```
<?xml version="1.0"?>
<!DOCTYPE rss SYSTEM
   "http://my.netscape.com/publish/formats/rss-0.91.dtd">
<rss version="0.91">
```

```
<channel>
  <copyright>Copyright 2005.</copyright>
  <pubDate>Wed, 14 Dec 2005 07:00:00 GMT</pubDate>
  <lastBuildDate>Mon, 12 Dec 2005 07:00:00 GMT</lastBuildDate>
  <docs>http://www.rssmaniac.com/steve/info.html</docs>
  <description>This feed contains news from Steve!</description>
  <link>http://www.rssmaniac.com/steve</link>
  <title>Steve's News!</title>
  <language>en-us</language>
  <image>
    <title>Steve's News</title>
    <url>http://www.rssmaniac.com/steve/Image.jpg</url>
    <link>http://www.rssmaniac.com/steve</link>
    <description>Steve's News</description>
    <width>144</width>
    <height>36</height>
  </image>
            .
            .
            .
```

The <image> element has no attributes, but it can have a number of child elements. The required child elements are the following:

- <title>

- <url>

- <link>

And here are the optional child elements:

- <description>

- <width>

- <height>

Let's take a look at some of these elements next. Some of them, such as <width> and <height>, have particular restrictions you should know about.

### The <image> element's <title> element

The <title> element gives a title to the image.

```
<image>
  <title>Steve's News</title>
     .
     .
     .
</image>
```

RSS readers often show this title if for some reason the image can't be displayed. The <title> element, which is required in the <image> element, has no child elements or attributes.

### The <image> element's <url> element

The <url> element's function is no surprise: It holds the URL of the image, and is a required child element of the <image> element.

```
<image>
  <title>Steve's News</title>
  <url>http://www.rssmaniac.com/steve/Image.jpg</url>
     .
     .
     .
</image>
```

This element doesn't have any child elements or attributes. Note that URLs must begin with either *http://* or *ftp://*, not *www*.

### The <image> element's <link> element

The <link> element is a required child element of the <image> element, and contains the URL the RSS reader brings up if the user clicks the link.

```
<image>
  <title>Steve's News</title>
  <url>http://www.rssmaniac.com/steve/Image.jpg</url>
  <link>http://www.rssmaniac.com/steve</link>
     .
     .
     .
</image>
```

A URL in a `<link>` element must begin with *http://* or *ftp://*. Usually, this URL points to your main page, or to a page that explains more about your feed.

### The `<image>` element's `<description>` element

The `<description>` element is an optional `<image>` element, and, as you can guess, is designed to include a description of your feed that you usually put into the image's (required) `<title>` element.

```
<image>
  <title>Steve's News</title>
  <url>http://www.rssmaniac.com/steve/Image.jpg</url>
  <link>http://www.rssmaniac.com/steve</link>
  <description>Steve's News</description>
      .
      .
      .
</image>
```

### The `<image>` element's `<width>` element

You can let the RSS reader know the width of an image, but, as with Web browsers, you don't have to, because the RSS reader can figure it out after the image is fully loaded.

```
<image>
  <title>Steve's News</title>
  <url>http://www.rssmaniac.com/steve/Image.jpg</url>
  <link>http://www.rssmaniac.com/steve</link>
  <description>Steve's News</description>
  <width>144</width>
      .
      .
      .
</image>
```

The text contained in this element is a positive integer that gives the width of the feed's image in pixels, and its value must be between 1 and 144, inclusive (yep, 144 is the maximum). So you can't use an image 800 pixels wide in your feed. Some readers use a default value if you don't specify the width of your image, and that, for some reason, is 88 pixels.

This element has no child elements and no attributes.

### The `<image>` element's `<height>` element

The image's `<height>` element is an optional child element of the `<image>` element, and specifies the image's height in pixels.

```
<image>
    <title>Steve's News</title>
    <url>http://www.rssmaniac.com/steve/Image.jpg</url>
    <link>http://www.rssmaniac.com/steve</link>
    <description>Steve's News</description>
    <width>144</width>
    <height>36</height>
</image>
```

The text contained in this element should correspond to a positive integer between 1 and 400, inclusive—meaning images can be quite a bit higher than they are wide. The default value for 0.91 RSS documents, for some reason, is set at 31 pixels.

This element has no child elements and no attributes.

## The `<managingEditor>` element

The `<managingEditor>` element gives your feed's readers someone to contact. An optional element, it's a child element of the `<channel>` element.

```
<?xml version="1.0"?>
<!DOCTYPE rss SYSTEM
   "http://my.netscape.com/publish/formats/rss-0.91.dtd">
<rss version="0.91">
  <channel>
    <copyright>Copyright 2005.</copyright>
    <pubDate>Wed, 14 Dec 2005 07:00:00 GMT</pubDate>
    <lastBuildDate>Mon, 12 Dec 2005 07:00:00 GMT</lastBuildDate>
    <docs>http://www.rssmaniac.com/steve/info.html</docs>
    <description>This feed contains news from Steve!</description>
    <link>http://www.rssmaniac.com/steve</link>
```

```
<title>Steve's News!</title>
<language>en-us</language>
<image>

    .

    .

    .

</image>
<managingEditor>steve@rssmaniac.com (Steve)</managingEditor>

    .

    .

    .
```

Formally speaking, this element should contain the email address of the managing editor of your feed, not just a name. If anyone wants to get in touch, they should be able to use this email address. This element doesn't have any child elements or attributes.

## The <webMaster> element

The <webMaster> element, another child element of the <channel> element, holds the email address of the person responsible for handling any technical problems with your feed. This is to be distinguished from the <managingEditor> element, which holds the email address of the person responsible for the content of your site.

```
<?xml version="1.0"?>
<!DOCTYPE rss SYSTEM
   "http://my.netscape.com/publish/formats/rss-0.91.dtd">
<rss version="0.91">
  <channel>
    <copyright>Copyright 2005.</copyright>
    <pubDate>Wed, 14 Dec 2005 07:00:00 GMT</pubDate>
    <lastBuildDate>Mon, 12 Dec 2005 07:00:00 GMT</lastBuildDate>
    <docs>http://www.rssmaniac.com/steve/info.html</docs>
    <description>This feed contains news from Steve!</description>
    <link>http://www.rssmaniac.com/steve</link>
    <title>Steve's News!</title>
    <language>en-us</language>
    <image>
```

*(code continues on next page)*

```
        .
        .
        .
    </image>
    <managingEditor>steve@rssmaniac.com (Steve)</managingEditor>
    <webMaster>steve@rssmaniac.com (Steve)</webMaster>
        .
        .
        .
```

This element has no child elements or attributes.

## The <rating> element

In practice, the <rating> element is rarely used, so it's not included in our example RSS 0.91 document. The <rating> element, an optional child element of the <channel> element, gives a third-party Platform for Internet Content Selection (PICS) rating of your RSS feed. Among other things, the rating system is designed to avoid allowing access to adult content by minors. (You can find a list of PICS rating organizations at www.w3.org/PICS/raters.htm, but most of the links are defunct.)

If you're going to use this element, the text you place in it usually starts with "PICS-1.1", then includes the URL of the rating agency and its rating, resulting in something like the following:

```
    <rating>(PICS-1.1 "http://www.picswatcher.org/"  (A+))</rating>
```

## The <skipHours> element

The <skipHours> element lets you set the hours your feed will *not* be updated, if you choose to specify them. This element is not in big-time use these days, but when RSS was first developed, people assumed that feeds would be updated hourly. Accordingly, this element was designed to give you some time off by specifying what hours you will not be updating your feed.

```
    <?xml version="1.0"?>
    <!DOCTYPE rss SYSTEM
      "http://my.netscape.com/publish/formats/rss-0.91.dtd">
    <rss version="0.91">
```

```
<channel>
  <copyright>Copyright 2005.</copyright>
  <pubDate>Wed, 14 Dec 2005 07:00:00 GMT</pubDate>
  <lastBuildDate>Mon, 12 Dec 2005 07:00:00 GMT</lastBuildDate>
  <docs>http://www.rssmaniac.com/steve/info.html</docs>
  <description>This feed contains news from Steve!</description>
  <link>http://www.rssmaniac.com/steve</link>
  <title>Steve's News!</title>
  <language>en-us</language>
        .
        .
        .

  <skipHours>
        .
        .
        .

  </skipHours>
        .
        .
        .
```

The <skipHours> element has no attributes, but you must include at least one <hour> child element.

## The <skipHours> element's <hour> element

The <hour> element, a child element of the <skipHours> element, contains an hour of the day, measured in Greenwich Mean Time (GMT), when your feed will not be updated.

```
<?xml version="1.0"?>
<!DOCTYPE rss SYSTEM
  "http://my.netscape.com/publish/formats/rss-0.91.dtd">
<rss version="0.91">
  <channel>
    <copyright>Copyright 2005.</copyright>
    <pubDate>Wed, 14 Dec 2005 07:00:00 GMT</pubDate>
    <lastBuildDate>Mon, 12 Dec 2005 07:00:00 GMT</lastBuildDate>
    <docs>http://www.rssmaniac.com/steve/info.html</docs>
    <description>This feed contains news from Steve!</description>
```

*(code continues on next page)*

```
<link>http://www.rssmaniac.com/steve</link>
<title>Steve's News!</title>
<language>en-us</language>
              .

              .

              .

<skipHours>
  <hour>8</hour>
  <hour>9</hour>
  <hour>10</hour>
</skipHours>

          .

          .

          .
```

## The <skipDays> element

Like the <skipHours> element, the <skipDays> element lets you indicate what days of the week your feed won't be updated.

```
<?xml version="1.0"?>
<!DOCTYPE rss SYSTEM
  "http://my.netscape.com/publish/formats/rss-0.91.dtd">
<rss version="0.91">
  <channel>
    <copyright>Copyright 2005.</copyright>
    <pubDate>Wed, 14 Dec 2005 07:00:00 GMT</pubDate>
    <lastBuildDate>Mon, 12 Dec 2005 07:00:00 GMT</lastBuildDate>
    <docs>http://www.rssmaniac.com/steve/info.html</docs>
    <description>This feed contains news from Steve!</description>
    <link>http://www.rssmaniac.com/steve</link>
    <title>Steve's News!</title>
    <language>en-us</language>
    <image>
          .

          .

          .

    <skipDays>
          .
```

```
        •
        •
</skipDays>
<item>

        •
        •
        •
```

The `<skipDays>` element has no attributes, but if you use it, you must
include at least one child `<day>` element.

## The `<skipDays>` element's `<day>` element

You indicate a day of the week in the `<day>` element, in English (the
specification says you should use English for day names). For example,
if your feed isn't updated on Sundays, you can include a `<skipDays>`
element with a `<day>` child element like this:

```
<?xml version="1.0"?>
<!DOCTYPE rss SYSTEM
    "http://my.netscape.com/publish/formats/rss-0.91.dtd">
<rss version="0.91">
  <channel>
    <copyright>Copyright 2005.</copyright>
    <pubDate>Wed, 14 Dec 2005 07:00:00 GMT</pubDate>
    <lastBuildDate>Mon, 12 Dec 2005 07:00:00 GMT</lastBuildDate>
    <docs>http://www.rssmaniac.com/steve/info.html</docs>
    <description>This feed contains news from Steve!</description>
    <link>http://www.rssmaniac.com/steve</link>
    <title>Steve's News!</title>
    <language>en-us</language

        •
        •
        •

    <skipDays>
      <day>Sunday</day>
    </skipDays>
    <item>

        •
        •
        •
```

You can include up to seven `<day>` elements inside a `<skipDays>` element, each corresponding to a different day of the week. The `<day>` element has no child elements and no attributes.

## The `<item>` element

Here's the big one, the `<item>` element, which is meant to represent a Web page or a section of a Web page. As you know, you use this element to create items in your feed. In RSS 0.91, there is a limit of 15 `<item>` child elements in the `<channel>` element.

```
<item>
  <title>Steve shovels the snow</title>
  <description>It snowed once again.
    Time to shovel!>
  </description>
  <link>http://www.rssmaniac.com/steve</link>
</item>
      .
      .
      .
```

The `<item>` element has two required child elements:

- `<title>`

- `<link>`

And it has one optional child element:

- `<description>`

### The `<item>` element's `<title>` element

As you know from Chapter 3, an item's `<title>` element contains the title for the item, and its text will appear in the titles window in an RSS reader.

```
<item>
  <title>Steve shovels the snow</title>
    .
```

```
        .
        .
</item>
```

This element has no attributes or child elements. Note that it's required within an `<item>` element.

## The `<item>` element's `<description>` element

The `<description>` element contains a description of the item and usually includes part of the full text of the item. Even though this is an optional child element in the `<item>` element, you'll see a description in nearly all RSS items in your RSS reader.

```
<item>
    <title>Steve shovels the snow</title>
    <description>It snowed once again.
      Time to shovel!>
    </description>
    <link>http://www.rssmaniac.com/steve</link>
</item>
```

## The `<item>` element's `<link>` element

The `<link>` element is also required inside an `<item>` element, and as you know, it contains the URL of the full item.

```
<item>
    <title>Steve shovels the snow</title>
        .
        .
        .
    <link>http://www.rssmaniac.com/steve</link>

</item>
```

The item's link appears below the item's description in the RSS reader, and the user can click the link for more information on the item itself. As with other URLs, the URL you use here must start with *http://* or *ftp://*.

# The <textinput> element

RSS 0.91 provides for an optional <textinput> element that readers can use to ask you questions, search your site, provide feedback, and so on. This <textinput> element appears as a text field; readers can enter text and send it, with a click, to a URL you provide. This element is an optional child element of the <channel> element, and is not in general use today—you won't find many RSS readers that support it, because it's become standard to handle this kind of interaction with your readers on your Web site.

```
<textinput>
  <title>Search for other items</title>
  <description>What do you want to find?</description>
  <name>search</name>
  <link>http://www.rssmaniac.com/find.cgi</link>
</textinput>
      .
      .
      .
```

The <textinput> element doesn't have any attributes, but it does have four required child elements.

- <title>
- <description>
- <name>
- <link>

## The <textinput> element's <title> element

The <title> element lets you display a title for the <textinput> control. The title of the <textinput> control in our example is "Search for other items."

```
<textinput>
  <title>Search for other items</title>
      .
      .
      .
</textinput>
```

This element doesn't have any child elements or attributes.

### The <textinput> element's <description> element

The <textinput> control's <description> element lets you display a description, such as a prompt, for the <textinput> control.

```
<textinput>
  <title>Search for other items</title>
  <description>What do you want to find?</description>
      .
      .
      .
</textinput>
```

This element doesn't have any child elements or attributes.

### The <textinput> element's <name> element

When you send data to an online program, the data in an HTML control is associated with the name of the control. Online scripts and programs can then recover the data using that name. In our example, the name of the text-input control is *search*.

```
<textinput>
  <title>Search for other items</title>
  <description>What do you want to find?</description>
  <name>search</name>
      .
      .
      .
</textinput>
```

Thus, for example, if you were sending your data to a PHP script on the server, you could recover the data the user entered into the text-input control with the PHP expression $_REQUEST["search"]. This element also has no child elements or attributes.

### The <textinput> element's <link> element

The <textinput> control's <link> element holds a URL. You want the text the user enters into the control to be sent to this URL. This is the URL of the online script or program that handles that text, such as the program that runs a search for the user. In our example RSS 0.91 document, the text data the user enters will be sent to a PHP script named find.php:

```
<textinput>
   <title>Search for other items</title>
   <description>What do you want to find?</description>
   <name>search</name>
   <link>http://www.rssmaniac.com/find.php</link>
</textinput>
```

As usual, the URL must begin with *http://* or *ftp://* (and because you're passing data to an online script, you'll probably want to use *http://*). This element has no child elements or attributes.

That completes the RSS 0.91 syntax. Not bad—you're on your way to being an RSS pro.

# Writing RSS 1.0 Documents

RSS version 1.0 was quite a departure from RSS 0.91. Here's what our sample RSS 0.91 document looks like in RSS 1.0.

```
<?xml version="1.0"?>

<rdf:RDF
   xmlns:rdf="http://www.w3.org/1999/02/22-rdf-syntax-ns#"
   xmlns="http://purl.org/rss/1.0/"
>

   <channel rdf:about="http://www.rssmaniac.com/steve">
      <title>Steve's News</title>
      <link>http://www.rssmaniac.com/steve</link>
      <description>
         This feed contains news from Steve!
      </description>
```

```
<image rdf:resource="http://www.rssmaniac.com/steve/
Image.jpg" />

<items>
  <rdf:Seq>
    <rdf:li resource=
    "http://xml.com/pub/2000/08/09/xslt/xslt.html" />
  </rdf:Seq>
</items>

</channel>

<image rdf:about="http://www.rssmaniac.com/steve/Image.jpg">
  <title>Steve's News</title>
  <link>http://www.rssmaniac.com/steve</link>
  <url>http://www.rssmaniac.com/steve/Image.jpg</url>
</image>

<item rdf:about="http://www.rssmaniac.com/steve/about.html">
  <title>Steve shovels the snow</title>
  <link>http://www.rssmaniac.com/steve</link>
  <description>
  It snowed once again. Time to shovel!
  </description>
</item>

</rdf:RDF>
```

You can see this document opened in RSSReader (**Figure 4.2**).

As you see, an RSS 1.0 document varies greatly from an RSS 0.91 document. For one, the organization of the data is different: the <channel> element is closed before you list the <item> elements, for example. And you list a summary of the items in an <items> element, in <rdf:li> elements. For that matter, the document element itself is different—it begins with <rdf:RDF>, not <rss>. The very name of the <rdf:RDF> element emphasizes RSS 1.0's connection to RDF, the Resource Description Format.

**Figure 4.2**

Here's our sample RSS 1.0 document opened in RSSReader.

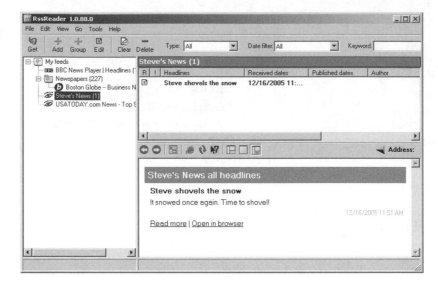

But why do some element names start with "rdf:"? That prefix represents a namespace in XML. Because you make up your own element names in XML, there's a good chance a name you make up may conflict with a name made up by someone else, so namespaces were introduced. Namespaces correspond to prefixes in XML documents. So, even if you have an element named <address> and someone else uses the same element name, you can use a namespace prefix such as <mine:address>, and they can use a different namespace prefix like <theirs:address>, and the elements won't conflict.

You set up a namespace in the document element by associating it with a unique text string (because your text string is unique, the elements in your namespace will be different and so you will have no conflict). A URL is usually used as this unique text string, because a Web resource has to have a unique URL. The URL can be your home page, for example.

In the <rdf:RDF> document element, an RSS 1.0 document connects the prefix *rdf* with the standard set of RDF elements, and sets up a default namespace for the rest of the document. (If you omit the prefix in an element, RSS readers will assume that element is in the default namespace.)

```
<rdf:RDF
   xmlns:rdf="http://www.w3.org/1999/02/22-rdf-syntax-ns#"
   xmlns="http://purl.org/rss/1.0/"
>
```

Now that you've used the `<rdf:RDF>` element, if you omit any prefix, your elements are assumed to be in the default namespace, which corresponds to the RSS 1.0 namespace (which in our example has been defined to correspond to the URL http://purl.org/rss/1.0/). When you use namespaces, your XML elements won't conflict with anyone's, and that namespace has a distinct advantage—you can create and add your own XML elements to RSS 1.0 documents. All you have to do is define a new namespace prefix; then you can make up and add your own elements to the document, as long as you preface them with the new prefix. For example, you might add the date to various elements, showing when they were created.

```
<rdf:RDF
   xmlns:rdf="http://www.w3.org/1999/02/22-rdf-syntax-ns#"
   xmlns:steve="http://www.rssmaniac.com/steve/about.html"
   xmlns="http://purl.org/rss/1.0/"
>

   <channel rdf:about="http://www.rssmaniac.com/steve">
     <steve:date>2005-03-01</steve:date>
     <title>Steve's News</title>
     <link>http://www.rssmaniac.com/steve</link>
     <description>
        This feed contains news from Steve!
     </description>

     <image rdf:resource="http://www.rssmaniac.com/steve/
     Image.jpg" />

     <items>
       <rdf:Seq>
```

*(code continues on next page)*

```
        <rdf:li resource=
        "http://xml.com/pub/2000/08/09/xslt/xslt.html" />
      </rdf:Seq>
    </items>

  </channel>

  <image rdf:about="http://www.rssmaniac.com/steve/Image.jpg">
    <title>Steve's News</title>
    <link>http://www.rssmaniac.com/steve</link>
    <url>http://www.rssmaniac.com/steve/Image.jpg</url>
  </image>

  <item rdf:about="http://www.rssmaniac.com/steve/about.html">
    <title>Steve shovels the snow</title>
    <steve:date>2006-09-01</steve:date>
    <link>http://www.rssmaniac.com/steve</link>
    <description>
    It snowed once again. Time to shovel!
    </description>
  </item>

</rdf:RDF>
```

In fact, there is an existing extension to RDF named the Dublin Core, and it already has many built-in elements you can add to RDF, including a <date> element. So when you give the Dublin Core elements their usual prefix of dc, and you connect that prefix to the defined Dublin Core namespace (which is "http://purl.org/dc/elements/1.1/"), you can add dates to any element in RSS 1.0.

```
<rdf:RDF
    xmlns:rdf="http://www.w3.org/1999/02/22-rdf-syntax-ns#"
    xmlns:dc="http://purl.org/dc/elements/1.1/"
    xmlns="http://purl.org/rss/1.0/"
  >

  <channel rdf:about="http://www.rssmaniac.com/steve">
    <dc:date>2005-03-01</steve:date>
```

```
<title>Steve's News</title>
<link>http://www.rssmaniac.com/steve</link>
<description>
  This feed contains news from Steve!
</description>

<image rdf:resource="http://www.rssmaniac.com/steve/
Image.jpg" />

<items>
  <rdf:Seq>
    <rdf:li resource=
    "http://xml.com/pub/2000/08/09/xslt/xslt.html" />
  </rdf:Seq>
</items>

</channel>

<image rdf:about="http://www.rssmaniac.com/steve/Image.jpg">
  <title>Steve's News</title>
  <link>http://www.rssmaniac.com/steve</link>
  <url>http://www.rssmaniac.com/steve/Image.jpg</url>
</image>

<item rdf:about="http://www.rssmaniac.com/steve/about.html">
  <title>Steve shovels the snow</title>
  <dc:date>2006-09-01</steve:date>
  <link>http://www.rssmaniac.com/steve</link>
  <description>
  It snowed once again. Time to shovel!
  </description>
</item>

</rdf:RDF>
```

As you can see, RSS 1.0 is based heavily on RDF—not the way the most popular version, RSS 2.0, was written. Many RSS authors wanted to reclaim RSS as its own language, not as an RDF sublanguage.

# Writing RSS 2.0 Documents

Now here's our RSS document in RSS 2.0 format, as created by NewzAlert Composer in Chapter 3. Note that NewzAlert Composer surrounds text with the XML markup `<!CDATA and ]]>` to hide that text from sensitive XML-parsing software. You don't need to use that markup in your RSS 2.0 documents; just place the text you want stored directly in your document.

```xml
<?xml version="1.0"?>
<rss version="2.0">
 <channel>
  <generator>NewzAlert Composer v1.70.6, Copyright (c) 2004-2005
   Castle Software Ltd, http://www.NewzAlert.com</generator>
  <lastBuildDate>Thu, 08 Dec 2005 14:01:27 -0500</lastBuildDate>
  <pubDate>Thu, 08 Dec 2005 14:01:34 -0500</pubDate>
  <title>Steve's News</title>
  <description><![CDATA[This feed contains news from
   Steve!]]></description>
  <link>http://www.rssmaniac.com/steve</link>
  <language>en-us</language>
  <copyright>(c) 2006</copyright>
  <managingEditor>Steve</managingEditor>
  <image>
   <title>Steve's News</title>
   <url>http://www.rssmaniac.com/steve/Image.jpg</url>
   <link>http://www.rssmaniac.com/steve</link>
   <description>Steve's News</description>
   <width>144</width>
   <height>36</height>
  </image>
    <item>
      <title>Steve shovels the snow</title>
      <description><![CDATA[It snowed once again.
       Time to shovel!]]></description>
      <pubDate>Thu, 08 Dec 2005 08:39:51 -0500</pubDate>
      <link>http://www.rssmaniac.com/steve</link>
    </item>
 </channel>
</rss>
```

RSS 2.0 is really the successor to RSS 0.91 and 0.92, not to RSS 1.0. Here's what's different in RSS 2.0:

- Channels are no longer limited to 15 items: there is no limit to the number of items in a channel.

- RSS places restrictions on the first non-whitespace characters of the data in `<link>` and `<url>` elements. The URLs in `<link>` and `<url>` elements must begin with *http://*, *https://*, *news://*, *mailto:*, or *ftp://* (no longer just *http://* or *ftp://*).

- The `<!DOCTYPE>` element is no longer required.

- You use `<rss version="2.0">` instead of `<rss version="0.91">` as the document element.

- There are new elements and attributes.

Read on for an in-depth look at the new elements and attributes in RSS 2.0.

## The `<channel>` element

Here's a list of the required channel elements in RSS 2.0. Note that the `<language>` element, which was required in RSS 0.91, is now an optional child element in the `<channel>` element.

- `<title>`

- `<link>`

- `<description>`

Here are the optional `<channel>` child elements in RSS 2.0:

- `<language>`

- `<copyright>`

- `<managingEditor>`

- `<webMaster>`

- `<pubDate>`

- `<lastBuildDate>`

- `<category>`

- `<generator>`

- `<docs>`

- `<cloud>`

- `<ttl>`

- `<image>`

- `<rating>`

- `<textInput>`

- `<skipHours>`

- `<skipDays>`

Of these optional elements, the `<category>`, `<generator>`, `<cloud>`, and `<ttl>` elements are new and did not appear in version 0.91.

## The `<channel>` element's `<category>` element

As you subscribe to more and more feeds in an RSS reader, you might want a reader that lets you organize your feeds into various folders or categories, as RSSReader does. The `<category>` element lets you suggest a category for your feed, and you can include as many `<category>` elements as you want. Here's a category element in our RSS 2.0 document:

```
<?xml version="1.0"?>
<rss version="2.0">
 <channel>
  <generator>NewzAlert Composer v1.70.6, Copyright (c) 2004-2005
   Castle Software Ltd, http://www.NewzAlert.com</generator>
  <lastBuildDate>Thu, 08 Dec 2005 14:01:27 -0500</lastBuildDate>
  <pubDate>Thu, 08 Dec 2005 14:01:34 -0500</pubDate>
  <title>Steve's News</title>
  <category>Newspapers</category>
       .
       .
       .
```

This element functions something like the categories on the back of books that are used for filing purposes in bookstores (Fiction/Mystery and the like).

This element is optional in the `<channel>` element, and has one optional attribute, `<domain>`, which usually gives a URL that lets you add more information about the category.

## The `<channel>` element's `<generator>` element

The optional `<generator>` element holds text identifying the program that was used to create the file. For example, our RSS 2.0 document was created by NewzAlert Composer.

```
<?xml version="1.0"?>
<rss version="2.0">
 <channel>
  <generator>NewzAlert Composer v1.70.6, Copyright (c) 2004-2005
   Castle Software Ltd, http://www.NewzAlert.com</generator>
  <lastBuildDate>Thu, 08 Dec 2005 14:01:27 -0500</lastBuildDate>
  <pubDate>Thu, 08 Dec 2005 14:01:34 -0500</pubDate>
  <title>Steve's News</title>
        .
        .
        .
```

This element is an optional child element of the `<channel>` element and has no attributes.

## The `<channel>` element's `<cloud>` element

The `<cloud>` element lets you interact with a Web application (also called a cloud) that supports the rssCloud interface. At its fastest, RSS feeds are assumed to be updated hourly, but sometimes that's not fast enough. For that reason, you can register with a cloud for faster updates. Programs that are registered with the cloud are notified immediately of updates. You can learn more about clouds at http://blogs.law.harvard.edu/tech/soapMeetsRss#rsscloudInterface.

There are five required attributes in this element: domain, the domain of the cloud; port, the server port over which communication should take place; path, the directory of the registering application on the server; registerProcedure, the name of the registering application; and protocol, the online communication protocol, which is usually XML-RPC (RPC stands for Remote Procedure Call) or SOAP (Simple Object Access Protocol).

```
<?xml version="1.0"?>
<rss version="2.0">
 <channel>
  <generator>NewzAlert Composer v1.70.6, Copyright (c) 2004-2005
    Castle Software Ltd, http://www.NewzAlert.com</generator>
  <lastBuildDate>Thu, 08 Dec 2005 14:01:27 -0500</lastBuildDate>
  <pubDate>Thu, 08 Dec 2005 14:01:34 -0500</pubDate>
  <title>Steve's News</title>
  <cloud domain="rssmaniac.com" port="80" path="/RPC2"
    registerProcedure="register" protocol="soap"/>
       .
       .
       .
```

## The <channel> element's <ttl> element

The last new optional element is the <ttl> element. TTL stands for "time to live," which is the number of minutes a channel can be cached before it should be refreshed from the source. It has always been assumed that channels are refreshed hourly, but if you're writing your own feed, that's going to be a tough one (unless you're a total fanatic, of course).

Here's how you might set the time for refreshes to two hours (120 minutes) in an RSS 2.0 document:

```
<?xml version="1.0"?>
<rss version="2.0">
 <channel>
  <generator>NewzAlert Composer v1.70.6, Copyright (c) 2004-2005
    Castle Software Ltd, http://www.NewzAlert.com</generator>
  <lastBuildDate>Thu, 08 Dec 2005 14:01:27 -0500</lastBuildDate>
  <pubDate>Thu, 08 Dec 2005 14:01:34 -0500</pubDate>
```

```
<title>Steve's News</title>
<ttl>120</ttl>
            .
            .
            .
```

## The <item> element

There are also changes to the RSS 2.0 <item> element. These are the required child elements of the <item> element:

- <title>
- <link>

The optional child elements of the <item> element are the following:

- <description>
- <author>
- <category>
- <comments>
- <enclosure>
- <guid>
- <pubDate>
- <source>

Which ones are new? The optional <author>, <category>, <comments>, <enclosure>, <guid>, and <source> elements.

### The <item> element's <author> element

The <author> element encloses not the author's name, but his or her email. The idea is that readers of your feed can get in touch with the author of a particular item, especially if that author is not the author of the whole channel.

```
<item>
```

*(code continues on next page)*

```
<title>Steve shovels the snow</title>
<author>steve@rssmaniac.com</author>
<description><![CDATA[It snowed once again.
 Time to shovel!]]></description>
<pubDate>Thu, 08 Dec 2005 08:39:51 -0500</pubDate>
<link>http://www.rssmaniac.com/steve</link>
</item>
```

This is a much-needed element if you have a number of people writing for the same feed, as is the case more and more. If a reader has contact information only for the channel, he or she would have to contact the channel staff in order to reach a particular individual. Providing the author's email on an item-by-item basis is a better idea.

This optional element has no child elements or attributes.

## The <item> element's <category> element

The <category> child element of the <item> element lets you list a category for the item, thus making it a snap to organize the items in your feed. This optional element might hold a category such as <category>Music</category> that lets you give information about where your item fits in. You can have as many <category> items as you like.

```
<item>
 <title>Steve shovels the snow</title>
 <author>steve@rssmaniac.com</author>
 <description><![CDATA[It snowed once again.
  Time to shovel!]]></description>
 <pubDate>Thu, 08 Dec 2005 08:39:51 -0500</pubDate>
 <link>http://www.rssmaniac.com/steve</link>
 <category>Snow</category>
 <category>Labor</category>
 <category>Weather</category>
</item>
```

The <category> element has one optional attribute, <domain>. This attribute is usually a URL that lets you add more information about the category.

### The <item> element's <comments> element

You might think that the <item> element's <comments> element contains comments about an item, but that's not the way it was designed. Instead, this element is supposed to contain a URL to a page of comments for this item.

```
<item>
 <title>Steve shovels the snow</title>
 <author>steve@rssmaniac.com</author>
 <description><![CDATA[It snowed once again.
  Time to shovel!]]></description>
 <pubDate>Thu, 08 Dec 2005 08:39:51 -0500</pubDate>
 <link>http://www.rssmaniac.com/steve</link>
 <comments>http://www.rssmaniac.com/steve/comments.html
 </comments>
</item>
```

This optional element has no child elements and no attributes.

### The <item> element's <enclosure> element

The <enclosure> child element of the <item> element is a critical one. This is the element that makes podcasting possible (see Chapter 7, "Podcasting: Adding Multimedia to Your Feeds").

```
<item>
 <title>Steve shovels the snow</title>
 <author>steve@rssmaniac.com</author>
 <description><![CDATA[It snowed once again.
  Time to shovel!]]></description>
 <pubDate>Thu, 08 Dec 2005 08:39:51 -0500</pubDate>
 <link>http://www.rssmaniac.com/steve</link>
 <enclosure url="http://www.rssmaniac.com/steve/shoveling.mp3"
   length="4823902" type="audio/mpeg" />
</item>
```

This optional child element lets you include MP3 files, for example, in your feed. There are three required attributes in this element. The url attribute gives the online location of the enclosure, the `length` attribute gives its length in bytes, and the `type` gives its MIME type, such as `"audi/mpeg"` for MP3 files (for a list of the possible MIME types, see http://www.iana.org/assignments/media-types/).

In this element, the URL must begin with `"http://"`.

### The <item> element's <guid> element

It's possible—especially if you have multiple authors writing for your feed—that you could send out two items with the same title. Some RSS readers might just look at the title and decide that they've already read the item and go on to the next. What can you do to prevent this?

You can give each item in your feed a *globally unique identifier*, or guid. A `<guid>` element is composed of a text string that uniquely identifies an item. RSS readers can check an item's `<guid>` and know for certain which items are different.

A `<guid>` element can contain any text string, as long as it's unique. For example, it could be an URL on your Web site (and because URLs are unique, they work fine—as long as you don't reuse them). You place your guid in a `<guid>` element.

```
<item>
 <title>Steve shovels the snow</title>
 <author>steve@rssmaniac.com</author>
 <description><![CDATA[It snowed once again.
  Time to shovel!]]></description>
 <pubDate>Thu, 08 Dec 2005 08:39:51 -0500</pubDate>
 <link>http://www.rssmaniac.com/steve</link>
 <guid>http://www.rssmaniac.com/48393.html</guid>
</item>
```

Another possibility is simply a large random number (that's the way Microsoft creates guids used in the volume labels of newly formatted disks) or a large random string of characters. If there are enough random digits or letters in your guid, the odds are high that your guid will not match any other guid.

```
<item>
 <title>Steve shovels the snow</title>
```

```
<author>steve@rssmaniac.com</author>
<description><![CDATA[It snowed once again.
 Time to shovel!]]></description>
<pubDate>Thu, 08 Dec 2005 08:39:51 -0500</pubDate>
<link>http://www.rssmaniac.com/steve</link>
<guid>JFWE0-F980D-V04MV-WVR05-9E0FK-EV3R3-TIVK4</guid>
</item>
```

There are no rules for creating your own guid in RSS 2.0; it just must be a unique text string.

The `<guid>` element has an attribute named isPermaLink, which you can set to "true" or "false." If you set this attribute to "true," the RSS reader knows that the guid string is a URL, and a *permalink* at that (a URL that won't change over time—at least, not as rapidly as other URLs).

## The `<item>` element's `<source>` element

In RSS 2.0, items can also contain a `<source>` element. Containing the title of the RSS channel that originated the item, this element is useful when one feed contains items from a variety of feeds (for example, when you create a new feed based on search terms). Anytime your feed contains items from other feeds or sources, it's a good idea to use the `<source>` element.

```
<item>
 <title>Steve shovels the snow</title>
 <author>steve@rssmaniac.com</author>
 <description><![CDATA[It snowed once again.
  Time to shovel!]]></description>
 <pubDate>Thu, 08 Dec 2005 08:39:51 -0500</pubDate>
 <link>http://www.rssmaniac.com/steve</link>
 <source url="http://www.rssmaniac.com/steve/news.xml">
   Steve's News
 </source>
</item>
```

This element has a required attribute: the url attribute, which gives the XML file source of the feed (in other words, the URL you can use to read the feed). So if you use this element, you can list not just the title of the feed the item came from, but also the URL of that feed (of course, ask permission before including other people's items in your feed).

## Extending RSS 2.0

Just as with RSS 1.0, you can extend RSS 2.0. If you want to create and add your own XML elements to an RSS 2.0 document, that's fine—you just have to make sure that your new elements are in their own namespace.

For example, I might want to add a new namespace that uses the prefix steve to an RSS document. Here's how that would work (remember that you have to assign a unique string to your namespace prefix).

```
<?xml version="1.0"?>
<rss version="2.0"
  xmlns:steve="http://www.rssmaniac.com/steve/about.html">
 <channel>
  <generator>NewzAlert Composer v1.70.6, Copyright (c) 2004-2005
   Castle Software Ltd, http://www.NewzAlert.com</generator>
  <lastBuildDate>Thu, 08 Dec 2005 14:01:27 -0500</lastBuildDate>
  <pubDate>Thu, 08 Dec 2005 14:01:34 -0500</pubDate>
  <title>Steve's News</title>
  <description><![CDATA[This feed contains news from
   Steve!]]></description>
            .
            .
            .
</rss>
```

Now you're free to create and add your own elements, as long as you use your new namespace's prefix:

```
<?xml version="1.0"?>
<rss version="2.0"
  xmlns:steve="http://www.rssmaniac.com/steve/about.html">
 <channel>
  <generator>NewzAlert Composer v1.70.6, Copyright (c) 2004-2005
   Castle Software Ltd, http://www.NewzAlert.com</generator>
  <lastBuildDate>Thu, 08 Dec 2005 14:01:27 -0500</lastBuildDate>
```

```
<pubDate>Thu, 08 Dec 2005 14:01:34 -0500</pubDate>
<steve:affiliation>RSS MegaGigaCo, Inc.</steve:affiliation>
<title>Steve's News</title>
<description><![CDATA[This feed contains news from
  Steve!]]></description>
<link>http://www.rssmaniac.com/steve</link>
<language>en-us</language>
<copyright>(c) 2006</copyright>
<managingEditor>Steve</managingEditor>
<image>
  <title>Steve's News</title>
  <url>http://www.rssmaniac.com/steve/Image.jpg</url>
  <link>http://www.rssmaniac.com/steve</link>
  <description>Steve's News</description>
  <width>144</width>
  <height>36</height>
</image>
<item>
  <title>Steve shovels the snow</title>
  <description><![CDATA[It snowed once again.
    Time to shovel!]]></description>
  <pubDate>Thu, 08 Dec 2005 08:39:51 -0500</pubDate>
  <link>http://www.rssmaniac.com/steve</link>
</item>
</channel>
</rss>
```

Note that even though you can add new XML elements to RSS 2.0
elements this way, there is no guarantee that RSS readers will know
how to handle them. And if they can't, they'll just ignore your feeds,
unless you use your own specialized software, written to handle your
new elements.

**Unlike an RSS 1.0 document, an RSS 2.0 document does not define a
default namespace for the entire document. The reason is RSS 2.0's
backward compatibility with RSS 0.91 and 0.92, which do not contain a
default namespace. Thus an RSS 0.91 or 0.92 document is also a valid
RSS 2.0 document.**

# Writing Atom Documents

Atom documents take a little more thought to create from scratch, because the Atom specification is more complicated (it's more than 50 pages long). Here are some of the differences between RSS 2.0 and Atom:

- Atom items are called entries.

- There's no <channel> tag (not really of any use anyway).

- Use <id> tags instead of <guid> tags.

- All elements are in the default Atom namespace.

- Links should have rel, type, and href attributes.

Here's our sample RSS document translated into a valid Atom 1.0 document. Note the different elements compared with those in an RSS 2.0 document.

```
<?xml version="1.0"?>
  <feed xmlns="http://www.w3.org/2005/Atom">
    <title type="text">Steve's News</title>
    <subtitle type="html">
      News from Steve
    </subtitle>
    <updated>2005-09-01T18:00:00Z</updated>
    <id>tag:example.org,2003:3</id>
    <link rel="alternate" type="text/html"
     hreflang="en" href="http://www.rssmaniac.com/steve"/>
    <link rel="self" type="application/atom+xml"
     href="http://www.rssmaniac.com/steve/news.xml"/>
    <rights>Copyright 2006.</rights>
    <entry>
      <title>Steve shovels the snow</title>
      <link rel="alternate" type="text/html"
       href="http://www.rssmaniac.com/steve"/>
      <link rel="enclosure" type="audio/mpeg" length="353566"
       href="http://rssmaniac.com/steve/snow.mp3"/>
      <id>tag:example.org,2003:3.2397</id>
```

```
        <updated>2005-09-01T18:00:00Z</updated>
        <published>2005-09-01T16:00:00Z</published>
        <author>
          <name>Steve</name>
          <uri>http://rssmaniac.com/steve</uri>
          <email>steve@rssmaniac.com</email>
        </author>
        <contributor>
          <name>Nancy</name>
        </contributor>
        <content type="xhtml" xml:lang="en"
         xml:base="http://rssmaniac.com/">
          <div xmlns="http://www.w3.org/1999/xhtml">
            It snowed once again. Time to shovel!
          </div>
        </content>
      </entry>
      </entry>
    </feed>
```

Atom feeds are somewhat more complex and longer than RSS 2.0 documents, but if you take a look at what's going on in our sample document, it should be understandable—or at least familiar.

# 5

# Blogging with RSS

This chapter is all about working with RSS and Web logs, or blogs. Blogs are Web logs of news items that are read by interested people, and RSS feeds are streams of news items that are read by interested people. Together, they're a natural combination. Blogs are maintained by server-side software, and that software can be adapted to automatically create a new RSS feed every time you post to a blog.

Here's how it works. You come up with a great new thought and log on to your blogging site. You create your new blog entry and post it, using the site's blogging software. The new blog entry appears as it should, and you're satisfied.

Behind the scenes, however, there's more going on. Most blogging sites automatically add your new blog entries as new items for your RSS feed. You don't have to do anything at all. Anyone who has subscribed to your feed is notified of the new item when they start their RSS reader.

As you can see, blogging and RSS are a natural fit. This chapter explores how to get a blog going that also creates an RSS feed for you automatically.

# Blogging with Blogger

Blogger.com (www.blogger.com) was one of the earliest blogging sites (**Figure 5.1**), and may still be the best known among blogging sites today; in fact, its parent company was just bought by Google. You can set up your own blog at Blogger—which has more than 300,000 blogs—for free. And your blog will automatically be made available as an RSS feed—Blogger creates Atom feeds for you automatically.

**Figure 5.1**

Blogger.com is a famous blogging site.

Writing, creating, and maintaining your own blog is easy at Blogger. You can host your blog on your own Web site, or on Blogger's BlogSpot server.

How do you create your blog and then sign up for the automatic feed based on your blog? It's easy. After you click the Create Your Blog Now button, you enter your username, password, display name, and email address (**Figure 5.2**).

**Figure 5.2**

It's easy to create an account at Blogger.

Next, you can name your blog and set the URL your readers will enter to access your blog—in our example, http://rssmaniac.blogspot.com (**Figure 5.3**). Blogger then asks you to enter the word that appears in the wavy graphic (this step is to prevent online programs from creating blogs). If you plan to host your blog on your own site, click the Advanced Blog Setup link, but the vast majority of Blogger users host their blogs on BlogSpot.

**Figure 5.3**
Blogger uses a separate page for your blog's name and URL.

You can choose from a dozen templates for your blog to set its appearance. In our example, we will stick with the default choice, Minima (**Figure 5.4**).

**Figure 5.4**
Select your blog's template or create a new one.

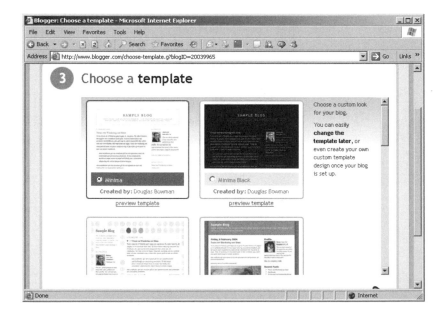

Then, if all goes as it should, Blogger creates your new blog (**Figure 5.5**). Very simple!

**Figure 5.5**

The new blog has been created.

## Posting with Blogger

Now you're ready to start posting to your new blog. Click the Start Posting button to open the new post-editing page. Simply enter the title and the text to your new post. When you're ready to publish your new post, select the Publish Post button located at the bottom of the page (**Figure 5.6**).

Blogger publishes your post and, if things work correctly, notifies you that everything went fine (**Figure 5.7**).

**Figure 5.6**

In the space provided, create a new post.

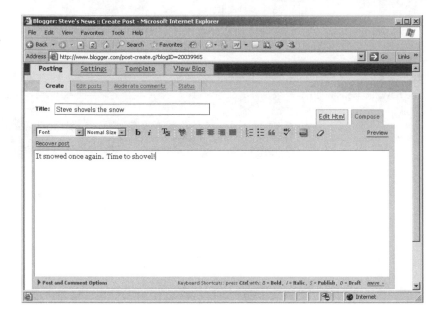

**Figure 5.7**

Your post has been published!

Want to see your new blog? Click the View Blog tab or link. Your newly created blog appears—very cool (**Figure 5.8**).

**Figure 5.8**

Your new blog at Blogger.com.

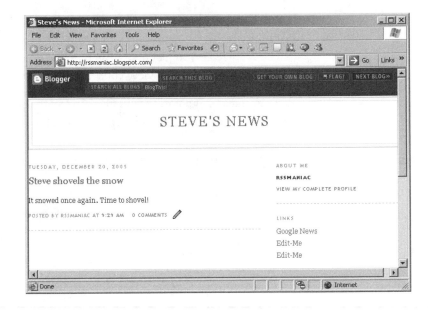

## Blogger's Atom feed

How can you grab your blog's Atom feed? Choose the Settings tab in your blog's main page, then click the Site Feed link to display the properties of your new Atom feed (**Figure 5.9**).

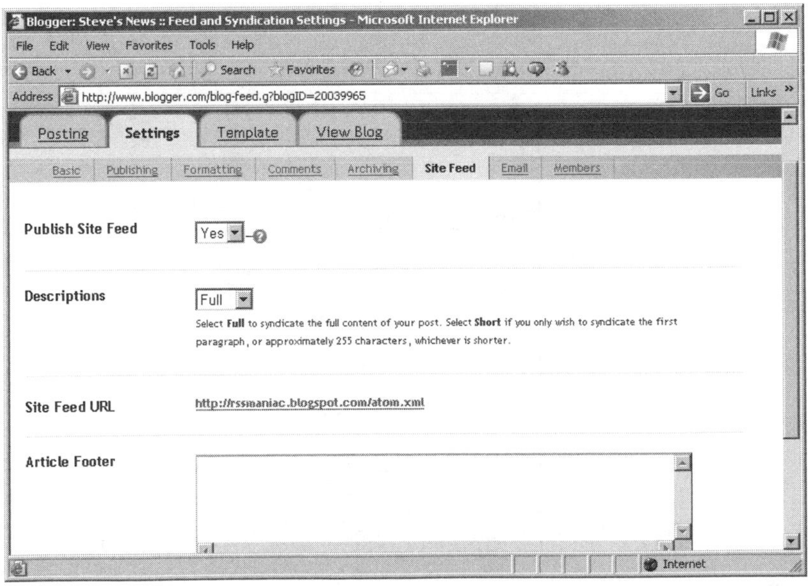

**Figure 5.9**

The Settings tab lists your Atom feed URL as well as options for displaying your feed.

Notice the URL of your automatically created Atom feed: http://rssmaniac.blogspot.com/atom.xml. That's how Blogger's Atom feeds can be accessed—you just add */atom.xml* to the end of your blog's URL. Now all you have to do is view your new feed in a reader (**Figure 5.10**).

Want to add another post to your blog? To create a new post, choose the Posting tab in your blog's main page, then click the Create link (**Figure 5.11**).

**Figure 5.10**
Here's your blog's Atom feed in RSSReader.

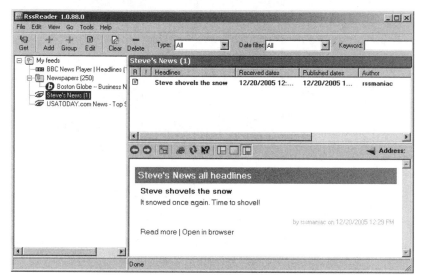

**Figure 5.11**
Click the Create link to add a new post to your blog.

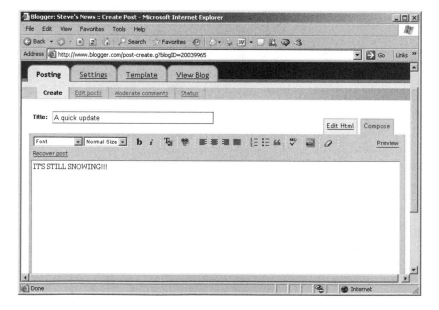

After you click the Publish Post button, wait just a minute or two and your new post will appear in the blog. That new post will also appear in your Atom feed for the blog, as you see in RSSReader (**Figure 5.12**).

**Figure 5.12**

You might have to wait a couple minutes to see the new blog post in your Atom feed.

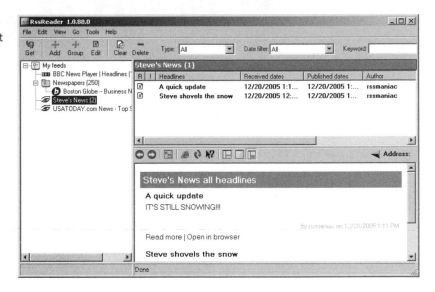

 By default, other users can add comments to your blog. Those comments, however, will not appear in your Atom feed for your blog.

Blogger has endless other options as well: You can post by email, post from any Web site with Blogger's Blog This button, create a group blog that people can post to, post photos if you use Blogger's Hello add-on, and even use AudioBlogger to post audio by telephone.

# Blogging with LiveJournal

LiveJournal (www.livejournal.com) is a blogging site that has an astounding 1,981,685 active users, according to its home page (**Figure 5.13**). Blogs you create at LiveJournal are automatically converted into Atom or RSS feeds.

**Figure 5.13**

LiveJournal has nearly 2 million active users.

To create a new blog, you click the Create link to open the Create New Journal page (**Figure 5.14**).

**Figure 5.14**

Simply follow the directions to create a new blog at LiveJournal.

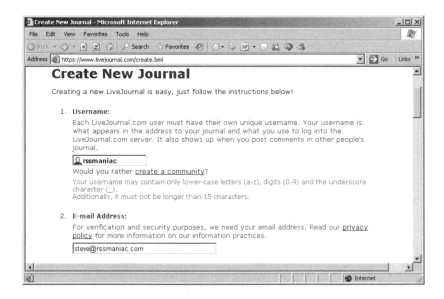

Next, enter your username (*rssmaniac* here), email address, date of birth, and account type. Leave the radio button next to Free Account selected, as it is by default, to create a free account, and read and accept the terms of use, which are listed in a text area control. Then, as with Blogger, you decipher a set of letters and numbers, enter them in a text field to prove you're an actual human, and click the Create Journal button.

LiveJournal emails a link to you that you have to click to complete the registration. This takes you to the success page (**Figure 5.15**).

**Figure 5.15**
LiveJournal validates your email address.

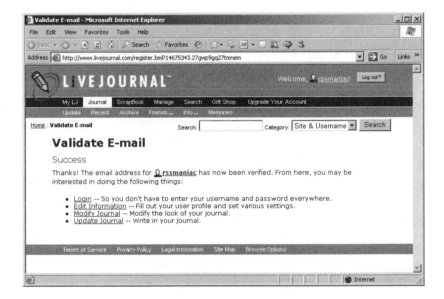

With *rssmaniac* as the username, your new blog will be accessible at www.livejournal.com/users/rssmaniac/.

## Posting with LiveJournal

After you enter a new subject for your post and the text in the Entry box, click the Update Journal button at the bottom of the page (**Figure 5.16**).

**Figure 5.16**

To post to your new blog, click the Update Journal button to open the Update Journal page.

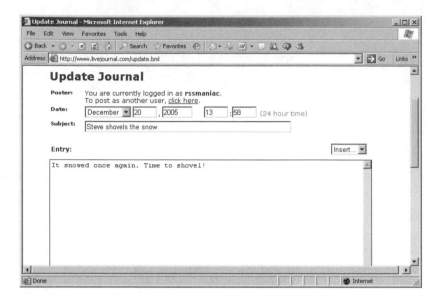

Doing so takes you back to the Update Journal page, where you click a link to see your new blog (**Figure 5.17**).

**Figure 5.17**

Take a look at your new blog at LiveJournal.

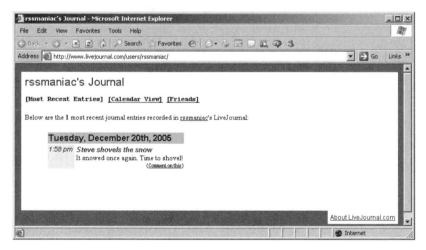

# LiveJournal's RSS and Atom feeds

At LiveJournal, you can get both RSS and Atom feeds for your blog. In general, here's the URL you'd use to gain access to the RSS or Atom feed for your LiveJournal blog:

www.livejournal.com/users/*username*/data/rss

www.livejournal.com/users/*username*/data/atom

Here's what the RSS 2.0 feed looks like at LiveJournal:

```
<?xml version="1.0" encoding="utf-8"?>
<!--    If you are running a bot please visit this policy page
outlining rules you must respect. http://www.livejournal.com/bots/
    -->
<rss version="2.0"
xmlns:lj="http://www.livejournal.org/rss/lj/1.0/">
<channel>
<title>rssmaniac</title>
<link>http://www.livejournal.com/users/rssmaniac/</link>
<description>rssmaniac - LiveJournal.com</description>
<managingEditor>steve@lightlink.com</managingEditor>
<lastBuildDate>Tue, 20 Dec 2005 19:09:54 GMT</lastBuildDate>
<generator>LiveJournal / LiveJournal.com</generator>
<item>
<guid isPermaLink="true">
http://www.livejournal.com/users/rssmaniac/362.html</guid>
<pubDate>Tue, 20 Dec 2005 19:09:54 GMT</pubDate>
<title>Steve shovels the snow</title>
<author>steve@lightlink.com</author>
<link>http://www.livejournal.com/users/rssmaniac/362.html</link>
<description>It snowed once again. Time to shovel!</description>
<comments>http://www.livejournal.com/users/rssmaniac/362.html
</comments>
</item>
</channel>
</rss>
```

You can see your new blog's RSS feed in FeedDemon (**Figure 5.18**).

**Figure 5.18**

View your new blog's RSS feed from LiveJournal in FeedDemon.

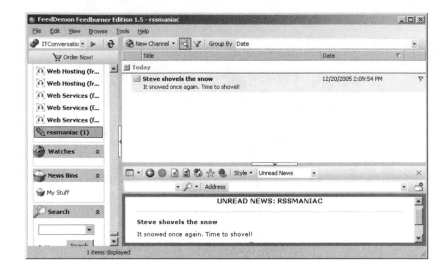

As with Blogger, when you update your blog in LiveJournal, your RSS and Atom feeds are automatically updated to match. One cool thing about LiveJournal is that you can post just about anything—including photos—using a cell phone from anywhere.

## Blogging with TypePad

TypePad (www.typepad.com) is another good place to host your blog (**Figure 5.19**). TypePad costs from $4.95 to $14.95 a month, depending on the option you select—and there's a 30-day free trial.

To create an account, click the Start Free Trial button. Signing up for a new account works much as it does with LiveJournal: Select and enter a member (user) name (again, *rssmaniac* in our example), password, your email address, and date of birth, then accept the Terms of Service (**Figure 5.20**).

**Figure 5.19**
Here's the TypePad home page.

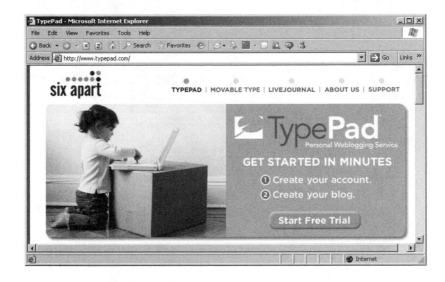

**Figure 5.20**
Create an account by selecting your account name and password.

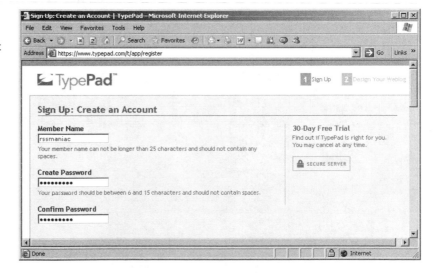

You can also select the URL of your blog (**Figure 5.21**).

When you're all set, click the Continue button, and select the billing plan you want. Whatever plan you get, you'll have a 30-day free trial. The current plans are Basic, at $4.95 per month or $49.50 per year; Plus, at $8.95 per month or $89.50 per year (allows you to build photo albums and maintain up to three blogs); and Pro, at $14.95 per month or $149.50 per year (lets you have guest authors and unlimited Web logs). A credit card is necessary.

**Figure 5.21**

Be careful when you select your domain name—you can't change it later.

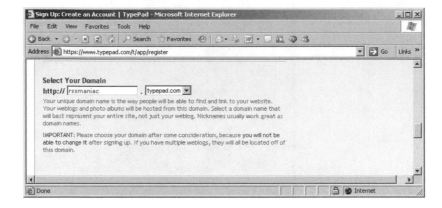

After entering all the necessary information, it's time to design your blog. First name your blog, then select your blog's layout and style from a bunch of templates (**Figure 5.22**).

**Figure 5.22**

TypePad has layouts for digital photos, audio, and video as well as class styles.

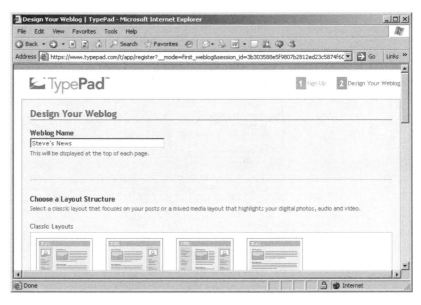

After you've finished your design, a confirmation page appears, followed by a Congratulations page, on your new account.

# Posting with TypePad

To get started, use the Post link next to your new blog's name. Doing so brings up an editing page much like the one you use with Blogger or LiveJournal (**Figure 5.23**).

After you've saved your blog, click the View Weblog link at the top-right corner of the page to see your new blog (**Figure 5.24**).

**Figure 5.23**

Create a new post by choosing the Post tab.

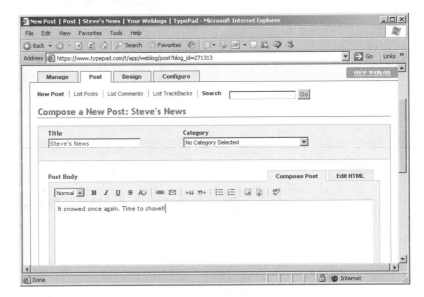

**Figure 5.24**

Here's how your new blog looks in TypePad.

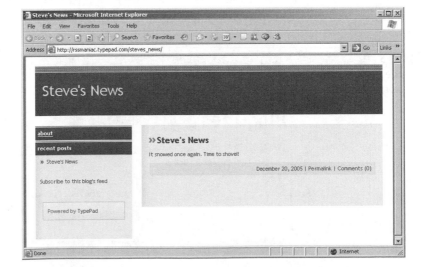

## TypePad's RSS feed

You can subscribe to your new RSS 1.0 feed in the usual way; just let your RSS reader know about the feed's URL (**Figure 5.25**).

**Figure 5.25**

View your new blog in SharpReader.

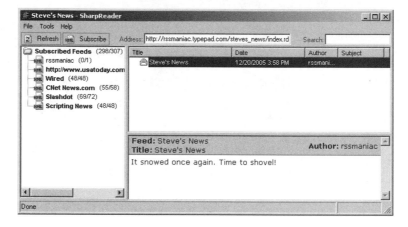

# Blogging with Bloglines

You've already seen Bloglines (www.bloglines.com) in Chapter 2, "Grabbing RSS with Readers," where it was used as an RSS reader. But as you can gather from its name, you can use Bloglines to create your own blog as well. In the main Bloglines page, sign in or create a new account and then click the My Blog tab and click the link on the right to set up your "clip blog" (**Figure 5.26**).

**Figure 5.26**

You need to set up a clip blog in Bloglines.

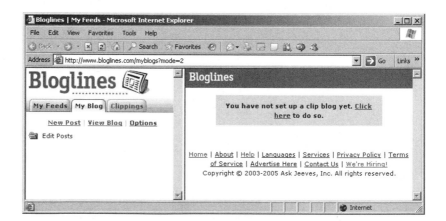

What's a clip blog? It's a blog you create from the good stuff you read in the blogs on Bloglines. You simply "clip" text and add it to your blog. Enter the user name you want to use for your blog, the blog's title and description, and select the privacy setting (**Figure 5.27**).

**Figure 5.27**

Enter the standard information for your new blog in Bloglines.

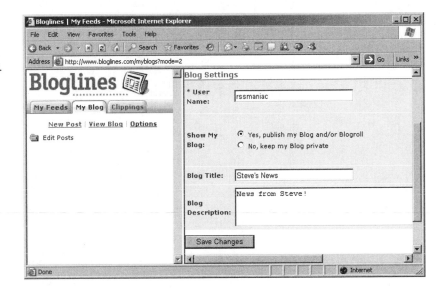

After filling in that information, save your changes. In the new page that appears, click the My Blog tab to display your new blog (**Figure 5.28**).

**Figure 5.28**

Your new blog displayed in Bloglines.

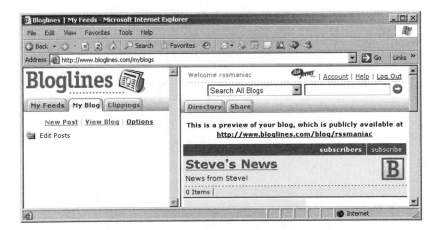

The new blog is available at www.bloglines.com/blog/rssmaniac. There's nothing in it yet—so to add a post, click New Post to open the post editor. You can choose from various font options for your new blog (**Figure 5.29**).

**Figure 5.29**
Bloglines lets you select the font, font style, and font size for the new blog.

After you've entered your new post, scroll down, click Publish to Blog and then navigate to the URL of your new blog (**Figure 5.30**).

**Figure 5.30**
Your new blog in Bloglines.

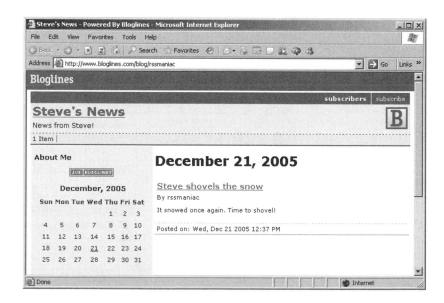

# Bloglines' RSS feed

To subscribe to your blog's new RSS feed, click the Sub button on the left.

To read your new feed from Bloglines itself (**Figure 5.31**), just subscribe to the feed as you would any feed using Bloglines—go to the Bloglines main page, log in if necessary, and click the My Feeds tab, followed by the Add link.

How do you clip news items and add them to your blog? When you see an RSS item you like, just click the Clip/Blog This link at the bottom of the RSS items (**Figure 5.32**).

**Figure 5.31**

Read your new blog using RSS in Bloglines.

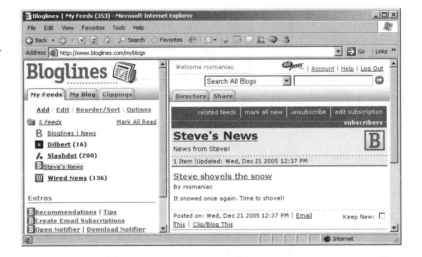

**Figure 5.32**

You can also read other RSS items in Bloglines.

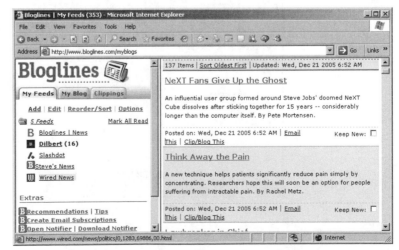

When you click the Clip/Blog This link, the RSS item opens in a new window (**Figure 5.33**).

**Figure 5.33**

It's easy to clip an item in Bloglines.

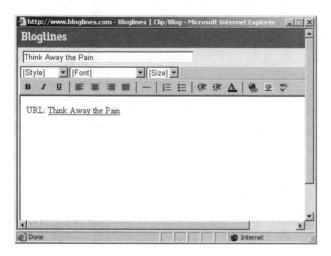

After you click Publish to Blog, a confirming message appears in the current window. Close that window and click the My Blogs button in the main Bloglines window. The newly-clipped item will now appear in your blog (**Figure 5.34**).

**Figure 5.34**

Here's the clipped item as it appears in your Bloglines blog.

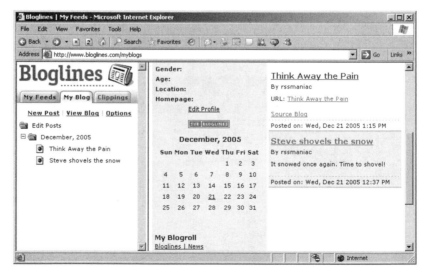

To add some text to the newly clipped item, just click the item to open the editing window (**Figure 5.35**).

**Figure 5.35**

Edit a clipped item in your Bloglines blog.

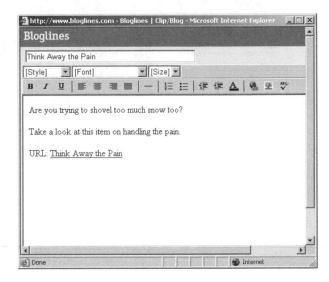

Make the edits you'd like, then resave your blog. When you go back to your blog, you'll see your comments added to the newly clipped blog item (**Figure 5.36**).

**Figure 5.36**

You can comment on a clipped item in your Bloglines blog.

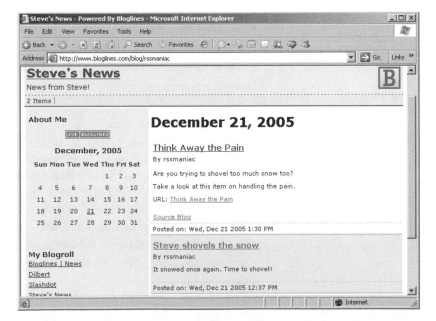

This new item will also appear in the RSS feed for your blog (**Figure 5.37**).

**Figure 5.37**

Here's the final version of the RSS feed for the Bloglines blog.

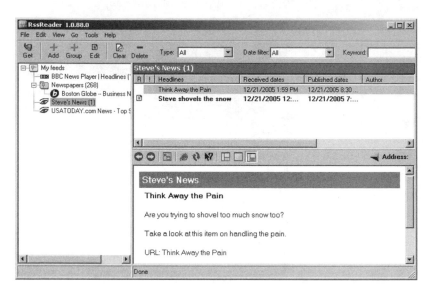

The final RSS 2.0 feed for your new blog looks like this:

```xml
<?xml version="1.0"?>
<rss version="2.0">
<channel>
<title>Steve's News</title>
<link>http://www.bloglines.com/blog/rssmaniac</link>
<description>News from Steve!</description>
<language>en-us</language>
<webMaster>support@bloglines.com</webMaster>
<item>
<title>Think Away the Pain</title>
<description><P>Are you trying to shovel too much snow too? </P>
<P>Take a look at this item on handling the pain.</P> <P>URL: <A
href="http://www.bloglines.com/preview?siteid=262&amp;itemid=5102"
target=_blank class=blines2 title="Link to another page in this
blog">Think Away the Pain</A> </P></description>
<pubDate>Wed, 21 Dec 2005 13:30:16 GMT</pubDate>
<guid>http://www.bloglines.com/blog/rssmaniac?id=2</guid>
<link>http://www.bloglines.com/blog/rssmaniac?id=2</link>
</item>
```

```
<item>
<title>Steve shovels the snow</title>
<description>It snowed once again. Time to shovel!</description>
<pubDate>Wed, 21 Dec 2005 12:37:11 GMT</pubDate>
<guid>http://www.bloglines.com/blog/rssmaniac?id=1</guid>
<link>http://www.bloglines.com/blog/rssmaniac?id=1</link>
</item>
</channel>
</rss>
```

Each time you clip an item and put it in your blog, a link appears to the source blog, and it seems that would be the perfect place to use the RSS 2.0 `<source>` element. However, as you can see by looking at the RSS feed for this blog, that source information doesn't appear in the RSS feed.

# Blogging with Yahoo

You can also create blogs on Yahoo (http://360.yahoo.com). Log in with a Yahoo username and password (or create a new Yahoo account), then click Create a Blog.

Enter your new blog title, description, and so on, and make sure you select the "Yes, publish my blog as an RSS 2.0 feed" check box (**Figure 5.38**).

**Figure 5.38**

Enter the title and description to create a Yahoo blog.

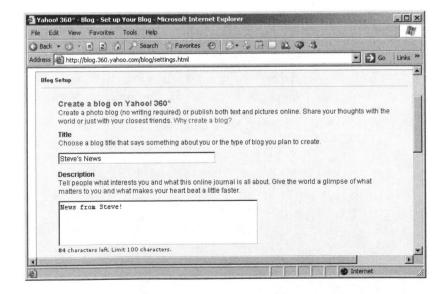

Your new blog will be at http://360.yahoo.com/*username*, where *username* is your Yahoo username.

## Posting with Yahoo

After creating your new blog, click Compose Blog Entry to post a new item to your blog (**Figure 5.39**).

**Figure 5.39**

You can use text, a photo, or both to post to your new blog.

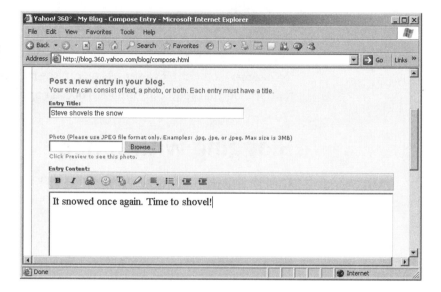

When you've finished entering the text (and optional photo) for your blog item, post the item to your blog.

To see your new blog, click the View Blog button. The new blog appears complete with your first post (**Figure 5.40**). Not bad.

To subscribe to the new RSS feed for your new blog, all you do is click the RSS button under the new blog post.

**Figure 5.40**

Click View Blog to see your new Yahoo blog.

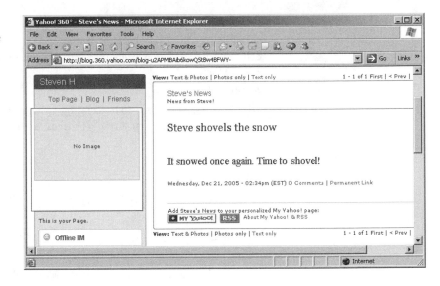

## Yahoo's RSS feed

Here's the RSS 2.0 Yahoo created for this first example blog:

```
<rss version="2.0">
<channel>
<title>
<![CDATA[ Steve's News
]]>
</title>
<link>http://blog.360.yahoo.com/blog-u2APMBAib6kowQStBw4BFWY-
</link>
<description>
<![CDATA[ News from Steve!
]]>
</description>
<language>en-us</language>
<lastBuildDate>Wed, 21 Dec 2005 19:34:23 GMT</lastBuildDate>
<item>
<title>
<![CDATA[ Steve shovels the snow
```

*(code continues on next page)*

```
]]>
</title>
<link>http://blog.360.yahoo.com/blog-u2APMBAib6kowQStBw4BFWY-
?p=1</link>
<description>
<![CDATA[ <span style="font-size:14pt; font-family:Palatino;
"><font face="Times New Roman">It snowed once again. Time to
shovel!</font></span>
]]>
</description>
<pubDate>Wed, 21 Dec 2005 19:34:23 GMT</pubDate>
</item>
</channel>
</rss>
<!-- feblg10.mgl.re2.yahoo.com uncompressed/chunked Wed Dec 21
11:38:26 PST 2005
-->
```

There you go—once again, your blog was automatically translated into a new RSS feed.

As you can see, you have plenty of options. And of course, there are other sites and downloadable tools you can use to create blogs and convert them into RSS feeds. Now all you have to do is to maintain your blog—it'll be disseminated automatically to all your readers using RSS.

# 6

# Automating Creation of RSS Feeds

You've seen how to create RSS feeds using RSS editors that can store XML files for you. And you've seen how to create those XML files yourself, from scratch.

Are there other options? Yes—you can let software create RSS feeds for you automatically, from a variety of sources including blogs, Web pages, email, and data stored in databases.

Many Web sites, such as USAToday.com, support a number of RSS feeds. Do you think the site employs a dozen RSS experts to update those feeds every day? No, it uses automatic RSS-creation tools. Some of those tools notice when a Web page (such as one that holds a new news item) changes, for example, and converts that page's content into an RSS item, which is added to an updated feed—automatically.

That's what this chapter is all about—the tools that let you create RSS feeds automatically from a variety of sources.

# Creating RSS with Blogging Tools

As you saw in Chapter 5, "Blogging with RSS," blogs and RSS go together naturally. When you update a blog, you're adding a new item to it—and spreading the word about such items is what RSS is all about.

It's hard to think of a better way to publish your blog than by creating an RSS feed. That's why so many blogging sites let you automatically convert your blog to RSS feeds.

Here are some of the blogging sites and the RSS feeds they'll create for you automatically:

- Blogger: Atom feeds
- BlogLines: RSS 2.0 feeds
- LiveJournal: RSS 2.0 and Atom feeds
- TypePad: RSS 2.0 and Atom feeds
- Yahoo: RSS 2.0 feeds

If you are already publishing your blog, in many cases you're all set to create your own RSS feed—your blogging site will do it for you.

But using a blogging Web site is only one way to create your RSS feed automatically. There are many other techniques—such as grabbing news content from Web pages.

# Scraping RSS from HTML

In the RSS world, the process of extracting data from a Web site is called *scraping*, and there are several ways to do it. Some software looks at a site and guesses what you want in an RSS feed, and other software requires that you set up your site in a certain way so it can scrape data off it easily. Both kinds are valid, so which software you choose is up to you.

**Don't start scraping Web sites and publishing the content in your own RSS feeds before you get permission.**

## RSS with FeedFire

FeedFire (www.feedfire.com) is an easy software package to start with (**Figure 6.1**).

**Figure 6.1**

Registration is free at FeedFire.com.

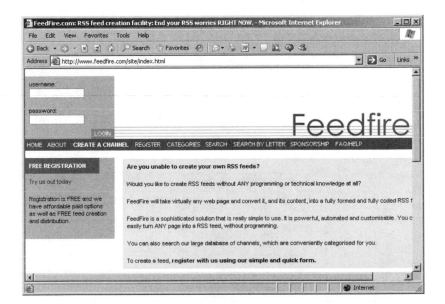

To log in you need to register first, and registration is free. After you've set your user name and password, log in, and it's time to create a new channel by scraping a Web page.

In this example, a sample feed for the USAToday.com home page was created to show how FeedFire works. The *USA Today*'s URL has been entered in FeedFire's Create a Channel page (**Figure 6.2**).

**Figure 6.2**

Creating a new channel at FeedFire.com is easy.

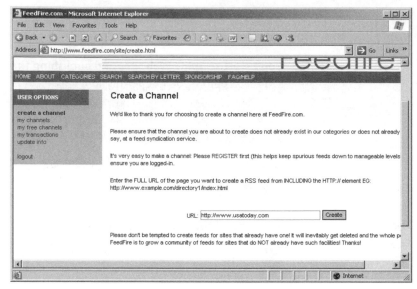

When you click the Create button, the new sample channel is created for you (**Figure 6.3**).

**Figure 6.3**

The new feed is based on the home page of USAToday.com.

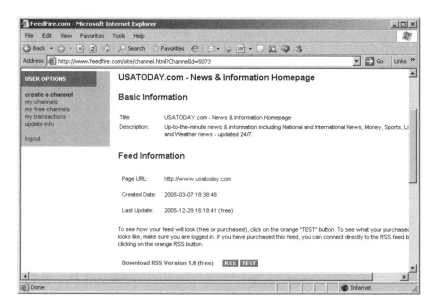

FeedFire creates RSS 1.0 feeds.

```
<?xml version="1.0" encoding="ISO-8859-1"?>
<rdf:RDF xmlns:rdf="http://www.w3.org/1999/02/22-rdf-syntax-ns#"
xmlns="http://purl.org/rss/1.0/"
xmlns:dc="http://purl.org/dc/elements/1.1/"
xmlns:ag="http://purl.org/rss/1.0/modules/aggregation/"
xmlns:dcterms="http://purl.org/dc/terms/"
xmlns:syn="http://purl.org/rss/1.0/modules/syndication/">
<channel rdf:about="http://www.usatoday.com">
<title>USATODAY.com    News &amp; Information Homepage</title>
<link>http://www.usatoday.com</link>
<description>Up-to-the-minute news & information including
National and International News, Money, Sports, Life,
Tech and Weather news   updated 24/7.   Created by
FeedFire.com</description>
<syn:updatePeriod>daily</syn:updatePeriod>
<syn:updateFrequency>1</syn:updateFrequency>
<dcterms:modified>2005-12-29T16:12:40+00:00</dcterms:modified>
<dcterms:created>2005-12-29T16:12:40+00:00</dcterms:created>
<items>
<rdf:Seq>
<rdf:li rdf:resource="http://www.usatoday.com/life/2005-12-28-
year-in-bad-news_x.htm" />
<rdf:li rdf:resource="http://www.usatoday.com/news/
interactive-media.htm" />
<rdf:li rdf:resource="http://www.usatoday.com/news/gallery/
2005/12-28-day/flash.htm" />
<rdf:li rdf:resource="http://www.usatoday.com/news/nation/2005-
12-27-oklahoma-fires_x.htm" />
<rdf:li rdf:resource="http://usatodaytv.feedroom.com/
?fr_story=FEEDROOM127556" />
<rdf:li rdf:resource="http://www.usatoday.com/news/health/2005-
12-28-smoking-limits_x.htm" />
<rdf:li rdf:resource="http://www.usatoday.com/news/world/2005-
12-29-israel-explosion_x.htm" />
<rdf:li rdf:resource="http://www.usatoday.com/money/economy/
housing/2005-12-29-existing-homes_x.htm" />
<rdf:li rdf:resource="http://www.usatoday.com/news/
washington/2005-12-28-corps-jeep_x.htm" />
```

*(code continues on next page)*

```
<rdf:li rdf:resource="http://www.usatoday.com/news/nation/2005-
12-28-young-moving_x.htm" />
            .

            .

            .
</rdf:Seq>
</items>
</channel>
<item rdf:about="http://www.usatoday.com/life/2005-12-28-year-
in-bad-news_x.htm">
<title>2005 seemed to validate Chicken Little's
pessimism</title>
<link>http://www.usatoday.com/life/2005-12-28-year-in-bad-
news_x.htm</link>
<dc:date>2005-12-29T16:12:40+00:00</dc:date>
</item>
<item rdf:about="http://www.usatoday.com/news/interactive-
media.htm">
<title>Interactive Media</title>
<link>http://www.usatoday.com/news/interactive-media.htm</link>
<dc:date>2005-12-29T16:12:40+00:00</dc:date>
</item>
            .

            .

            .
</rdf:RDF>
```

To subscribe to this new feed, use the XML button.

There are a couple of things you should notice about this *USA Today* feed (**Figure 6.4**). One is that it's simple, showing only links, not item content. Another is that the items in the RSS feed don't appear in the same order as on the original Web page. FeedFire also often puts ads in its free RSS feeds.

You can also pay for various other levels of RSS feed creation at FeedFire. In the paid levels, you can list keywords to specify what links you want to include in your feed, and you can "sponsor" a feed, which allows you to place your name at the beginning of the feed's name.

**Figure 6.4**

The new *USA Today* feed is displayed in the description window.

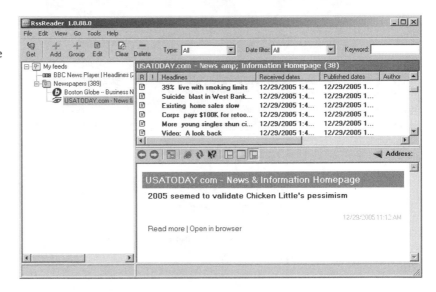

## RSS with myWebFeeds

Another Web-site scraper is myWebFeeds, at www.mywebfeeds.com (**Figure 6.5**).

**Figure 6.5**

You can turn any Web page into a feed with myWebFeeds.

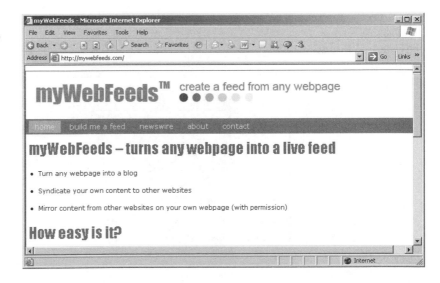

Select the Build Me a Feed link to create a new feed, and enter the URL (**Figure 6.6**)—here, http://www.usatoday.com.

**Figure 6.6**

Just follow the directions to build a new feed at myWebFeeds.

The Preview button lets you see the items in the new feed (**Figure 6.7**). However, setting up a new feed at myWebFeeds isn't free.

**Figure 6.7**

There is a fee to receive the code for a feed at myWebFeeds.

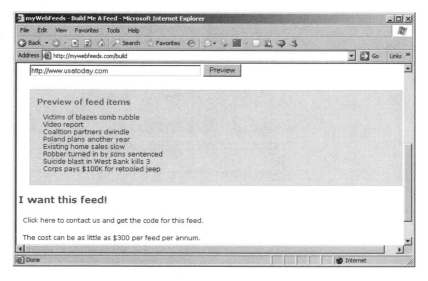

FeedFire and myWebFeeds are nice tools that let you scrape Web sites and publish RSS feeds from those sites. If you want to extract more detailed information, however, you have to customize the Web pages you're scraping for data.

## RSS with W3C's online service

The World Wide Web Consortium's online Web-site scraper gives you more power but at the price of more work (**Figure 6.8**). When something is from the W3C, as you might expect if you've ever worked with W3C specifications, things can get complex.

For starters, you can only scrape XHTML pages, not HTML. XHTML, which stands for Extensible Hypertext Markup Language, is the W3C's recasting of HTML 4.01—the final version of HTML—in XML 1.0. (You can read all about XHTML at www.w3.org/TR/xhtml1/.) In other words, XHTML documents are XML documents that look just like HTML to a browser.

**Remember that you can make up your own tags in XML.**

You use XML tags to match the standard HTML tags—for example, <html>, <head>, <body>, and so on, and they look like normal HTML tags to the browser. But since the tags are actually XML tags, the resulting document is an XML document even though its extension is .html.

XHTML has two advantages: First, it can be validated just like any XML document, and validating an XHTML document will show you any syntax errors in the document. Second, because it's XML, you can extend XHTML by creating your own tags. (However, you have to do some fancy footwork to make the browser understand what the new tag is supposed to do—usually, you use Cascading Style Sheets (CSS) styles to customize what a new tag does in the browser.)

There are plenty of rules that specify how to write XHTML, and as a result it's cumbersome and hasn't really caught on among the home page crowd, although it's popular on corporate Web sites.

**Still confused about XHTML? The W3C provides a tool to help convert XHTML into HTML. Read on.**

To scrape an XHTML Web page and create an RSS 1.0 feed, go to www.w3.org/2000/08/w3c-synd (Figure 6.8).

**Figure 6.8**

The W3C site gives directions on how to configure your XHTML page.

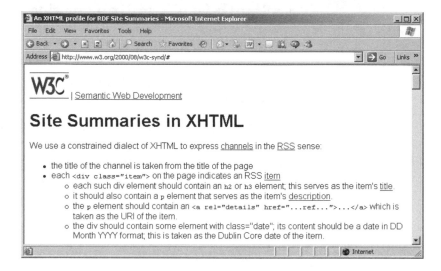

I used a simple XHTML page and scraped it to create an RSS feed (**Figure 6.9**). In order to be scraped, an XHTML page has to use a lot of special XHTML behind the scenes. For example, you can see some of the directions on how to configure your XHTML page in Figure 6.9.

**Figure 6.9**

Here's a sample XHTML page.

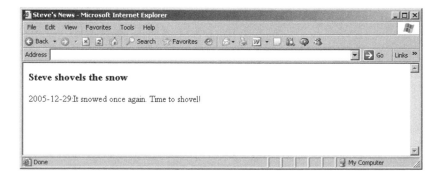

How do you build an XHTML page that can be scraped? Let's create news.html, an XTHML page, to show how this works. You start news.html like any XML document, with an XML declaration:

```
<?xml version="1.0" encoding="utf-8"?>
        .

        .

        .
```

There are three main types of XHTML: strict, transitional, and frameset. Strict XHTML 1.0 will be used in this example. To indicate to the browser that you're using strict XHTML 1.0, use a <!DOCTYPE> element that points to the strict XHTML 1.0 DTD (recall from Chapter 4, "Creating RSS Feeds from Scratch," that DTDs let you check an XML document's validity and make sure there are no syntax errors). Here's the strict XHTML 1.0 <!DOCTYPE> element:

```
<?xml version="1.0" encoding="utf-8"?>
<!DOCTYPE html PUBLIC "-//W3C//DTD XHTML 1.0 Strict//EN"
"http://www.w3.org/TR/xhtml1/DTD/xhtml1-strict.dtd">
        .

        .

        .
```

Now you can add the <html> element, giving it the standard XHTML namespace of http://www.w3.org/1999/xhtml.

```
<?xml version="1.0" encoding="utf-8"?>
<!DOCTYPE html PUBLIC "-//W3C//DTD XHTML 1.0 Strict//EN"
"http://www.w3.org/TR/xhtml1/DTD/xhtml1-strict.dtd">
<html xmlns="http://www.w3.org/1999/xhtml" xml:lang="en-US"
lang="en-US">
        .

        .

        .
```

You also specify how you're going to work with XHTML so that the W3C tool can convert the document into RSS (with <div> elements and class attributes to set up an RSS item, for example) using the profile

attribute of the <head> element. The profile attribute should be set to
http://www.w3.org/2000/08/w3c-synd/#, as you see in news.html:

```
<?xml version="1.0" encoding="utf-8"?>
<!DOCTYPE html PUBLIC "-//W3C//DTD XHTML 1.0 Strict//EN"
"http://www.w3.org/TR/xhtml1/DTD/xhtml1-strict.dtd">
<html xmlns="http://www.w3.org/1999/xhtml" xml:lang="en-US"
lang="en-US">
  <head profile="http://www.w3.org/2000/08/w3c-synd/#">
      .
      .
      .
```

The name of the new RSS channel is taken from the XHTML document's <title> element; that title in our example is Steve's News.

**In XHTML, each <head> element must contain one, and only one, <title>
element.**

```
<?xml version="1.0" encoding="utf-8"?>
<!DOCTYPE html PUBLIC "-//W3C//DTD XHTML 1.0 Strict//EN"
"http://www.w3.org/TR/xhtml1/DTD/xhtml1-strict.dtd">
<html xmlns="http://www.w3.org/1999/xhtml" xml:lang="en-US"
lang="en-US">
    <head profile="http://www.w3.org/2000/08/w3c-synd/#">
      <title>Steve's News</title>
    </head>
        .
        .
        .
```

So far, so good; you've named your new channel. To create items for
your RSS feed, you use the <body> element of the document. To create a
new item, you use a <div> element with a class attribute set to "item".

```
<?xml version="1.0" encoding="utf-8"?>
<!DOCTYPE html PUBLIC "-//W3C//DTD XHTML 1.0 Strict//EN"
"http://www.w3.org/TR/xhtml1/DTD/xhtml1-strict.dtd">
<html xmlns="http://www.w3.org/1999/xhtml" xml:lang="en-US"
lang="en-US">
    <head profile="http://www.w3.org/2000/08/w3c-synd/#">
```

```
    <title>Steve's News</title>
  </head>

  <body>

    <div class="item">
        .

        .

        .
```

Using a `<div>` opening tag with a `class` attribute set to `"item"` starts a new item. To set the title of the item you must use an `<h3>` XHTML element. The title of this item is set to "Steve shovels the snow."

```
<?xml version="1.0" encoding="utf-8"?>
<!DOCTYPE html PUBLIC "-//W3C//DTD XHTML 1.0 Strict//EN"
"http://www.w3.org/TR/xhtml1/DTD/xhtml1-strict.dtd">
<html xmlns="http://www.w3.org/1999/xhtml" xml:lang="en-US"
lang="en-US">
  <head profile="http://www.w3.org/2000/08/w3c-synd/#">
    <title>Steve's News</title>
  </head>

  <body>

    <div class="item">
      <h3>Steve shovels the snow</h3>
        .

        .

        .
```

At this point, then, a new item has been created and given a title. Now it's time to add a description using a `<p>` element.

```
<?xml version="1.0" encoding="utf-8"?>
<!DOCTYPE html PUBLIC "-//W3C//DTD XHTML 1.0 Strict//EN"
"http://www.w3.org/TR/xhtml1/DTD/xhtml1-strict.dtd">
<html xmlns="http://www.w3.org/1999/xhtml" xml:lang="en-US"
lang="en-US">
  <head profile="http://www.w3.org/2000/08/w3c-synd/#">
```

*(code continues on next page)*

```
      <title>Steve's News</title>
    </head>

    <body>

      <div class="item">
        <h3>Steve shovels the snow</h3>
        <p>

          .

          .

          .

        </p>
      </div>

    </body>
  </html>
```

To set the date of an item, you can use a `<span>` element with a class attribute set to `"date"`.

```
    <?xml version="1.0" encoding="utf-8"?>
    <!DOCTYPE html PUBLIC "-//W3C//DTD XHTML 1.0 Strict//EN"
    "http://www.w3.org/TR/xhtml1/DTD/xhtml1-strict.dtd">
    <html xmlns="http://www.w3.org/1999/xhtml" xml:lang="en-US"
    lang="en-US">
      <head profile="http://www.w3.org/2000/08/w3c-synd/#">
        <title>Steve's News</title>
      </head>

      <body>

        <div class="item">
          <h3>Steve shovels the snow</h3>
          <p>
            <span class="date">2005-12-29</span>

            .

            .

            .

          </p>
```

```
          </div>

        </body>
      </html>
```

Now you can add the text for the item.

```
<?xml version="1.0" encoding="utf-8"?>
<!DOCTYPE html PUBLIC "-//W3C//DTD XHTML 1.0 Strict//EN"
"http://www.w3.org/TR/xhtml1/DTD/xhtml1-strict.dtd">
<html xmlns="http://www.w3.org/1999/xhtml" xml:lang="en-US"
lang="en-US">
  <head profile="http://www.w3.org/2000/08/w3c-synd/#">
    <title>Steve's News</title>
  </head>

  <body>

    <div class="item">
      <h3>Steve shovels the snow</h3>
      <p>
        <span class="date">2005-12-29:</span>
        It snowed once again. Time to shovel!
        .
        .
        .
      </p>
    </div>

  </body>
</html>
```

Finally, you can add a link to the full text of the document using an `<a>` element with a `rel` attribute set to `"details"` and an `href` attribute set to the URL of the item's full text.

```
<?xml version="1.0" encoding="utf-8"?>
<!DOCTYPE html PUBLIC "-//W3C//DTD XHTML 1.0 Strict//EN"
"http://www.w3.org/TR/xhtml1/DTD/xhtml1-strict.dtd">
```

*(code continues on next page)*

```
<html xmlns="http://www.w3.org/1999/xhtml" xml:lang="en-US"
lang="en-US">
  <head profile="http://www.w3.org/2000/08/w3c-synd/#">
    <title>Steve's News</title>
  </head>

  <body>

    <div class="item">
      <h3>Steve shovels the snow</h3>
      <p>
        <span class="date">2005-12-29:</span>It snowed once again.
        Time to shovel!
          <a rel="details" title="Snow Item"
            href="http://www.rssmaniac.com/news.html"></a>
      </p>
    </div>

  </body>
</html>
```

In order to give the W3C converter access to your XHTML Web page, that page has to be online. (In general, that's not a big problem because Web pages are supposed to be online, but it would have been nice if the W3C had provided a way to read the Web page from your hard drive or allowed you to paste it into its converter to make testing and development of your Web pages a lot easier.)

So to see how to convert your XHTML page to RSS, first upload the page so it is available online. Then go to the W3C converter page and enter the URL of your XHTML page (don't change the XSL file URL—XSL stands for Extensible Stylesheet Language, and it's used to convert your XHTML into RSS). When you're ready, click the Get Results button (**Figure 6.10**).

If all goes well, a new page appears displaying your RSS items. That's what you want.

 **tip**   If all doesn't go well when you try to convert your file, check your Web page's XHTML with the W3C validator at http://validator.w3.org/. It'll tell you if there's something wrong with your XHTML.

**Figure 6.10**

Fill in the information about the XHTML page you want to scrape.

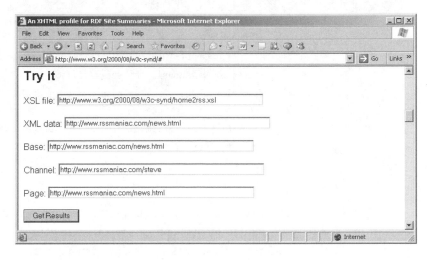

Now view the page source in the browser (select View > Source in Internet Explorer or View > Page Source in Firefox) to see the XML for the page. That XML is the RSS 1.0 version of your RSS feed.

Here's what the RSS 1.0 looks like for our example, as created by the W3C converter:

```
<?xml version="1.0" encoding="utf-8"?>
<?xml-stylesheet href="http://www.w3.org/2000/08/w3c-
synd/style.css" type="text/css"?>
<rdf:RDF xmlns:dc="http://purl.org/dc/elements/1.1/"
xmlns:h="http://www.w3.org/1999/xhtml"
xmlns:hr="http://www.w3.org/2000/08/w3c-synd/#"
xmlns:rdf="http://www.w3.org/1999/02/22-rdf-syntax-ns#"
xmlns:rdfs="http://www.w3.org/2000/01/rdf-schema#"
xmlns="http://purl.org/rss/1.0/">
<channel rdf:about="http://www.rssmaniac.com/steve">
<title>Steve's News</title>
<description/>
<link>http://www.rssmaniac.com/steve</link>
<dc:date/>
<items>
<rdf:Seq>
<rdf:li rdf:resource="http://www.rssmaniac.com/news.html"/>
</rdf:Seq>
```

*(code continues on next page)*

```
</items>
</channel>
<item rdf:about="http://www.rssmaniac.com/news.html">
<title>Steve shovels the snow</title>
<description>2005-12-29:It snowed once again. Time to
shovel!</description>
<link>http://www.rssmaniac.com/news.html</link>
<dc:date>2005-12-29</dc:date>
</item>
</rdf:RDF>
```

There you go—your Web page has been scraped and turned into RSS 1.0. It's a fairly quick process if you write your Web pages in XHTML, but the XHTML part can be a problem for many people.

## Converting HTML to XHTML

The W3C has another online tool that can convert HTML pages into XHTML; that tool, at http://cgi.w3.org/cgi-bin/tidy, is named Tidy (**Figure 6.11**). The original purpose was to "tidy up" the HTML in Web pages. (There's a great deal of sloppy HTML on the Internet—nesting errors, no closing tags, and so on; by some estimates, nearly half the code in browsers is there to deal with problematic HTML.)

**Figure 6.11**

Use the W3C's Tidy tool to convert HTML pages to XHTML.

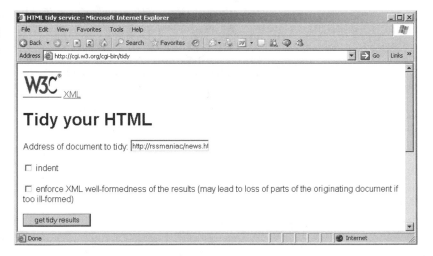

Say you've written an HTML—not XHTML—page that uses the conventions that the W3C converter needs to turn a page into RSS, such as using a `profile` attribute in the `<head>` opening tag, a `class` attribute set to `"item"` in a `<div>` opening tag to create an RSS item, and so on. Your HTML file might look like the following:

```
<html>
    <head profile="http://www.w3.org/2000/08/w3c-synd/#">
      <title>Steve's News</title>
    </head>

    <body>
      <div class="item">
        <h3>Steve shovels the snow</h3>

        <p>
          <span class="date">2005-12-29:</span>It snowed once again.
          Time to shovel!
          <a rel="details" title="Snow Item"
          href="http://www.rssmaniac.com/news.html"></a>
        </p>
      </div>

    </body>
</html>
```

You can convert the HTML file into XHTML by uploading this document, entering the URL into the Tidy page (click the indent check box if you want the results to be indented), and then clicking the Get Tidy Results button. You can see the results as they appear in Internet Explorer (**Figure 6.12**).

**Figure 6.12**

The HTML page was converted to XHTML.

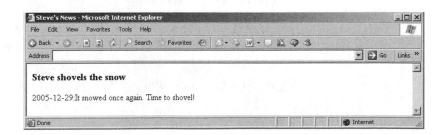

To get the XHTML source, go to View > Source or View > Page Source as before, and copy the XHTML.

```
<!DOCTYPE html PUBLIC "-//W3C//DTD XHTML 1.0 Strict//EN"
    "http://www.w3.org/TR/xhtml1/DTD/xhtml1-strict.dtd">

<html xmlns="http://www.w3.org/1999/xhtml">
<head profile="http://www.w3.org/2000/08/w3c-synd/#">
  <meta name="generator" content=
  "HTML Tidy for Linux/x86 (vers 12 April 2005), see www.w3.org" />

  <title>Steve's News</title>
</head>

<body>
  <div class="item">
    <h3>Steve shovels the snow</h3>

    <p><span class="date">2005-12-29:</span>It snowed once again.
    Time to shovel!
    <a rel="details" title="Snow Item" href=
    "http://www.rssmaniac.com/news.html"></a></p>
  </div>
</body>
</html>
```

Tidy is a useful tool if you want to use the W3C converter to scrape XHTML pages into RSS, and you can create HTML pages if you're not familiar with XHTML.

# RSS from Email

Here's another option: You can automatically create RSS feeds from email. That's a cool way of creating RSS feeds, and we'll take a look at how it works here. This technique is especially useful if you have regular mass mailings and you want to make the content available via RSS feed.

# RSS with NewslettersByRSS

Using NewslettersByRSS (www.newslettersbyrss.com/pubDefault.aspx), you can create RSS feeds automatically from email (**Figure 6.13**). First sign up at the site by filling in your name, email address, newsletter title, description of your feed, Web site URL, and the other requested information.

**Figure 6.13**

Click the Learn More links on Newsletters-ByRSS site to get additional information about sending and using newsletters.

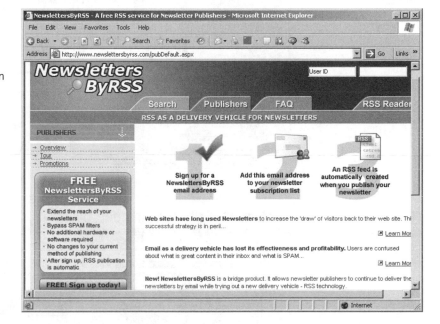

 After you sign up at NewslettersByRSS, you're given an email address where you can send your news (**Figure 6.14**). When you want to send email to an email list—or just add an item to your RSS feed—make sure you send it to the address you're given. NewslettersByRSS will generate an RSS 2.0 feed for you, based on your email.

You'll next see a confirming Web page that lists ways to publicize your feed (**Figure 6.15**). Note the link to the RSS Link Page, which gives you the URL for your created feed.

**Figure 6.14**

You've successfully created an account.

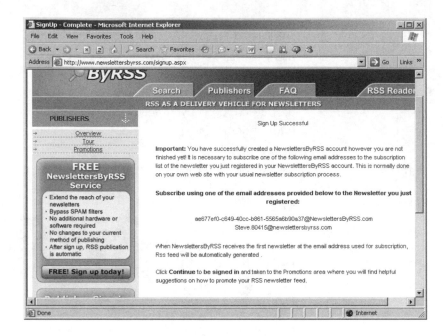

**Figure 6.15**

Copy any of the RSS graphics to use for your newsletter.

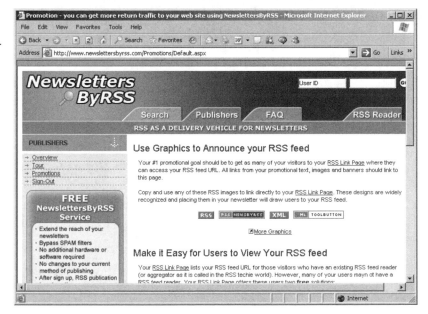

NewslettersByRSS gives interested readers an easy way to subscribe to the content of your newsletter as a feed instead of receiving it via email (**Figure 6.16**).

**Figure 6.16**

NewslettersByRSS makes it easy for your subscribers to read your feed.

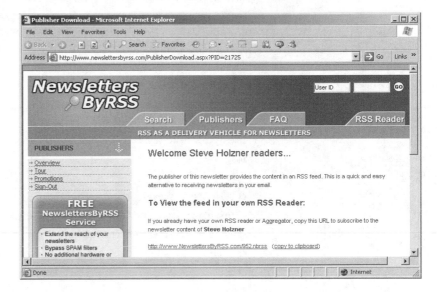

The URL for the new feed will also be sent to you in a confirming email, as well as your publisher ID and password, and the email address to add to your email list. When you send out a mailing to your email list, make sure that you also send the email address NewslettersByRSS gives you so that it can publish the email in your RSS feed.

The subject line of your newsletter email will become a new item's title in your RSS feed, and the date of your email will become the date of your new item. It's that simple—just sign up with NewslettersByRSS, get an email address and URL for your new feed, send your email to that email address, and NewslettersByRSS publishes your feed.

Here's the RSS 2.0 that was created when an email was sent to NewslettersByRSS.

```
<?xml version="1.0" encoding="us-ascii"?>
<rss version="2.0">
<channel>
```

*(code continues on next page)*

```
<title>Steve's News</title>
<link>http://www.NewslettersByRSS.com/952.nbrss</link>
<description>News from Steve!</description>
<generator>NewslettersByRSS v1.0</generator>
<atom:link xmlns:atom="http://www.w3.org/2005/Atom" rel="self"
href="http://www.newslettersbyrss.com/Feed/952.xml"
type="application/rss+xml" />
<image>
<title>Steve's News</title>
<url>http://www.newslettersbyrss.com/images/powered_by_rss.gif
</url>
<link>http://www.NewslettersByRSS.com</link>
</image>
<item>
   <title>Steve shovels the snow</title>
   <link>http://www.NewslettersByRSS.com/30594.952.nbrss</link>
   <description>It snowed once again. Time to shovel!</description>
   <pubDate>Fri, 30 Dec 2005 11:55:03 GMT</pubDate>
</item>
</channel>
</rss>
```

## RSS with iUpload

Besides dedicated email-to-RSS utilities like NewslettersByRSS, many blog sites let you post blog entries by email, and they'll create an RSS feed for you. In other words, you just email your items to the blogging site and it'll create your RSS feed for you. One such site is iUpload at www.iuplog.com (**Figure 6.17**).

To create a blog that you can email to, enter your information, the name of your new blog, a description, and other information requested. Click Submit to create your new, empty blog (**Figure 6.18**).

**Figure 6.17**

iUplog.com can create an RSS feed for you.

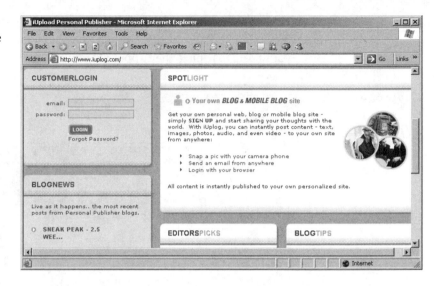

**Figure 6.18**

Although not available in this empty blog, the iUpload site provides viewer stats for each blog.

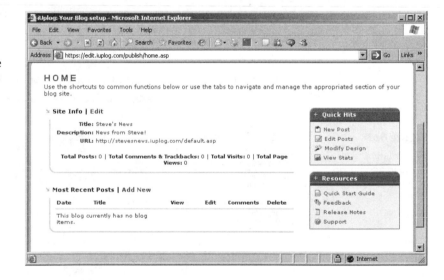

When your new blog is created, you get a confirming email that includes an email address for where to send your posts. After emailing your posts to iUplog, they appear in your blog (**Figure 6.19**).

**Figure 6.19**

Here's a new post with my blog.

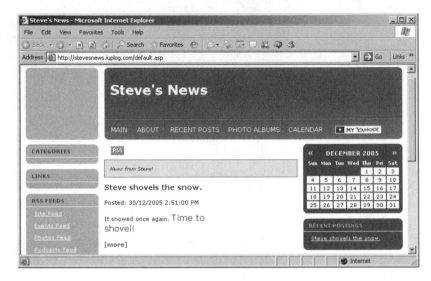

You can use the RSS button to subscribe to your new RSS feed, which can then be read in RSS readers such as SharpReader (**Figure 6.20**).

**Figure 6.20**

A new feed from iUpload appears in SharpReader.

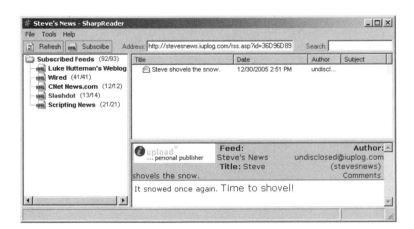

# RSS with Automatic Software

There's also free software available that works on Web servers and can scrape or create RSS feeds for you. If you want to use a software package to scrape Web sites and create RSS, be sure that your Web site can run Perl, Python, Java, or whatever language the package you want to use needs. For more information, check the Web sites for the software package you're interested in using. Here's a starter list of available RSS-scraping software:

- Grouper (www.geckotribe.com/rss/grouper) handles Web pages and Web searches and converts them to RSS. Uses the Java programming language on the Web server.

- MySQL-to-RSS 2.0 PHP script (www.cadenhead.org/workbench/ gems/rss_2_php_script.txt) is a PHP script that lets you convert data to RSS 2.0 in an MySQL database.

- RSSHarvest (www.bitworking.org/RssHarvest.html) supports custom Web page scraping.

- RSS.py (www.mnot.net/python/RSS.py) is a tool written in the Python programming language that can create RSS for you.

- Script2rss (http://sourceforge.net/projects/script4rss) creates scripts using the Perl scripting language to convert HTML pages to RSS.

- XML::RSS (http://sourceforge.net) is a Perl module that is capable of creating RSS from a Perl data structure.

- xpath2rss (www.mnot.net/xpath2rss) uses the Python programming language and XPath expressions to scrape RSS for you. (XPath is an XML specification that lets you target individual locations in an XML document.)

# 7

# Podcasting: Adding Multimedia to Your Feeds

You've probably seen a POD button but what are podcasts and how are they tied to RSS?

As you may recall from Chapter 1, "Gotta Get My RSS," podcasts revolve mainly around the `<enclosure>` element that was added to RSS in version 0.92. Your RSS file's `<enclosure>` element is a URL pointing to a binary-file resource—such as sound, image, or video—on the Internet. You can record audio or video files as podcasts, and download them when you subscribe to a feed. You see more and more podcasts on the Internet these days, and all you have to do is subscribe to the feed when you see a podcast button (**Figure 7.1**).

**Figure 7.1**

Podcasts from CNN.

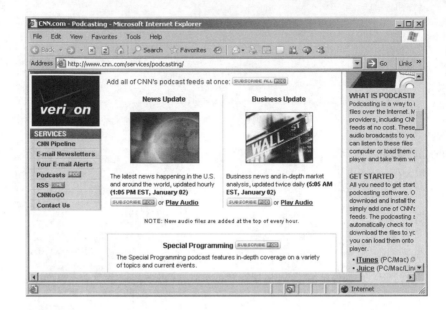

After you've subscribed to a podcast, what happens next is up to your software. If you have an RSS reader that can handle podcasts, you'll see a link to an enclosure in each RSS item that contains a podcast; clicking that link lets you hear the podcast. If you have dedicated podcast software, the RSS item won't appear at all—you'll just hear the podcast after it's been downloaded.

This chapter examines the whole process of adding multimedia to your feeds, starting with an overview of podcasting, then explaining how to create podcasts, put them into your feeds, and download them.

# All About Podcasting

The term *podcasting* comes from combining the words *iPod* and *broadcasting*. Podcasts are largely MP3 files like the ones played on the Apple iPod, and they're available for free or broadcast over the Web.

In fact, you don't need an iPod to listen to podcasts (the term *podcast* is misleading because it suggests that you do). You don't even need a portable player if you have a computer that plays audio. The truth is that experiments with video enclosures in RSS date back to 2000. Some people, who don't like the name *podcasting* because it suggests a connection to Apple, call it *blogcasting*, *audioblogging*, *RSScasting*, or *Webcasting*.

A podcast is simply an RSS feed on the Internet that includes audio and/or video files and that can be publicly subscribed to. It's different from the other type of online audio or video distribution—streaming audio or video—because when you stream audio or video, you download the data and there's no file involved; if you want to save the data, you have to capture it and store it in a file. With podcasting, your computer downloads the entire file first, then plays it (unlike with streaming, where the playback can begin as soon as you start downloading data). Podcasts can't be used to broadcast live events, as streaming can. Instead, podcasts are meant to distribute subscribed content.

The popularity of podcasting is enormous. According to online encyclopedia Wikipedia, blogger Doc Searls has been keeping track of the number of *podcast* entries in Google since September 28, 2004. At that point, he found 24. On September 30, there were 526. Three days later, there were 2,750. By October 18, there were over 100,000. A year later, Google listed more than 100,000,000 entries for *podcast*.

It's also worth noting that although podcasts are usually MP3 sound files or MPG or MP4 video files, they can be any file type, such as PDF. XML files, such as RSS files, can't contain binary data such as the data stored in audio or video files—they can contain only text. However, they can *point* to binary files (such as MP3 files) with the URL of those files, and that's exactly what happens with podcasting.

This example includes an enclosure named snow.mp3:

```
<item>
 <title>Steve shovels the snow</title>
 <author>steve@rssmaniac.com</author>
 <description><![CDATA[It snowed once again.
  Time to shovel!]]></description>
 <pubDate>Thu, 08 Dec 2005 08:39:51 -0500</pubDate>
 <link>http://www.rssmaniac.com/steve</link>
 <enclosure url="http://www.rssmaniac.com/steve/snow.mp3"
   length="4823902" type="audio/mpeg" />
</item>
```

# Creating a Podcast

To create your own podcast and get it out to the world, you have to design your feed and then record your audio or video. We will look at how to create an audio podcast, since that's much more common than video podcasts these days.

To design your feed, it is helpful to write a mission statement of some kind or a set of guidelines. It's especially important to outline the tone and direction of your podcast if you have a number of people recording the audio and you plan to host different authors. What topic or topics do you want to discuss? Which topic or topics do you want to avoid (such as touchy political topics)? Setting your goals in a mission statement can save you a lot of time and trouble if you need to ask your contributors to re-record their contributions.

## The equipment

In the standard scenario, you need a computer with a sound card and speakers, as well as a microphone.

Most computers come with sound cards and speakers these days, and it's easy to pick up a microphone if your computer doesn't have one (many do now as well).

Instead of a simple microphone, however, I recommend a headset with both earphones and a built-in microphone. The sound quality is generally much higher and extraneous noises are kept to a minimum. You can buy headsets very cheaply at most of the popular electronics stores like Best Buy or Radio Shack.

## The software

After you have the hardware you need, you'll need recording software that can create and store the MP3 files to enclose in your podcasts.

Your operating system most likely contains sound-recording software such as Windows XP Sound Recorder (**Figure 7.2**).

**Figure 7.2**

The Windows XP Sound Recorder is showing the snow podcast.

To record audio, you only have to click the red disk button (shown in Figure 7.2, on the far right, where it appears in glorious black and white). When you're finished recording, select the square stop button. That's all it takes.

By default, Windows XP Sound Recorder records in the Windows WAV format. To change to MP3, select the File > Properties menu item, then click the Convert Now button. You can select the MP3 format for your files in the resulting dialog (**Figure 7.3**).

**Figure 7.3**

Windows XP Sound Recorder lets you select the podcast file format.

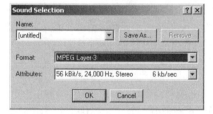

Using built-in audio-recording software such as Sound Recorder is an easy way to create podcasts, but it doesn't always work. In particular, Sound Recorder can be unreliable. For some people it doesn't record at all, for unknown reasons; and for others, it displays a generic error with the incorrect message that memory is full.

There are plenty of reliable audio-recording programs available, and many are free. You can find a list of audio-recording software for the

Mac and Windows at www.podcastalley.com/forum/links.php?id=15. Here's a sampling of the available audio-recording software:

- Audacity (http://audacity.sourceforge.net) is free software for recording and editing sounds for Mac OS X, Microsoft Windows, GNU/Linux, and other operating systems.

- BlogMatrix Sparks (www.blogmatrix.com) lets you record, mix, share, publish, store, and listen to recordings. It also makes it easy to upload podcasts to the Blogmatrix.com site (about $5 per month for hosting a podcasting).

- CastBlaster podcast-recording software ($50, www.castblaster.com) lets you record and mix recordings. It requires Windows XP.

- Digidesign Pro Tools LE (www.digidesign.com) lets you record, edit, mix, and master recording. Works on PC or Mac.

- MixCast Live ($12, www.mixcastlive.com) lets you record, encode, and tag recordings. It even handles Skype recording.

- Propaganda 1.0 ($49.95, www.makepropaganda.com) lets you record or import voice, music, sound effects, and other audio sources. You can also reorder and mix clips. With a simple click you can upload the podcast to your Web site, complete with RSS, XML, and HTML support.

- Sound Forge Audio Studio ($69.95, www.sonymediasoftware.com/Products) lets you record sounds; just connect a microphone or instrument and click Record.

- SoundEdit Pro (www.rmbsoft.com/sep.asp) lets you record, mix, edit, and analyze sound. It can convert audio files into different formats, including MP3, WMA, WAV, Ogg Vorbis, and many others.

One of the most popular sound recorders for podcasts is BlogMatrix Sparks 2.0 (**Figure 7.4**).

BlogMatrix Sparks 2.0 is a powerful software package that lets you not only record podcasts, but also upload them. To make an audio recording, you simply click the Record button at the upper-left (**Figure 7.5**).

**Figure 7.4**

BlogMatrix Sparks 2.0 is one of the most popular sound recorders for podcasts.

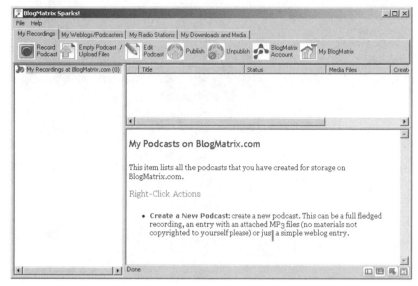

**Figure 7.5**

Click the Record button with BlogMatrix Sparks to record your podcast.

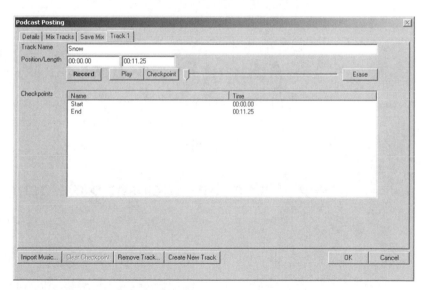

After you click the Record button and it changes to Stop, you start the recording. When you're finished, click the Stop button to stop recording. It's that easy. BlogMatrix Sparks lets you record multiple tracks, as you'd find on a CD, but in this case, a single podcast is all you need. To save your recording in an MP3 file, choose the Save Mix tab (**Figure 7.6**).

**Figure 7.6**

It's easy to record and save an MP3 file with BlogMatrix Sparks.

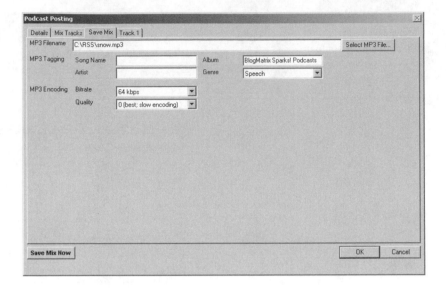

You then select a name and directory for your new MP3 file, and click the Save Mix Now button.

# Adding Enclosures to RSS Items

Excellent, you've created your MP3 file and packed everything you want into it. You're ready to distribute your podcast. And you can do that with a little help from RSS.

## Using the <enclosure> element

Podcasts are all about the <enclosure> element, which was first introduced in RSS 0.92. This element is a child element of the RSS <item> element. There are three required attributes in this element:

- The url attribute gives the online location of the enclosure. Don't forget, URLs must start with http://.

- The length attribute gives the length of the enclosure in bytes.

- The type attribute gives the MIME type of the enclosure, such as "audio/mpeg" for MP3 files. (For a list of the possible MIME types, go to www.iana.org/assignments/media-types/.)

All these items are pretty self-explanatory, except perhaps the MIME type enclosure. MIME, which stands for Multipurpose Internet Mail Extension, originally specified the type of data sent with email so computers would know what to do with that data. In time, MIME types evolved to describe hundreds of types of data; now, when you use the `<enclosure>` element, you have to specify the MIME type of the enclosure so the software you're using knows what to do. Some MIME types include `audio/mpeg` (which you use for MP3 files), `video/mpeg` (MPEG and MP4 video files), `image/jpeg` (JPEG files), and so on. You can see the full list of available types at www.iana.org/assignments/media-types/. The MIME type for podcast enclosures is usually `audio/mpeg`.

Here's an example of the `<enclosure>` element in an RSS 0.92 or 2.0 item:

```
<item>
 <title>Steve shovels the snow</title>
 <author>steve@rssmaniac.com</author>
 <description>It snowed once again. Time to
 shovel!</description>
 <pubDate>Thu, 08 Dec 2005 08:39:51 -0500</pubDate>
 <link>http://www.rssmaniac.com/steve</link>
 <enclosure url="http://www.rssmaniac.com/steve/snow.mp3"
   length="4823902" type="audio/mpeg" />
</item>
```

You can also use enclosures in RSS 1.0, although the syntax is different and the enclosure would look like this:

```
<rss:item>
        .
        .
        .
   <enc:enclosure>
     <enc:Enclosure>
       <enc:type>audio/mpeg</enc:type>
       <enc:length>4823902</enc:length>
       <enc:url>http://www.rssmaniac.com/steve/snow.mp3</enc:url>
     </enc:Enclosure>
   </enc:enclosure>
</rss:item>
```

That's what the <enclosure> element looks like. Now let's put it to work.

## Adding enclosures by hand

There are many ways to add enclosures to your RSS feeds. For example, you could start with a feed, news.xml:

```
<?xml version="1.0"?>
<rss version="2.0">
 <channel>
  <lastBuildDate>Thu, 08 Dec 2005 14:01:27 -0500</lastBuildDate>
  <pubDate>Thu, 08 Dec 2005 14:01:34 -0500</pubDate>
  <title>Steve's News</title>
  <description>This feed contains news from Steve!</description>
  <link>http://www.rssmaniac.com/steve</link>
  <language>en-us</language>
  <copyright>(c) 2006</copyright>
  <managingEditor>Steve</managingEditor>
  <image>
   <title>Steve's News</title>
   <url>http://www.rssmaniac.com/steve/Image.jpg</url>
   <link>http://www.rssmaniac.com/steve</link>
   <description>Steve's News</description>
   <width>144</width>
   <height>36</height>
  </image>
   <item>
    <title>Steve shovels the snow</title>
    <description>It snowed once again. Time to
    shovel!</description>
    <pubDate>Thu, 08 Dec 2005 08:39:51 -0500</pubDate>
    <link>http://www.rssmaniac.com/steve</link>
   </item>
   <item>
    <title>Now it's raining</title>
    <description>It's raining out there and the sump pump is
    going in here.</description>
    <pubDate>Thu, 18 Dec 2005 08:39:51 -0500</pubDate>
    <link>http://www.rssmaniac.com/steve</link>
```

```
      </item>
    </channel>
  </rss>
```

Each <item> element can contain an <enclosure> element, so you can just place an <enclosure> element in an item by hand.

```
<?xml version="1.0"?>
<rss version="2.0">
 <channel>
  <lastBuildDate>Thu, 08 Dec 2005 14:01:27 -0500</lastBuildDate>
  <pubDate>Thu, 08 Dec 2005 14:01:34 -0500</pubDate>
  <title>Steve's News</title>
  <description>This feed contains news from Steve!</description>
  <link>http://www.rssmaniac.com/steve</link>
  <language>en-us</language>
  <copyright>(c) 2006</copyright>
  <managingEditor>Steve</managingEditor>
  <image>
   <title>Steve's News</title>
   <url>http://www.rssmaniac.com/steve/Image.jpg</url>
   <link>http://www.rssmaniac.com/steve</link>
   <description>Steve's News</description>
   <width>144</width>
   <height>36</height>
  </image>
    <item>
     <title>Steve shovels the snow</title>
     <description>It snowed once again. Time to shovel!
     </description>
     <pubDate>Thu, 08 Dec 2005 08:39:51 -0500</pubDate>
     <link>http://www.rssmaniac.com/steve</link>
     <enclosure url="http://www.rssmaniac.com/steve/snow.mp3"
     length="673920" type="audio/mpeg" />
    </item>
    <item>
     <title>Now it's raining</title>
     <description>It's raining out there and the sump pump is
```

*(code continues on next page)*

```
      going in here.</description>
      <pubDate>Thu, 18 Dec 2005 08:39:51 -0500</pubDate>
      <link>http://www.rssmaniac.com/steve</link>
    </item>
  </channel>
</rss>
```

That's all it takes to do a podcast. Now you have to upload your RSS feed file, news.xml, to a Web server so it has a URL and is available to RSS. You also need to upload your MP3 file to the URL you gave in news.xml (that is, http://www.rssmaniac.com/steve/snow.mp3) so that podcast-enabled software can download the podcast and read it.

 **You can upload your podcast with an FTP program. To find FTP software, go to www.tucows.com and search for *FTP*. You'll find more than 100 FTP software packages, many of them free, designed for various operating systems.**

As you can see, if you write your RSS feeds from scratch, it's not difficult to add an enclosure. You can add an enclosure to any RSS item (only one enclosure per item, however) in version 0.92 or later RSS documents.

 **Different Web servers have different ways of handling files and making them available for download. By default, the files you upload should be available for download publicly, but if not, you might need to change the protection setting of your enclosure files on the server. If you have trouble downloading an enclosure when you test your podcast, check with your server's tech staff. You might also want to increase the protection of your podcasts; on many servers, stored files can be overwritten by anyone by default.**

## NewzAlert Composer

NewzAlert Composer is an RSS creator program that lets you create feeds (see Chapter 3, "Creating RSS Feeds"). And it's one of the programs that will let you add enclosures to your feed as well.

**Figure 7.7**
NewzAlert Composer, an RSS creator program, also lets you create podcasts.

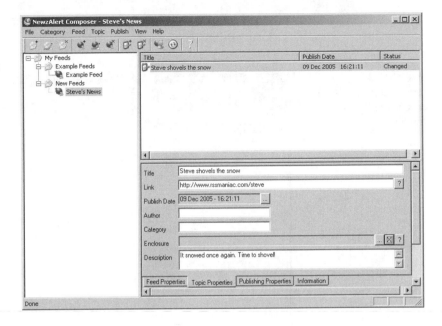

To add an enclosure to a particular RSS item in a feed, just select that feed item in the main window, and the item's details appear automatically when you choose the Topic Properties tab (**Figure 7.7**).

Adding an enclosure is easy, but that enclosure has to already be available online, because you need a URL to create an enclosure in NewzAlert Composer. To create that enclosure, just click the button displaying an ellipsis (...) next to the Enclosure text box. Doing so opens the Enclosure Information dialog (**Figure 7.8**).

 **Click the ellipsis button next to the File Size text box and navigate to your enclosure file. NewzAlert Composer will tell you the file's size in bytes.**

**Figure 7.8**
Enter the URL for your enclosure, its size in bytes, and its MIME type (audio/MPEG here) in the NewzAlert Composer's Enclosure Information dialog.

After you click OK, NewzAlert Composer reappears, displaying the new enclosure's data (**Figure 7.9**).

**Figure 7.9**

NewzAlert Composer is displaying an item with an enclosure.

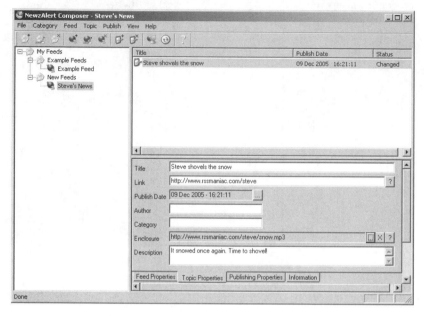

When you're ready to publish your new feed, select Publish > Publish Feed (as discussed in Chapter 3) to upload the RSS file, but not the enclosure. You're responsible for uploading the enclosure yourself, so use a good FTP program (such as the ones you can find at www.tucows.com).

Here's the actual RSS 2.0 created by NewzAlert Composer, including the new enclosure:

```
<?xml version="1.0" encoding="ISO-8859-1"?>
<rss version="2.0">
 <channel>
  <generator>NewzAlert Composer v1.70.6, Copyright (c) 2004-2005
  Castle Software Ltd, http://www.NewzAlert.com</generator>
  <lastBuildDate>Mon, 02 Jan 2006 11:46:23 -0500</lastBuildDate>
  <pubDate>Mon, 02 Jan 2006 11:47:43 -0500</pubDate>
  <title>Steve's News</title>
```

```
<description><![CDATA[This feed contains news from
Steve!]]></description>
<link>www.rssmaniac.com.com/steve</link>
<language>en-us</language>
<copyright>(c) 2006</copyright>
<managingEditor>Steve</managingEditor>
<image>
  <title>Steve's News</title>
  <url>http://www.rssmaniac.com/steve/Image.jpg</url>
  <link>www.rssmaniac.com/steve</link>
  <description>Steve's News</description>
  <width>144</width>
  <height>36</height>
</image>
    <item>
      <title>Steve shovels the snow</title>
      <description><![CDATA[It snowed once again.
        Time to shovel!]]></description>
      <pubDate>Fri, 09 Dec 2005 16:21:11 -0500</pubDate>
      <link>http://www.rssmaniac.com/steve</link>
      <enclosure url="http://www.rssmaniac.com/steve/snow.mp3"
        length="673920" type="audio/mpeg" />
    </item>
  </channel>
</rss>
```

NewzAlert Composer is a good product and gets the job done nicely. But one of the drawbacks is that you have to upload the podcast file yourself. There are some dedicated podcast programs that take care of that for you; those programs will be covered later in this chapter.

## FeedForAll

FeedForAll is an RSS creator that lets you add enclosures to feeds easily (**Figure 7.10**).

**Figure 7.10**

Title, description, link, and publication date are required fields in the Feeds tab of RSS creator FeedForAll.

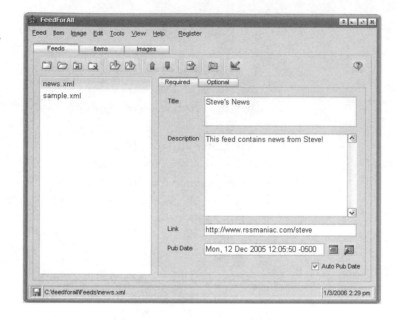

To add an enclosure to an item, choose the Items tab and select the item you want to add an enclosure to (**Figure 7.11**).

**Figure 7.11**

Select an item under the Items tab to add an enclosure in FeedForAll.

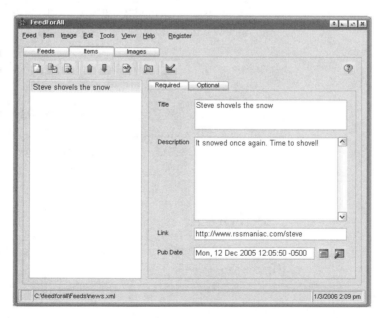

Now, because enclosures are optional in RSS items, select the Optional tab and enter your enclosure's data (**Figure 7.12**).

**Figure 7.12**
Add information about your enclosure in the Optional tab in FeedForAll.

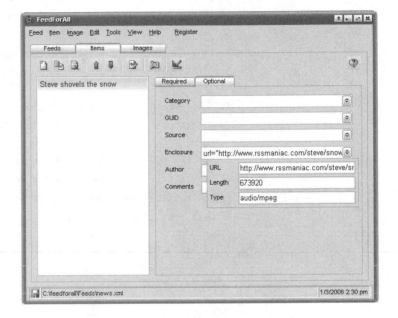

As before, you have to enter the URL of the enclosure, its size in bytes, and its MIME type. (NewzAlert Composer gives you a drop-down menu that lists the MIME types, but in FeedForAll, you have to enter the MIME type by hand, so be sure you know the MIME type of your enclosure first.)

With FeedForAll, you choose File > Upload to upload your RSS file. And as with NewzAlert Composer, you have to upload your enclosure separately.

Here's the RSS 2.0 file created by FeedForAll, complete with the new enclosure.

```
<?xml version="1.0" encoding="windows-1252"?>
<rss version="2.0">
  <channel>
    <title>Steve&apos;s News</title>
```

*(code continues on next page)*

```
<description>This feed contains news from Steve!</description>
<link>http://www.rssmaniac.com/steve</link>
<docs>http://blogs.law.harvard.edu/tech/rss</docs>
<lastBuildDate>Mon, 2 Jan 2006 12:49:23 -0500</lastBuildDate>
<pubDate>Mon, 12 Dec 2005 12:05:50 -0500</pubDate>
<generator>FeedForAll v1.0 (1.0.2.0) unlicensed
version</generator>
<item>
   <title>Steve shovels the snow</title>
   <description>It snowed once again. Time to
   shovel!</description>
   <link>http://www.rssmaniac.com/steve</link>
   <enclosure url="http://www.rssmaniac.com/steve/snow.mp3"
   length="673920" type="audio/mpeg"></enclosure>
   <pubDate>Mon, 12 Dec 2005 12:05:50 -0500</pubDate>
</item>
  </channel>
</rss>
```

Like NewzAlert Composer, FeedForAll is a useful tool that makes it easy to create RSS feeds with enclosures. But if you're just going to be creating podcasts, take a look at some of the dedicated podcast software.

# Using Dedicated Podcast Software

Podcasts have become so popular that you can find a good number of software packages designed especially for developing and uploading them. In many cases you don't have to touch the RSS. Here's a starter list of dedicated podcast software:

- BlogMatrix Sparks (www.blogmatrix.com) lets you record, mix, share, publish, store, and listen to recordings. It also makes it easy to upload podcasts to the Blogmatrix.com site. Hosting a podcasting starts at about $5 per month.

- ePodcast Creator (www.industrialaudiosoftware.com/products) lets you record, edit, create your RSS feed, and upload your podcast. The current list price is $89.95.

- ePodcast Producer (www.industrialaudiosoftware.com/products) lets you record, edit, and create RSS tags, then upload your podcast from one program. The current list price is $249.95.

- Podomatic (www.podomatic.com) lets you create, mix, store, search, and download podcasts. There's even an on-site recorder and mixer that you can use without downloading. And it's all free.

- PodProducer (www.podproducer.net/en/) is free software that lets you produce and record podcasts. It requires Windows XP.

BlogMatrix Sparks is a superb software package not just for recording podcasts, as we saw earlier in this chapter, but also for the dedicated podcaster (hosting packages for your podcasts begin at $5/month as of this writing). After you've made a number of recordings in BlogMatrix Sparks, it's easy to upload them to Blogmatrix.com.

**Figure 7.13**

Here are several recordings made in BlogMatrix Sparks.

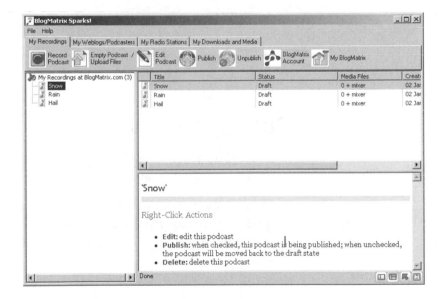

To configure a podcast, select it in BlogMatrix Sparks and click the Edit Podcast button in the toolbar to open the Podcast Posting dialog, where you can add HTML to your podcast (**Figure 7.14**).

**Figure 7.14**

Configure your recording in the Edit Podcast dialog in BlogMatrix Sparks.

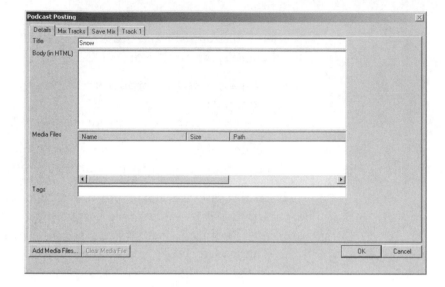

To publish your podcast to Blogmatrix.com, click the Publish button or right-click the recording and select the Publish item. The first time you do so, BlogMatrix Sparks signs you up with Blogmatrix.com and you're on your way.

## Downloading Podcasts

After you've uploaded and published podcasts, how exactly do you *download* and listen to them?

For some podcasts, you don't need additional software, not even an RSS reader, to download and listen to them. That's the case when there's a direct link to the podcast's MP3 file, and you can simply click the link in your browser to play that file (clicking a link to an MP3 file plays that MP3 file in browsers like Internet Explorer and Firefox).

At www.itconversations.com, for example, the Download MP3 link, when clicked, downloads and plays the podcast (**Figure 7.15**). Or in some browsers, you can use the audio controls to play the file directly.

**Figure 7.15**

At www.itconversations.com, you can click the Download MP3 link to play a podcast.

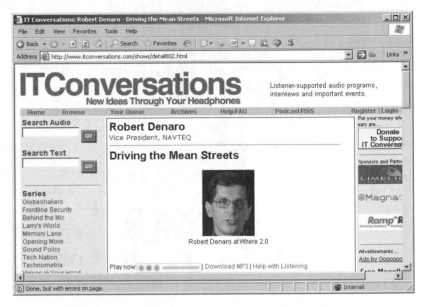

 **tip**

**Want to save a podcast's MP3 file to disk instead of just playing it? Right-click the link to the MP3 file and select the appropriate browser option—for example, in Internet Explorer it's Save Target As, and in Firefox it's Save Link As.**

You don't need any software at all except that which comes with your operating system (assuming it includes a browser and a media player that plays MP3 files).

However, that's not the way podcasts are usually distributed—usually, you would need an RSS reader or dedicated podcast software to listen to (or view) podcasts.

The following two sites have lists of software available specifically for downloading podcasts:

- www.podcastalley.com/forum/links.php?id=1

- www.ipodder.org/directory/4/ipodderSoftware

## Podcast.net

A great way to listen to podcasts is to go to www.podcast.net, where you can search among hundreds of podcasts by title or description—no software to download. You can also browse through podcast categories as you please (**Figure 7.16**).

When you want to hear a podcast, just click the play button next to the podcast. That's all there is to it.

**You can't reach a podcast directly by URL using www.podcast.net, but it's easy to add a podcast to its database. Just click the Add a Podcast link, which appears in the logo at the top of each page on the site. To add a new podcast, give its URL, its title, and some keywords you think people might use to find it, and you're set. Now you can use www.podcast.net to listen to the podcast you want.**

## Bloglines

Another online podcast package is Bloglines, at www.bloglines.com (also discussed in Chapter 2 and Chapter 5). Bloglines isn't specially built to handle podcasts, but it's an online RSS reader that lets you listen to podcasts.

After you create an RSS feed with an enclosure, you can subscribe to that feed at www.bloglines.com. The link to the enclosure is about two-thirds down the page. To listen to or view enclosures using Bloglines, just click the Enclosure link in the description window (**Figure 7.17**).

**Figure 7.17**

An enclosure at www.bloglines.com lets you listen to or view an RSS feed.

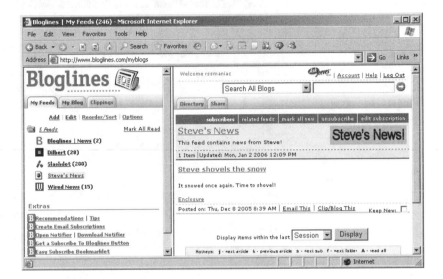

All of which is to say that Bloglines is a good option if you want to read RSS feeds, search them, and listen to podcasts. Now that online access is faster with cable and other connections, using an online reader like Bloglines to read feeds and listen to podcasts is hardly any different from using an application on your computer—except that you don't have to install any software.

## Juice Receiver

Juice (formerly iPodder) is a dedicated podcast reader that you can download for free at http://juicereceiver.sourceforge.net. You can subscribe to RSS feeds that include podcasts by clicking the Add button (the one with the plus sign), or go to Tools > Add a Feed menu item (**Figure 7.18**).

**Figure 7.18**
Juice Receiver boasts that you can listen to a podcast anytime, anywhere.

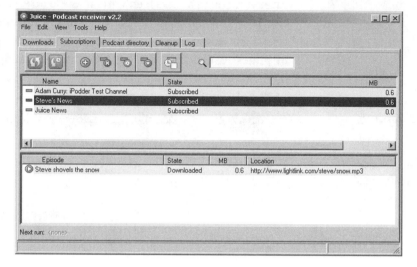

**Figure 7.18**
Juice Receiver boasts that you can listen to a podcast anytime, anywhere.

After you've subscribed to a feed with a podcast, Juice downloads that podcast and you can listen to it simply by clicking the arrow icon next to the item's title. The item's enclosure, such as an MP3 file, is launched using whatever default software you have on your computer.

Juice is designed primarily as a podcast receiver, not as an RSS reader, but if it's podcasts you want, it's a good choice.

## RSSRadio

Want to download an RSS feed's podcast? RSSRadio (www.dorada.co.uk/) is another podcast reader that can help. If you know the URL of the RSS feed, use Actions > Add a New Subscription > By URL and enter the URL. Your new subscription will appear on the left, and the items in the feed on the right. RSSRadio downloads the podcast for an RSS item and displays a clickable icon. Audio podcasts display an icon labeled AUD (**Figure 7.19**).

If you right-click the icon and select Play Program from the menu, RSSRadio launches the podcast using the software on your computer that usually handles files of the podcast's type.

**Figure 7.19**

RSSRadio displays an AUD icon for all audio podcasts.

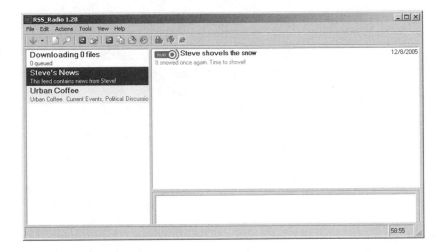

## BlogMatrix Sparks

BlogMatrix Sparks, which has already been discussed in this chapter, is a good podcast player (**Figure 7.20**). It goes to some effort to extract the items in an RSS feed and present the data in a nice format.

**Figure 7.20**

BlogMatrix Sparks is very easy to use.

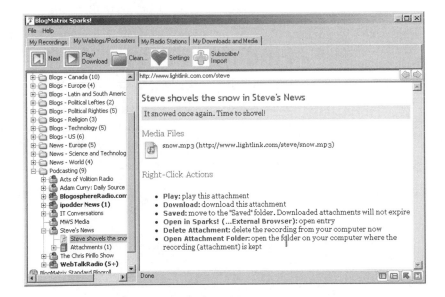

Besides displaying the text from the feed, BlogMatrix Sparks also lists your podcast options. For example, to play a podcast, you can right-click its icon (in the left window, the small icon labeled "Steve shovels the snow" in the Steve's News folder) and select one of the Play items, such as Play in Sparks or Play in Media Player (or whatever operating-system utility BlogMatrix Sparks chooses) to play the podcast.

## iPods and MP3 players

Of course, there are other ways of listening to podcasts, given that the MP3 format is very popular. Apple's iPods and other MP3 players can easily play MP3 podcasts.

Apple's iTunes 6 software makes it easy to work with podcasts (for more about iTunes, go to www.apple.com/itunes/podcasts/). Here's an overview of what it can do:

- Browse more than 25,000 podcasts in the iTunes Music Store

- Listen to full podcasts before deciding to subscribe or not

- Synchronize podcasts to an iPod

- Synchronize video podcasts to iPods that support video

# Finding Podcasts

There are various techniques you can use to find podcasts out there. Some podcast readers, such as RSSRadio, let you search podcast directories. In RSSRadio, you can search by choosing Actions > Add a New Subscription > By URL, to open the Subscription Centre dialog, which gives you access to various podcast directories (**Figure 7.21**).

You can also search podcast directories directly; here's a starter list:

- www.podcast.net

- www.podcastbunker.com

- www.podcastcentral.com (**Figure 7.22**)

- www.ipodder.org/directory/4/podcasts

- www.podcastalley.com

**Figure 7.21**

RSSRadio lets you search podcast directories.

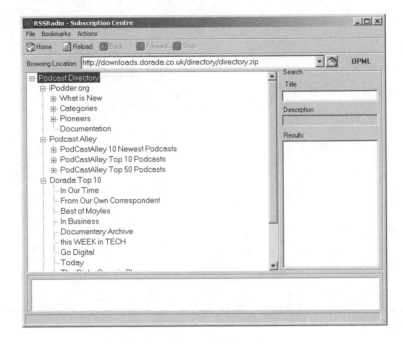

**Figure 7.22**

Podcast Central's directory includes podcast descriptions and update information.

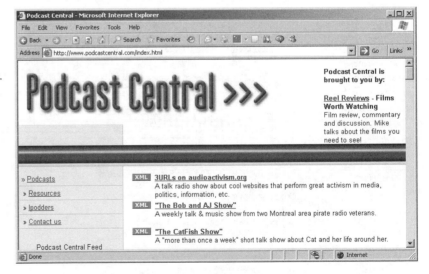

An especially cool one is www.podscope.com, which is sort of like Google for podcasts (**Figure 7.23**). Podscope actually listens to podcasts for you, and lets you search for the podcast you want based on a keyword.

**Figure 7.23**

Podscope is an audio and visual search engine.

For example, searching for the keyword *weather* gives you a multitude of podcasts to choose from (**Figure 7.24**).

**Figure 7.24**

Choose from the results of a podcast search at www.podscope.com.

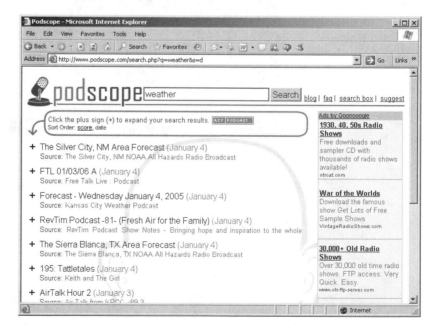

That's pretty cool—now you can search for podcasts based on keyword.

# 8

# Publicizing Your Feeds

Your feed is up-to-date, you've been making sure its items are timely and engaging, and you're staying on top of the latest RSS formats.

But not enough people are reading your feed. Sure, you're doing better than when you set up that email newsletter—because it was caught in spam filters or ignored by people swamped with email each day—but you still want more readers. You've worked hard on your feed, and you want to get your news out there.

This chapter is all about publicizing your RSS feed. Let's look at the best ways to get your feed noticed.

# Using the XML Button

Probably the most basic and usual way to get your feed noticed is to add an XML or RSS button to your Web page. That's the way hundreds of thousands of RSS feeds get noticed and subscribed to.

Here's the setup for a page on hamsters and their benefits, including an XML button to an RSS feed on hamsters:

```
<html>
  <head>
    <title>My Hamster Page</title>
  </head>

  <body>
    <center>
      <h1>Welcome to my hamster page!</h1>
      <img src="hamster.jpg">
      <br>
      Yes, it's true, everyone loves hamsters.
      <br>
      How could you not?
      <br>
      I write a lot on hamsters,
      <br>
      would you like to subscribe
      <br>
      to my super hamster RSS feed?
      <br>
      (What's RSS? Click <a href="http://en.wikipedia.org/wiki/Rss">
      here</a> for more info.)
      <br>
      Just use the XML button below to subscribe.
      <br>
      <a href="http://rssmaniac.com/hamster.xml">
      <img src="xml.gif" height="11" width="24" border = "0"></a>
    </center>
  </body>

</html>
```

The XML button appears in a browser, ready for readers to subscribe to your feed (**Figure 8.1**).

**Figure 8.1**

Here's the hamster page, complete with XML button.

When you add a subscription button to your Web page, keep in mind that these days, the XML button is the most popular. If you're targeting a specific version of RSS, such as 2.0, by all means use an RSS 2.0 button.

In general it's a good idea to include links with your feed. For the newbies among your readers, it's helpful to have a link to the Wikipedia page that explains what RSS is (that page also includes links showing where to get RSS readers). A link can catch all the hamster lovers who have no idea what RSS is. In fact, you might consider adding a page of instructions that tell your readers how to use the XML button to subscribe to your feed, a list of links to the RSS readers you prefer, and so on.

You can use the standard XML button, or you can get creative and use one of the many RSS buttons available on the Internet. A good site for finding feed buttons is http://gtmcknight.com/buttons/feeds.php (**Figure 8.2**).

**Figure 8.2**

Choose from a wide array of RSS feed buttons.

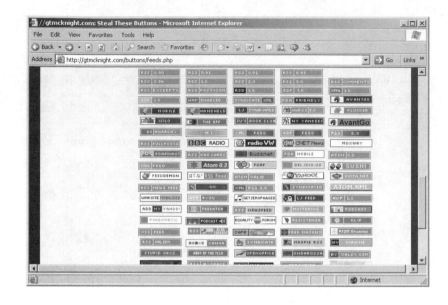

You're not limited to the standard buttons, of course. For example, the site www.derekfranklin.com uses a really big RSS button (**Figure 8.3**).

**Figure 8.3**

This site sports a jumbo-size RSS feed button.

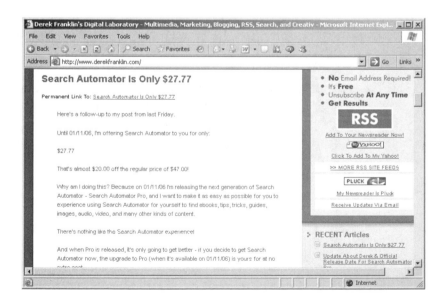

If you plan to have many RSS feeds, make sure you label each one, as you see at www.usatoday.com (**Figure 8.4**).

**Figure 8.4**

USAToday.com uses color coding as well as text to label its RSS feed buttons.

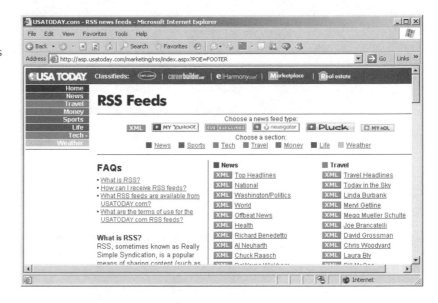

Now that you've added the XML button to your Web page, it's time to draw readers in.

# Getting Links to Your Page

One way to drive traffic to your Web site is to link your site to other sites, and then to ask those sites to link to your site. Here's an example link to another hamster page, called Hamster Hideout (**Figure 8.5**).

```
<html>
  <head>
    <title>My Hamster Page</title>
  </head>

  <body>
    <center>
      <h1>Welcome to my hamster page!</h1>
      <img src="hamster.jpg">
      <br>
      Yes, it's true, everyone loves hamsters.
      <br>
      How could you not?
```

*(code continues on next page)*

```
<br>
I write a lot on hamsters,
<br>
would you like to subscribe
<br>
to my super hamster RSS feed?
<br>
(What's RSS? Click <a href="http://en.wikipedia.org/wiki/Rss">
here</a> for more info.)
<br>
Just use the XML button below to subscribe.
<br>
<a href="http://rssmaniac.com/hamster.xml">
<img src="xml.gif" height="11" width="24" border = "0"></a>
<br>
Here's a great hamster page:
   <a href="http://www.hamsterhideout.com/">
   Hamster Hideout</a>
     </center>
   </body>

</html>
```

**Figure 8.5**

Notice the link to a similar site on hamsters.

Another way to get links to your site is to see which sites have links to sites that compete with yours, and asking those sites to add a link to your site. How can you find which sites link to your competitors? Use an online search engine like Google to search your competitors' URLs (in Google, enclose the URL you're searching for in quotation marks or you won't get any matches to your search).

For that matter, you can set up an RSS search feed to watch who is discussing your competitors' sites. Just use the URL of a competitor's site and create an RSS search feed (see Chapter 2, "Grabbing RSS with Readers").

To get more hits, you can also subscribe to services that connect similar sites, such as WebRing, at http://dir.webring.com/rw (**Figure 8.6**).

**Figure 8.6**

Subscribing to WebRing lets you link to sites that are similar to yours.

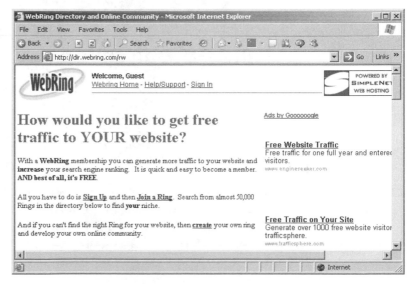

When you register your site on WebRing, it's added to the list of sites for the "ring," or category, that you choose. When people click the links in various pages in the ring, sometimes they'll come to your page. WebRing will send you HTML to include in your page so that people who come to your page can go to other ring sites as well (**Figure 8.7**).

**Figure 8.7**

Here's what the HTML looks like in a browser for the Blogger Webring, which is designed for bloggers who want to drive more traffic to their blogs.

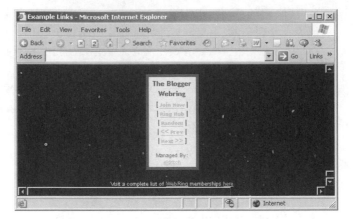

Visitors to your Web page can go to any of the sites in the ring—very useful for getting traffic to your site.

## Using Autodiscovery

A number of RSS readers and, increasingly, browsers, can discover RSS feeds on your page. Typically your feed displays an icon to let the visitor to your page subscribe to your feed. But to let an RSS reader or browser discover your feed automatically—a feature called *autodiscovery*—you include a <link> element in the <head> section of your page.

Here's how this works for the hamster page. Note that the href attribute should contain the URL of your feed, the rel attribute should contain "alternate", and the type attribute should contain "application/rss+xml" (what the title attribute contains is up to you).

```
<html>
  <head>
    <link rel="alternate" type="application/rss+xml" title="RSS"
      href="http://rssmaniac.com/hamster.xml">
    <title>My Hamster Page</title>
  </head>

  <body>
    <center>
      <h1>Welcome to my hamster page!</h1>
```

```
            <img src="hamster.jpg">
            <br>
            Yes, it's true, everyone loves hamsters.
            <br>
            How could you not?
            <br>
            I write a lot on hamsters,
            <br>
            would you like to subscribe
            <br>
            to my super hamster RSS feed?
            <br>
            (What's RSS? Click <a href="http://en.wikipedia.org/wiki/Rss">
            here</a> for more info.)
            <br>
            Just use the XML button below to subscribe.
            <br>
            <a href="http://rssmaniac.com/hamster.xml">
            <img src="xml.gif" height="11" width="24" border = "0"></a>
            <br>
            Here's a great hamster page:
              <a href="http://www.hamsterhideout.com/">
              Hamster Hideout</a>
          </center>
        </body>

    </html>
```

If you have an Atom feed, you would use the following HTML code
instead:

```
    <html>
      <head>
        <link rel="alternate" type="application/atom+xml" title="Atom"
          href="http://rssmaniac.com/hamster.xml">
        <title>My Hamster Page</title>
      </head>

            .

            .

            .
```

Search engines, including Google, that search for RSS and Atom feeds use autodiscovery, so it's a great idea to add this feature to your site. For more information, take a look at www.google.com/feedfetcher.html, which explains how Google searches for RSS feeds and makes them searchable.

# Optimizing for Search Engines

Search engines hunt through the Web for pages to list, and you can help them (and get better rankings) by listing the keywords you want associated with your page. By listing those keywords, you tell search engines what keywords should bring up your page.

## Publicizing your search terms

To list search-engine keywords, you use one of the `<meta>` elements in your page's `<head>` element. There are usually two `<meta>` elements— one with its name attribute set to `"description"`, where you can give a description of your page in the `<meta>` element's content attribute. You set the name attribute of the other `<meta>` element to `"keywords"`, and then give a comma-separated list of keywords that describe the content of your page to the content attribute of the `<meta>` element.

Here's an example for the hamster page:

```
<html>
  <head>
    <meta name="description" content="All about hamsters!">
    <meta name="keywords" content="hamster,hamsters, rodents, pets">
    <link rel="alternate" type="application/rss+xml" title="RSS"
      href="http://rssmaniac.com/hamster.xml">
    <title>My Hamster Page</title>
  </head>

  <body>
    <center>
      <h1>Welcome to my hamster page!</h1>
      <img src="hamster.jpg">
```

```
<br>
Yes, it's true, everyone loves hamsters.
<br>
How could you not?
<br>
I write a lot on hamsters,
<br>
would you like to subscribe
<br>
to my super hamster RSS feed?
<br>
(What's RSS? Click <a href="http://en.wikipedia.org/wiki/Rss">
here</a> for more info.)
<br>
Just use the XML button below to subscribe.
<br>
<a href="http://rssmaniac.com/hamster.xml">
<img src="xml.gif" height="11" width="24" border = "0"></a>
<br>
Here's a great hamster page:
  <a href="http://www.hamsterhideout.com/">
  Hamster Hideout</a>
</center>
</body>

</html>
```

Selecting the right keywords is an art. Bear in mind that if you select keywords in common use, your feed will be buried in the list of results.

People usually search for more than one keyword at once (*hamster* and *nutrition*, for example), so it pays to try and come up with good keyword combinations.

## Finding the right search terms

You can do some research into what the best terms or combination of terms would be for your Web page. A good place to start is Yahoo's marketing help page, http://searchmarketing.yahoo.com/rc/srch/ (**Figure 8.8**).

**Figure 8.8**

Yahoo's marketing help page includes tools to help you select the best keywords.

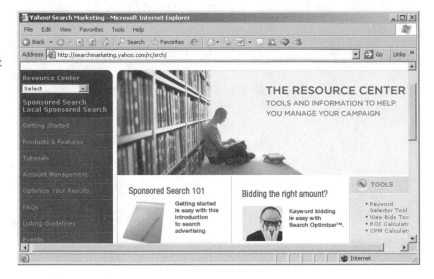

This help page has many resources, including the Keyword Selector Tool (**Figure 8.9**).

**Figure 8.9**

Use the Keyword Selector Tool at yahoo.com to start a list of the best search terms for your site.

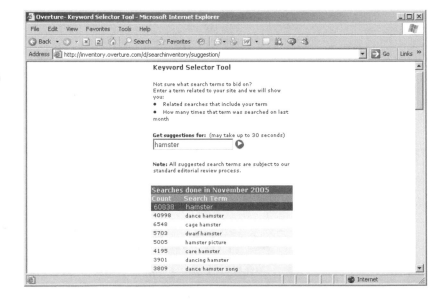

Enter the search term you're interested in using, and this tool tells you how popular it is. Not only that, you'll also see what search-term combinations are popular.

After you find a number of popular combinations, you'll want to include those keywords in your page. This will give you an enormous edge over someone who doesn't list keywords at all.

The search terms people use change all the time, so if you're serious about increasing traffic to your site and the number of subscribers to your RSS feed, try to keep on top of the most current search terms. As of this writing, for example, *avian flu* is a search term being entered by more and more people.

**tip**  **Avoid using trademarked terms in your list of keywords in your Web pages. Using such terms without permission could get you into trouble, especially if it looks like you're claiming ownership of those trademarks when they actually belong to someone else.**

Google gauges the importance of your site in part by how many sites link to your site. Accordingly, some people think Google has devalued the use of `<meta>` elements. To be considered a significant site in Google's estimation, at least, you should try to get as many legitimate sites as possible to link to yours. A little marketing work here, such as contacting the Webmasters of similar pages to get them to include a link to your site on their site, can pay off in a big way.

For more ideas to increase traffic to your Web site, go to Google's Webmaster help page at www.google.com/webmasters (**Figure 8.10**).

Among other things, Google discusses how it ranks pages—briefly (**Figure 8.11**). You can see such explanations at www.google.com/webmasters/4.html. Google uses a combination of 100 factors to rate a page, and that combination is always changing. In most cases, even Google is not certain how high a page will rank until its software has judged the page.

**Figure 8.10**

Use Google's Webmaster help page to get tips on marketing your Web site.

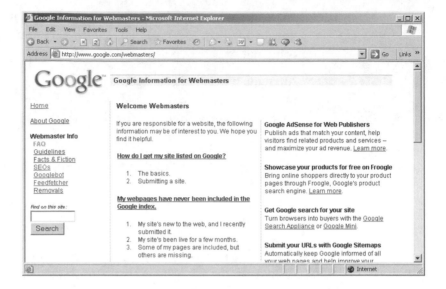

**Figure 8.11**

Google's Webmaster help page explains page rankings.

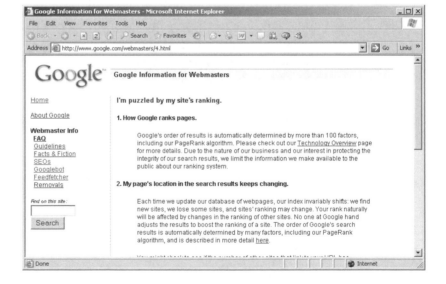

**tip**

If your page's title includes the keyword being searched for, Google often assumes your page is about that keyword and ranks it higher than other pages that only list the keyword in a <meta> element.

# Getting into Search Engines

Another way to improve your site's ranking is to submit it to one of the "big three" search engines: Google, Yahoo, or MSN Search. For example, to get into Google before Google finds your site during its routine Web searches, submit your site's URL to Google at www.google.com/addurl (**Figure 8.12**).

**Figure 8.12**

Follow the instructions to submit your site to Google.

You can do the same with Yahoo, at http://search.yahoo.com/info/submit.html (**Figure 8.13**). In order to submit your site, you must have a Yahoo ID, but getting one is easy and free.

How about MSN Search? The URL for submitting your site is http://search.msn.com/docs/submit.aspx (**Figure 8.14**).

Another search engine that's very useful is the Open Directory Project (http://dmoz.org/add.html), which other search engines search. Some say that if you list your site here, it will appear in Google not more than two months later.

**Figure 8.13**

Register before submitting your site to Yahoo.

**Figure 8.14**

Submit your site to MSN Search.

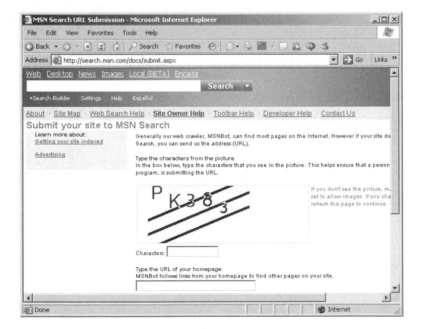

## Site-submission services and software

As more and more Webmasters want to improve their sites' rankings by submitting them to search engines, the market for such services has grown tremendously. As a result, there's an enormous number of software packages and services that can help, although you usually have to pay.

You can find site-submission services all over the Web, such as Engineseeker.com, at www.engineseeker.com (**Figure 8.15**), and Blast Engine, at www.blastengine.com (**Figure 8.16**), which claim they will submit your site to the major search engines.

**Figure 8.15**

Engineseeker.com is one of many services that will submit your site to the big search engines.

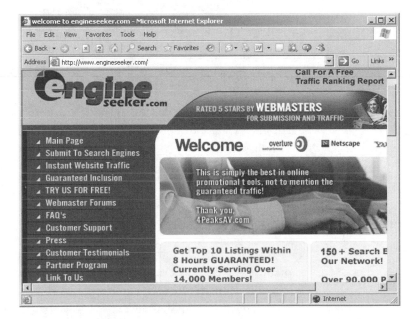

Before you subscribe to a site-submission service, check carefully to make sure it's not a scam. Webmasters who are desperate to get into search engines can fall prey to unscrupulous submission services. For example, some services use automated techniques to try to get your Web site into the search engines; if their efforts fail and no error messages are returned, those services may not know they failed.

**Figure 8.16**

Blast Engine is another Web service that helps you submit your site to the major search engines.

Also beware of site-submission services and software that claim they'll submit your site to 5,000 or so search engines. The truth is that most searches take place in Google, Yahoo, and MSN Search, and (as we've seen) you can register your site with them easily. So before you decide to pay for a submission service, give it some thought.

## Using search engine optimizers (SEOs)

Getting sites listed high in the search engines has become such big business that it is its own field—search engine optimization—and has spawned its own tool, the search engine optimizer (SEO). There are a multitude of SEO companies that promise to get your site listed high in many search engines. Indeed, if you search Google for *search engine optimization* or *search engine optimizer*, you'll get millions of results.

Unfortunately, like some site-submission services, some SEOs have behaved questionably (see, for example, the *Seattle Times* article at http://seattletimes.nwsource.com/html/businesstechnology/2002002970_nwbizbriefs12.html). There have been numerous scams as well, so recommendations will not be given here. In fact, some SEOs can get you into trouble with the search engines by doing the wrong thing. If an SEO spams the search engine with numerous submissions—deceptive text or hidden links, for example—your site can end up being banned by that search engine—probably not the result you envisioned.

**For more on what Google considers spam, and how to avoid it—and avoid being dropped from Google—take a look at www.google.com/ contact/spamreport.html. Google states the following: "Trying to deceive (spam) our Web crawler by means of hidden text, deceptive cloaking or doorway pages compromises the quality of our results and degrades the search experience for everyone."**

Most SEOs are honest, but you rarely get a guarantee of results. And if you do, the promise—such as getting your site among the top 10 similar sites on Google—might be too good to be true. Before you sign up with an SEO company, research several to see which one feels right, and ask for testimonials. If the SEO's firm seems overly secretive about its methods and refuses to offer testimonials, think twice. If you have to put a link to its service on your site, think twice. And if it demands a large amount of money without a substantive and realistic guarantee, definitely think twice.

**Google suggests you use caution before going with an SEO company that tries to get your business via spam email. Google says it routinely gets such spam emails too; can you imagine what that would look like? "Dear Google.com: Is Google ignoring you? How would you like to be listed No. 1 on Google.com?" Read more SEO hints from Google at www.google.com/webmasters/seo.html.**

Some sites rank a number of SEOs—162 on the SEO Consultants Directory site (www.seoconsultants.com), a service that may prove helpful (**Figure 8.17**).

**If you have a problem with an SEO that you can't resolve, you can take action. The Federal Trade Commission (FTC) handles complaints of unfair business practices. To file a complaint, go to www.ftc.gov or call 1-877-382-4357.**

**Figure 8.17**

SEO Consultants Directory ranks 162 (at press time) search engine optimization sites.

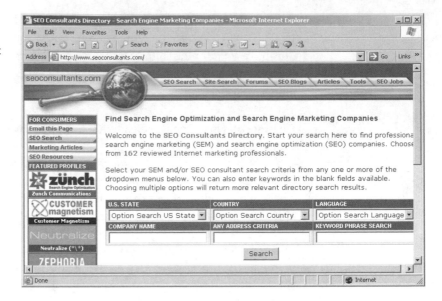

If you want to do some search engine optimization yourself, you can use resources online that discuss the procedure:

- http://searchenginewatch.com/searchday/article.php/2161191

- www.selfpromotion.com/search-engine-optimization.t

- http://websearch.about.com/od/keywordsandphrases/

SEO can be a powerful way of directing traffic to your Web site, and therefore to your RSS feed, but be careful. If you use what search engines consider abusive practices, you may end up being banned.

# Using RSS Feed Directories

Driving more traffic to your Web site isn't the only way to get more people to click your XML or RSS button. You can also submit your feed to RSS feed directories.

RSS directories are targeted to people who are looking for RSS feeds, so they're a great place to list your feed. Here's a starter list of directories (also in Chapter 2, "Grabbing RSS with Readers"):

- www.syndic8.com/feedlist.php

- www.blogstreet.com

- www.search4rss.com

- www.feedster.com

- www.completerss.com

- www.newsgator.com/ngs/default.aspx

- www.blogsearchengine.com (add *rss* after your search term)

- www.2rss.com/index.php

- www.rss-network.com

- www.rssfeeds.com

- www.shas3.com/RSS.html

Unfortunately, there are no "big three" RSS directories that correspond to Google, Yahoo, and MSN Search. To submit your feed to the RSS feed directories, you're usually stuck doing it yourself unless you want to use software to do it for you.

## Submitting a feed yourself

A good place to start submitting your RSS feed is www.syndic8.com, one of the most popular RSS directories (**Figure 8.18**). After you register, go to the submission page at www.syndic8.com/suggest_start.php.

You can also register at Search 4 RSS (www.search4rss.com), the RSS search engine (**Figure 8.19**). All you have to do is to supply the URL of your RSS feed (that is, the URL of your RSS feed's XML file).

**Figure 8.18**

After registering with Syndic8, you can submit your RSS feed.

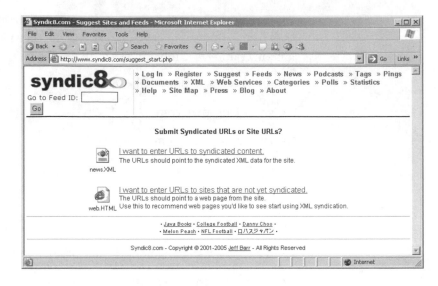

**Figure 8.19**

Adding a feed to Search 4 RSS is easy.

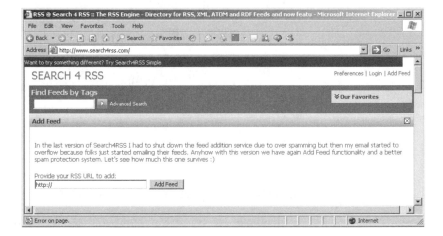

You can also submit your feed to a directory of RSS feeds at RSSfeeds.com (www.rssfeeds.com/suggest_wizzard.php). RSSfeeds.com doesn't like to receive automated submissions from software, so you're asked to enter not only your feed's URL, but also an anti-automation code that appears in a graphic (**Figure 8.20**).

RSS Network (www.rss-network.com), another directory site (**Figure 8.21**), lets you specify not only your feed's URL but also a category and a subcategory. These categories help the right people find your feed.

**Figure 8.20**

Simply fill out the fields to add a feed to www.rssfeeds.com.

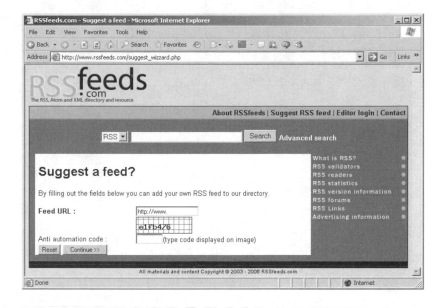

**Figure 8.21**

To add a feed in RSS Networks, start by selecting your feed's category.

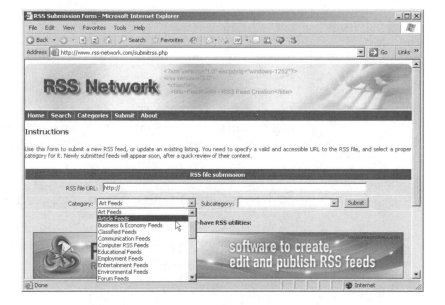

You can find another RSS directory at 2RSS.com (www.2rss.com). Scroll down the main page below the search area and you'll see a section for adding a new RSS feed (**Figure 8.22**).

**Figure 8.22**

In addition to the URL of your RSS feed, you can specify a category and description in 2RSS.com.

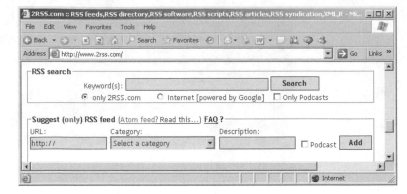

FeedBurner (www.feedburner.com) is another site that publicizes RSS feeds. FeedBurner also lets you track the number of hits your RSS feed received, which is useful.

Google now has a feature that lets you search blogs that have RSS feeds (http://blogsearch.google.com). As of this writing, there is no URL to submit your blog to this feature, but Google promises to add a URL in the future.

As you can see, there are many places to submit your RSS feed if you want to do it manually.

There are plenty of other RSS feed directories that you might want to use. You can find an excellent starter list of directories and the URLs to those directories at www.masternewmedia.org/rss/top55/.

## Submitting a feed using software

It can be a chore to submit your RSS feed to directories at multiple sites, so, as you might expect, you can try using software to rescue you from this chore. Here are some of the options (note that these are not recommendations).

RSS Submit, which you can buy at www.dummysoftware.com/rsssubmit.html, is supposed to submit your feed to 80 RSS and blog directories (**Figure 8.23**).

**Figure 8.23**

RSS Submit comes in three versions: Personal, Professional, and SEO.

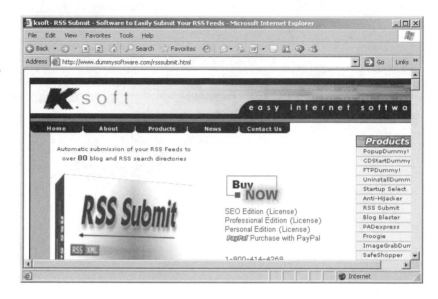

RSS Submit has various levels, starting with the Personal Edition ($44.95 as of this writing). RSS Submit's company, Ksoft, claims it is the most powerful RSS feed promotion tool available.

Another submission software package is RSS Planter ($29.95), at www.rssplanter.com/software/ (**Figure 8.24**).

**Figure 8.24**

RSS Planter offers a free trial so you can test it before you buy.

Feedshot (www.feedshot.com) is designed to publicize blogs with RSS feeds. It has a free option for submitting your feed to eight directories, and a $3 option to submit to 19 directories (**Figure 8.25**).

**Figure 8.25**

FeedShot is a blog-submission site.

Here's one that's free: RSS Announcer, which you can find at www.rssfornewbies.com (**Figure 8.26**).

**Figure 8.26**

RSS Announcer is free.

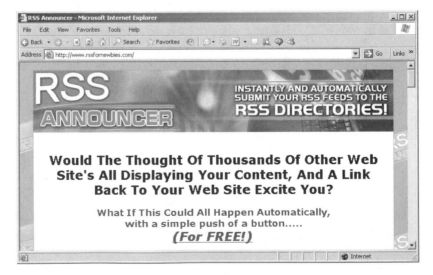

# Publicizing Your Podcast

How about publicizing your podcast? The first step is to add a podcast button to your Web page.

```
<html>
  <head>
    <title>My Hamster Page</title>
  </head>

  <body>
    <center>
      <h1>Welcome to my hamster page!</h1>
      <img src="hamster.jpg">
      <br>
      Yes, it's true, everyone loves hamsters.
      <br>
      How could you not?
      <br>
      I write a lot on hamsters,
      <br>
      would you like to subscribe
      <br>
      to my super hamster RSS feed?
      <br>
      (What's RSS? Click <a href="http://en.wikipedia.org/wiki/Rss">
      here</a> for more info.)
      <br>
      Just use the XML button below to subscribe.
      <br>
      <a href="http://rssmaniac.com/hamster.xml">
      <img src="xml.gif" height="11" width="24" border = "0"></a>
      <a href="http://rssmaniac.com/hamster.mp3">
      <img src="pod.gif" height="11" width="24" border = "0"></a>
    </center>
  </body>

</html>
```

**Figure 8.27**
A podcast button has been added to the hamster page.

You can use autodiscovery for podcasts, just as you can for RSS feeds. Just make sure that you use the right MIME type. For MP3 podcasts, that's `"audio/mpeg"`.

```
<html>
  <head>
    <link rel="alternate" type="audio/mpeg" title="podcast"
      href="http://rssmaniac.com/hamster.mp3">
    <title>My Hamster Page</title>
  </head>

  <body>
    <center>
      <h1>Welcome to my hamster page!</h1>
      <img src="hamster.jpg">
      <br>
      Yes, it's true, everyone loves hamsters.
      <br>
      How could you not?
      <br>
```

```
I write a lot on hamsters,
<br>
would you like to subscribe
<br>
to my super hamster RSS feed?
<br>
(What's RSS? Click <a href="http://en.wikipedia.org/wiki/Rss">
here</a> for more info.)
<br>
Just use the XML button below to subscribe.
<br>
<a href="http://rssmaniac.com/hamster.xml">
<img src="xml.gif" height="11" width="24" border = "0"></a>
<a href="http://rssmaniac.com/hamster.mp3">
<img src="pod.gif" height="11" width="24" border = "0"></a>
   </center>
  </body>

</html>
```

## Using podcast directories

There are also many podcast directories where you can submit your podcast. Here's a starter list of URLs of podcast directories to which you can add your podcast:

- www.podcastalley.com/add_a_podcast.php (**Figure 8.28**)

- www.podcast.net/addpodcast

- www.podcastbunker.com/Podcast/Podcast_Picks/Podcast_Submit_Form/

- http://audio.weblogs.com/pingform.html

- www.2rss.com (click the podcast check box; see Figure 8.22)

- www.feedburner.com (click the "I am a podcaster!" check box)

**Figure 8.28**

Complete the fields to add your podcast to Podcast Alley.

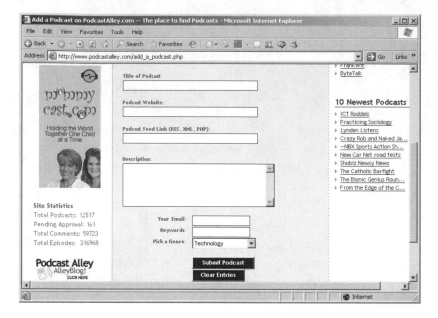

## Using ads

Another way to drive traffic to your Web site is to use online ads. One of the most effective ways to advertise online is on the search engines, where your ad appears when someone searches for one of the keywords you've associated with your site.

Here are two good sites for placing search engine ads:

- Google AdWords (https://adwords.google.com/select) places ads in Google.

- Overture (www.content.overture.com/d/) places ads in AltaVista, MSN Search, and Yahoo.

## Connecting to a bigger site

Finally, you can publicize your site and RSS feed by connecting your site to a larger one that already has a lot of traffic. Doing so can funnel thousands of readers your way. For example, you could write a blog for an online newspaper that gets a lot of traffic. You might also offer to write an online column for a major site that's connected to your interests.

# 9

# Converting RSS Feeds to a Web Site

You've seen many ways of creating RSS feeds so far. But what if you don't want to create an RSS feed, and instead you want to gather information from existing feeds? With thousands of feeds on the Web, there's no reason you need to create your own. Why not put together several feeds on a topic that interests you?

In fact, you can make those RSS feeds available to people who don't usually read RSS, by converting those feeds to RSS format.

 **When you start republishing other people's feeds, you might need to get permission first. At the very least, make sure you cite the sources of your information.**

# Why Convert RSS Feeds to a Web Site?

Believe it or not, many people don't read RSS feeds. So if you want to spread the word on your favorite topics with these folks, you can't use RSS. You can, however, display the items from an RSS feed on a Web page. When readers click a link for an item, they are redirected to the page associated with that RSS item.

All this cuts RSS out of the picture entirely as far as your page's readers are concerned. That's a good thing if you want to take information to the RSS-ignorant masses—you'll be handling the RSS yourself behind the scenes.

To put your RSS feed in a Web site, you need to convert the feed to a Web programming language—most likely JavaScript or HTML—and there are plenty of online services and software to help you do this.

All in all, it's easy to take RSS feeds and convert them into Web pages or display them in Web pages. Let's start with some online services that create JavaScript snippets you can add to your Web pages to display RSS channels.

# Converting RSS to JavaScript

The following are online services that create JavaScript you can embed in a Web page. That JavaScript calls a remote server that converts the RSS feed you've chosen into HTML, then displays the HTML on the Web page.

## RSS-xpress Lite

A good RSS-to-HTML converter is RSS-xpress Lite, at http://rssxpress. ukoln.ac.uk/lite/ (**Figure 9.1**).

To generate JavaScript for an RSS channel, just click the Include link, then the Try It link in the new page that appears (**Figure 9.2**).

**Figure 9.1**

RSS-xpress Lite converts RSS to HTML.

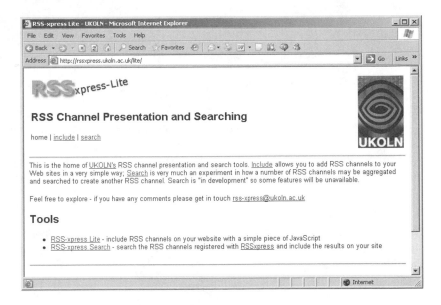

**Figure 9.2**

Follow RSS-xpress Lite's steps to convert RSS to HTML.

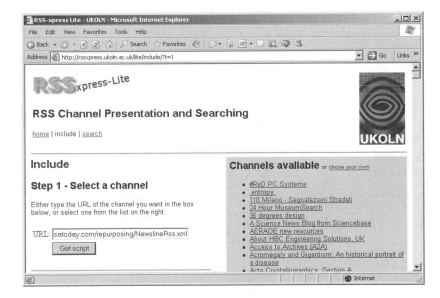

Enter the URL for the RSS feed you want to convert to HTML. In this example, it's the URL for an RSS feed from USAToday.com, at www.usatoday.com/repurposing/NewslineRss.xml.

When you select the Get Script button, what appears is the new JavaScript you can use to display the RSS channel in a Web page (**Figure 9.3**).

Here's the raw JavaScript that you get in this example:

```
<script src="http://rssxpress.ukoln.ac.uk/lite/viewer/
?rss=http%3A%2F%2Fwww.usatoday.com%2Frepurposing%2FNewslineRss.xml
"></script> <noscript><a
href="http://rssxpress.ukoln.ac.uk/lite/viewer/?rss=http%3A%2F%2Fw
ww.usatoday.com%2Frepurposing%2FNewslineRss.xml">View </a>
</noscript>
```

**Figure 9.3**

Simply cut and paste the code displayed to create JavaScript.

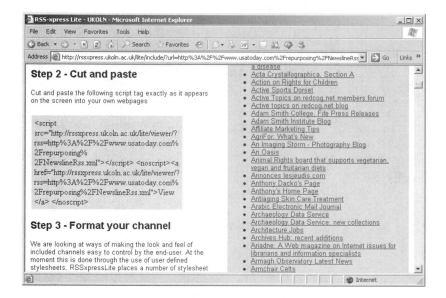

You can just paste the JavaScript into a Web page where you want the converted RSS feed's items to appear.

```
<html>
  <head>
    <title>
      The News
    </title>
  </head>
```

```
<body>
  <h1>Here's the news from USA Today</h1>
  <script src= "http://rssxpress.ukoln.ac.uk/lite/viewer/?rss=
  http%3A%2F%2Fwww.usatoday.com%2Frepurposing%2FNewslineRss.xml">
  </script>

  <noscript>
    <a href="http://rssxpress.ukoln.ac.uk/lite/viewer/?rss=
    http%3A%2F%2Fwww.usatoday.com%2Frepurposing%2FNewslineRss.
    xml">View </a>
  </noscript>
</body>
</html>
```

If you open this new page in a browser, you'll see the RSS feed
converted into HTML (**Figure 9.4**). Not bad.

**Figure 9.4**

The RSS feeds
have been converted
to HTML.

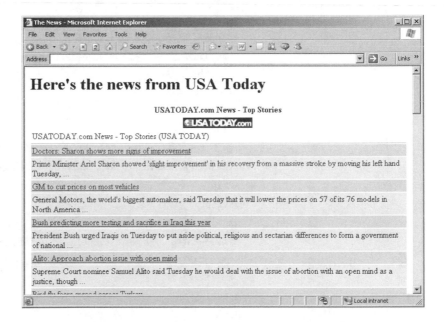

If you want to include other RSS feeds in your page, just create new JavaScript. For example, to include USAToday.com's world news as well as its top stories, you can add this JavaScript:

```html
<html>
  <head>
    <title>
      The News
    </title>
  </head>

  <body>
    <h1>Here's the news from USA Today</h1>
    <script src= "http://rssxpress.ukoln.ac.uk/lite/viewer/?rss=
    http%3A%2F%2Fwww.usatoday.com%2Frepurposing%2FNewslineRss.xml">
    </script>

    <noscript>
      <a href="http://rssxpress.ukoln.ac.uk/lite/viewer/?rss=
      http%3A%2F%2Fwww.usatoday.com%2Frepurposing%2FNewslineRss.
      xml">View </a>
    </noscript>

    <script
     src="http://rssxpress.ukoln.ac.uk/lite/viewer/?rss=
     http%3A%2F%2Fwww.usatoday.com%2Frepurposing%2FWorldRss.xml">
    </script>
    <noscript>
      <a
        href="http://rssxpress.ukoln.ac.uk/lite/viewer/?rss=
        http%3A%2F%2Fwww.usatoday.com%2Frepurposing%2FWorldRss.
        xml">View </a>
    </noscript>
  </body>
</html>
```

This code puts the two RSS feeds into the Web page, one after the other. Check out http://rssxpress.ukoln.ac.uk/lite/include for more on ways to arrange the RSS feeds on a Web page.

 **There's one drawback to creating HTML from RSS feeds on the fly like this—the resulting HTML is usually not readable in search engines.**

# RSS-to-JavaScript

RSS-to-JavaScript is another, fancier tool that converts RSS to JavaScript. You can find it at www.rss-to-javascript.com (**Figure 9.5**).

**Figure 9.5**
RSS-to-JavaScript is a free service.

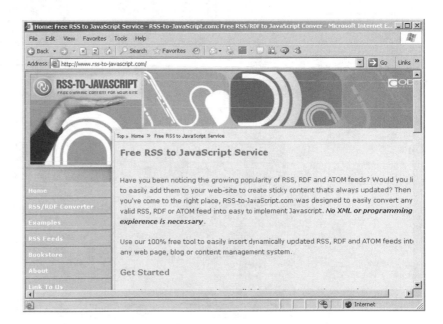

To get started, select the RSS/RDF/Atom Converter v4.0 link on the home page. You then enter the URL of your feed (**Figure 9.6**).

**Figure 9.6**

Fill in the appropriate information to convert an RSS feed to HTML.

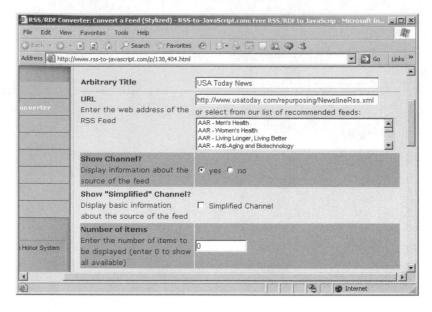

RSS-to-JavaScript provides many options to format your new HTML as you like (**Figure 9.7**).

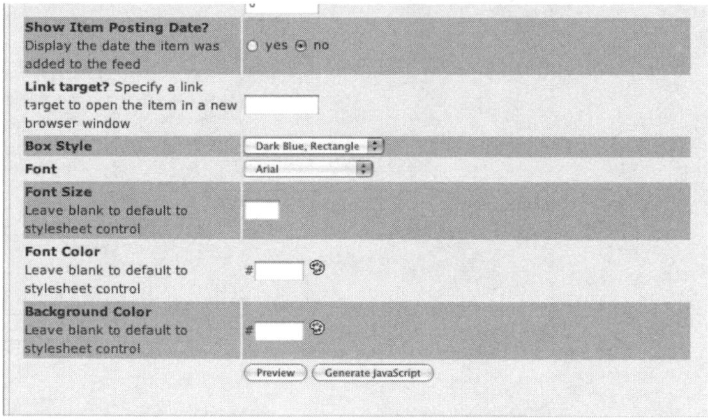

**Figure 9.7**

Here are more RSS feed formatting options.

When you select the Generate JavaScript button located at the bottom of the formatting options, the JavaScript for this feed is created (**Figure 9.8**).

**Figure 9.8**

Copy the JavaScript and paste it into your HTML document.

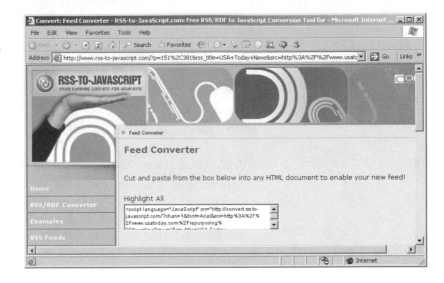

Then you simply paste this JavaScript into a Web page.

```
<html>
  <head>
    <title>
      The News
    </title>
  </head>

  <body>
    <h1>Here's the news from USA Today</h1>
    <script language="JavaScript" src=
      "http://convert.rss-to-javascript.com/?chan=1&font=Arial&src=
      http%3A%2F%2Fwww.usatoday.com%2Frepurposing%
      2FNewslineRss.xml&rss_title=USA Today News&box_list_id=413">
    </script>

    <noscript>Your browser does not support JavaScript.
      <a title='RSS-to-JavaScript.com: Free RSS to JavaScript
      Converter'
```

*(code continues on next page)*

```
            href=http://www.rss-to-javascript.com/
            ?p=151,381&chan=1&font=Arial
            &src=http%3A%2F%2Fwww.usatoday.com%2Frepurposing%
            2FNewslineRss.xml&rss_title=USA Today News&
            box_list_id=413&as_html=1>Click to read the latest
            news</a>.
    </noscript>

    <a href=http://www.rss-to-javascript.com target=_blank
      title='RSS-to-JavaScript.com: Free RSS to JavaScript
      Converter'>
      <img src=http://www.rss-to-javascript.com/images/rss-to-
      jss-small.gif alt='RSS to JavaScript' border=0></a>
    </body>
  </html>
```

This JavaScript creates a neat sidebar where your selected RSS feed is displayed (**Figure 9.9**).

**Figure 9.9**

The RSS feed is displayed in a sidebar.

# FeedRoll

FeedRoll (www.feedroll.com/rssviewer/) lets you create JavaScript from RSS feeds, but there's a catch—you can only select an RSS feed from FeedRoll's lists (**Figure 9.10**).

**Figure 9.10**

For JavaScript conversion, you must select an RSS feed from FeedRoll's list (on the right).

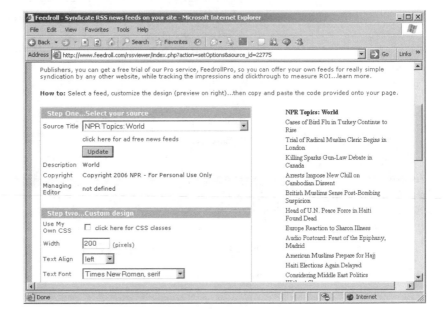

When you've formatted your HTML the way you want it, click the Update button, and copy the JavaScript that appears (below the HTML formatting options) into a Web page:

```
<html>
  <head>
    <title>
      The News
    </title>
  </head>

  <body>
    <h1>Here's the news from NPR</h1>
      <script language="javascript" type="text/javascript"
```

*(code continues on next page)*

```
          src="http://www.feedroll.com/rssviewer/view_rss.php?
          type=js&source_id=22775&feed_width=200&
          frame_color=black&title_textcolor=black&title_bgcolor=
          white&box_textcolor=black&box_bgcolor=
          white&feed_showborder=0&feed_spacing=2&
          feed_align=left&feed_textsize=12&feed_textfont=
          Times New Roman, serif&feed_maxitems=15&feed_desclimit=&
          feed_compact=1&feed_xmlbutton=0&link_openblank=1">
      </script>
   </body>
</html>
```

Like RSS-to-JavaScript, FeedRoll displays the items in the feed in a sidebar (**Figure 9.11**).

**Figure 9.11**

A FeedRoll-converted RSS feed from NPR appears on the page in a sidebar.

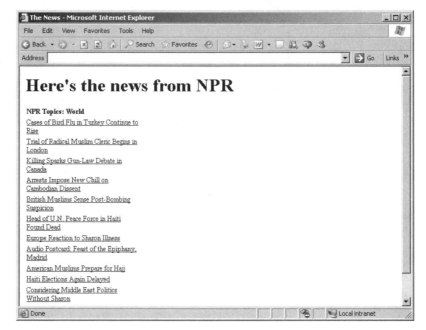

## Feed2JS

Feed2JS, at http://jade.mcli.dist.maricopa.edu/feed/, is a powerful service for creating HTML from RSS (**Figure 9.12**).

**Figure 9.12**

Feed2JS is a free service.

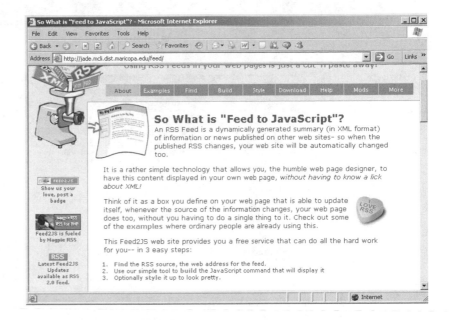

To create your own JavaScript for an RSS feed, click the Build link, and on the new page, enter your RSS feed's URL, then configure the HTML to be generated as you like it (**Figure 9.13**).

**Figure 9.13**

Feed2JS lets you preview your feed.

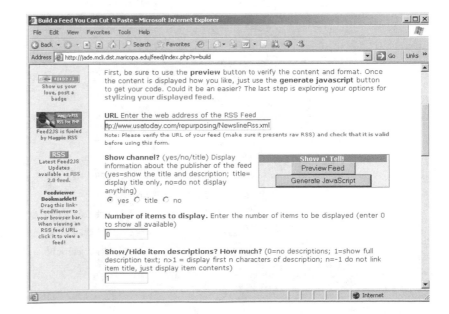

When you're ready, click the Generate JavaScript button to display the JavaScript for you to use (**Figure 9.14**).

**Figure 9.14**

Feed2JS generates the JavaScript for you.

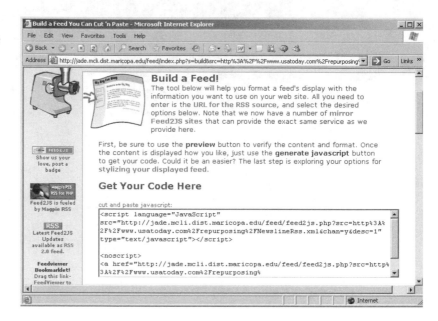

Copy your new JavaScript and paste it into a Web page.

```html
<html>
  <head>
    <title>
      The News
    </title>
  </head>

  <body>
    <h1>Here's the news from NPR</h1>
    <script language="JavaScript"
      src="http://jade.mcli.dist.maricopa.edu/feed/
      feed2js.php?src=http%3A%2F%2Fwww.usatoday.com%
      2Frepurposing%2FNewslineRss.xml&chan=y&desc=1"
      type="text/javascript">
    </script>
```

```
<noscript>
  <a href="http://jade.mcli.dist.maricopa.edu/feed/
    feed2js.php?src=http%3A%2F%2Fwww.usatoday.com%
    2Frepurposing%2FNewslineRss.xml&chan=y&desc=1&
    html=y"> View RSS feed
  </a>
</noscript>
</body>
</html>
```

Finally, take a look at the result (**Figure 9.15**).

**Figure 9.15**

Here's the news from USAToday.com.

## Jawfish

Another site that creates JavaScript from RSS feeds is Jawfish (www.geckotribe.com/rss/jawfish). In order to use this service, you need to create an account and log in (**Figure 9.16**).

**Figure 9.16**

Use the free trial
account to try Jawfish.

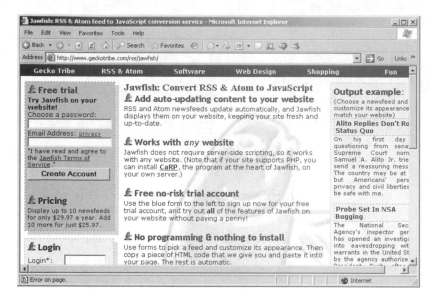

Unfortunately, the Jawfish site might complain that you need to turn on cookies in your browser—even if they are already on. Because of this problem, you might not be able to create JavaScript from scratch on this site.

On the other hand, the Jawfish site does give you a sample piece of JavaScript you can use to test its service. The following sample JavaScript will read an RSS feed from Washingtonpost.com (**Figure 9.17**).

```html
<html>
  <head>
    <title>
      The News
    </title>
  </head>

  <body>
    <h1>Here's the news from The Washington Post</h1>
    <script src="http://rss2js.geckotribe.com/jssample.php">
    </script>
  </body>
</html>
```

**Figure 9.17**

You can read Washingtonpost.com news using the sample script from Jawfish.

As you can see, there are a variety of sites that will produce JavaScript. You should be aware that because these sites rely on server-side code running on the service's server, performance is affected by server issues. For example, the UKOLN site's server, located in the United Kingdom, is quite slow for browsers in the United States to contact.

 **Want to check out more RSS-to-JavaScript options? Take a look at the list of services at www.rss-specifications.com/display-rss.htm.**

# Using Server-Side Software

The RSS-to-JavaScript Web sites described so far rely on server-side programming, and that programming resides on someone else's server. This means you're susceptible to changes on that server, server downtime, and so on.

Using a server-side software package allows you to avoid those problems, and there are plenty of packages to choose from. Most RSS-handling software uses the PHP language (although there are other, more innovative ways of doing things, such as using Java applets).

Your Web server may already support PHP; to find out, check with your server's tech staff. If it doesn't, you can find dozens of servers that do—just search on Google for *PHP server*.

**Installing PHP locally (on your own machine) is useful for testing and development purposes. You can get PHP for free from www.php.net.**

The PHP packages discussed in this chapter usually don't require much installation. Typically, you copy some PHP files over to the same directory in which you store your Web pages. Some packages involve substantial installation, however, and you may need to decide how much control you want to give them.

# Converting RSS to HTML

An alternative to converting your RSS feeds to JavaScript is converting them directly to HTML pages. You can load software for this purpose onto your Web server. These software packages use various programming languages on the Web server, most often PHP.

## RSSlib

RSSlib (www.2rss.com/software.php#rsslib) is a useful package for converting RSS feeds into HTML (**Figure 9.18**).

To install RSSlib, all you have to do is click the link rsslib-php.zip and unzip the file. Then copy the unzipped files over to the directory on your server where you want to use RSSlib—the same directory as the Web page in which you want the converted RSS feed to appear (**Figure 9.19**).

To get similar results for the RSS feed you choose, call the PHP script rss2html.php with the URL of the RSS feed you want to display. You pass the URL of the RSS feed using the rss_url parameter. In our example, the feed comes from USAToday.com's top stories.

**Figure 9.18**

RSSlib has parsers for
PHP and ASP.

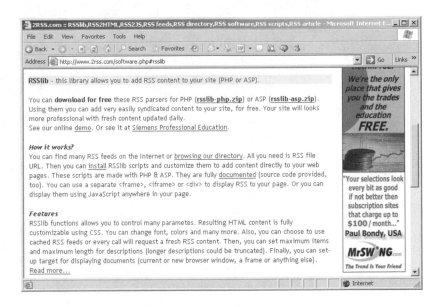

**Figure 9.19**

Here's an RSSlib demo
from CNET News.com.

There are various ways to insert the text for the RSS feed into a Web
page; here we will simply use only HTML and the <iframe> element to
create floating HTML frames.

To insert the HTML for the converted feed into a Web page, first create a 300-by-400–pixel floating frame without a border or scrollbar. The <iframe> element supports an <src> element, which lets you specify the source of the floating frame's content. And for the content in our example you would use this:

```
rss2html.php?rss_url=http://www.usatoday.com/repurposing/
NewslineRss.xml
```

Here's what it looks like in a Web page:

```
<html>
  <head>
    <title>
      The News
    </title>
  </head>

  <body>
    <h1>Here's the news from USA Today</h1>
    <iframe height="300" width="400" frameborder="0" scrolling="no"
    src="rss2html.php?rss_url=http://www.usatoday.com/repurposing/
    NewslineRss.xml">
    </iframe>
  </body>
</html>
```

**tip**   **You can also position** <iframe> **elements wherever you want them in a page by using cascading style sheet (CSS) styles. Take a look at any good HTML book for the details.**

The results appear in Internet Explorer, where it looks like the RSS feed's news items blend right into the page (**Figure 9.20**).

Although the <iframe> element used to be unique to Internet Explorer, all standard browsers support it now; you can see what this page looks like in Mozilla Firefox (**Figure 9.21**).

**Figure 9.20**
RSSlib displays USAToday.com's news in Internet Explorer.

**Figure 9.21**
RSSlib can display USAToday.com's news in Firefox as well.

# RSS2HTML

RSS2HTML, a PHP-based software package that converts RSS to HTML, is a free PHP script from FeedForAll. You can download this script at www.feedforall.com/free-php-script.htm (**Figure 9.22**).

**Figure 9.22**

FeedForAll offers a free PHP script.

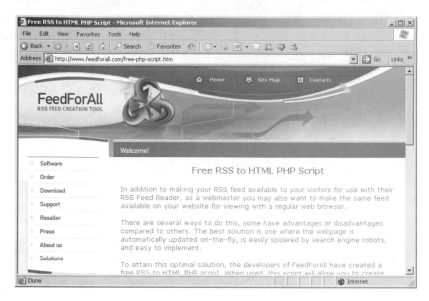

To download the script, click the download link, then select the Download button. This downloads a zip file with documentation, the PHP script rss2html.php, and a sample HTML template.

To use RSS2HTML call the rss2html.php script, passing it the parameters XMLFILE, TEMPLATE, and MAXITEMS. The XMLFILE parameter gives the name of a local RSS feed file (in the same directory as the rss2html.php script) or the URL to an RSS feed; TEMPLATE gives the name of the HTML template to use when formatting the HTML (we'll use the sample template that comes with RSS2HTML), and MAXITEMS specifies the maximum number of items to use.

Here's an example; navigating to this URL displays the RSS contents of news.xml, which is the RSS feed Steve's News:

```
http://www.rssmaniac.com/rss2html/rss2html.php?XMLFILE=news.xml&TE
MPLATE=sample-template.html&MAXITEMS=10
```

On the other hand, you may want to embed the HTML conversion of an RSS feed in a Web page, so you can use the same <iframe> technique you saw with RSSlib.

```
<html>
  <head>
    <title>
```

```
      The News
    </title>
  </head>

  <body>
    <h1>Here's the news from Steve</h1>
    <iframe height="300" width="400" frameborder="0" scrolling="no"
    src="rss2html.php?XMLFILE=news.xml&TEMPLATE=sample-
    template.html&MAXITEMS=10">
    </iframe>
  </body>
  </html>
```

RSS2HTML converts the RSS feed into HTML and displays it in a floating frame (**Figure 9.23**). Not bad.

**Figure 9.23**

Here's the page created with RSS2HTML.

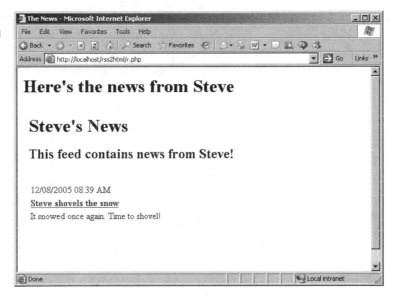

## Magpie

Magpie, at http://magpierss.sourceforge.net, is a powerful PHP-based package that lets you parse RSS and convert it into HTML (**Figure 9.24**).

**Figure 9.24**

Magpie is an XML-based RSS parser.

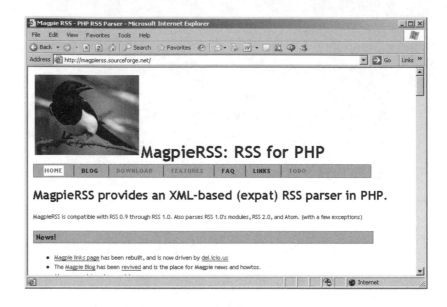

You'll have to get your hands into the PHP with Magpie, because it's really an RSS parser, not an HTML formatter like the previous two packages. Magpie reads—that is, parses—an RSS feed and stores it in a PHP object, and you're responsible for unpacking the feed's data and formatting it as you want.

Here's a little PHP to read the example feed from USAToday.com's top stories. You start PHP scripts with `<?php`, and in this case, the Magpie script `rss_fetch.inc` is included.

```php
<?php
  require 'rss_fetch.inc';

      .

      .

      .
```

Now you can call the Magpie PHP function `fetch_rss`, passing it the URL of the RSS feed you want to grab.

```php
<?php
  require 'rss_fetch.inc';

  $url = 'http://www.usatoday.com/repurposing/NewslineRss.xml';
```

```
$rss = fetch_rss($url);
          .
          .
          .
```

This code reads the RSS feed and stores it in the PHP variable $rss. You can display the title of the RSS feed this way:

```php
<?php
  require 'rss_fetch.inc';

  $url = 'http://www.usatoday.com/repurposing/NewslineRss.xml';
  $rss = fetch_rss($url);

  echo $rss->channel['title'], "<br>";
          .
          .
          .
```

You can also use a PHP foreach loop to display a hyperlink for the items in the feed, each on its own line.

```php
<?php
  require 'rss_fetch.inc';

  $url = 'http://www.usatoday.com/repurposing/NewslineRss.xml';
  $rss = fetch_rss($url);

  echo $rss->channel['title'], "<br>";

  foreach ($rss->items as $item) {
    $t = $item['title'];
    $u   = $item['link'];
    echo "<a href=$u>$t</a><br>";
  }
?>
```

**If you don't know PHP, you can use this PHP script to convert RSS to HTML using Magpie—just change the feed's URL to the URL of the feed you want to use.**

Now, when you use your browser to navigate to this script, called news.php in our example, you'll see your feed in HTML form (**Figure 9.25**). This is assuming the Magpie PHP script `rss_fetch.inc` is in the same directory as the news.php script.

**Figure 9.25**

Here's the feed from Magpie's output of the news.php script.

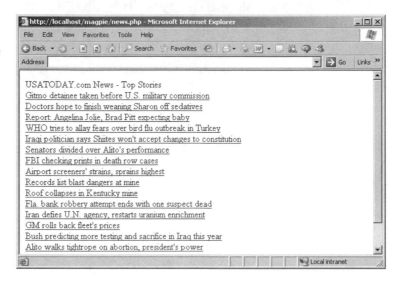

You can also embed `news.php` in another Web page using floating frames as before.

```
<html>
  <head>
    <title>
      The News
    </title>
  </head>

  <body>
    <h1>Here's the news from USA Today</h1>
    <iframe height="300" width="400" frameborder="0"
    scrolling="no"
      src="news.php">
    </iframe>
  </body>
</html>
```

The results of this HTML appear on a page in Internet Explorer, where you can see the feed that Magpie grabbed for you (**Figure 9.26**).

**Figure 9.26**

Created with Magpie, the top-stories feed appears in Internet Explorer.

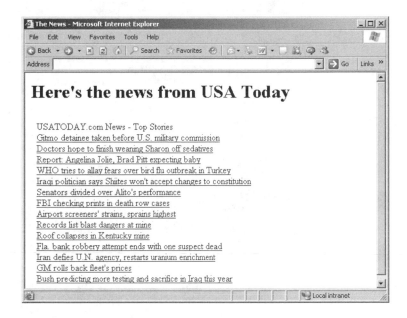

## DOMit

The DOMit software package has a parser that can put RSS in XML DOM (Document Object Model) form (**Figure 9.27**).

XML DOM is beyond the scope of this book, but if you're an accomplished XML and PHP person, DOMit may be the package for you. The DOMit RSS parser requires the DOMit XML parser, but you can download it for free at www.engageinteractive.com/mambo/index.php?option=content&task=view&id=3665&Itemid=20233.

You can see the DOMit RSS package at work in an example at www.engageinteractive.com/domitrss/testing_domitrss.php (**Figure 9.28**).

**Figure 9.27**

DOMit Uses a DOM
XML parser.

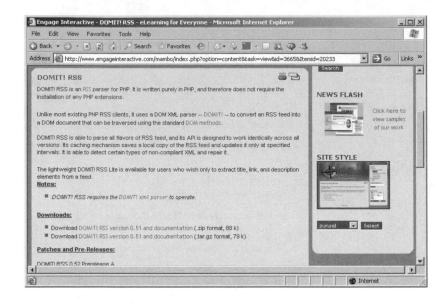

**Figure 9.28**

DOMit's testing
interface is easy to use.

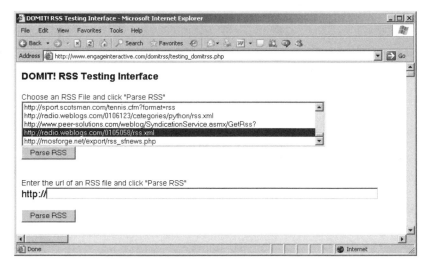

Select an RSS feed to convert to HTML, or enter the URL of a feed and
click the Parse RSS button to give you the RSS feed converted to HTML
(**Figure 9.29**).

**Figure 9.29**
Here's the RSS parsed by DOMit.

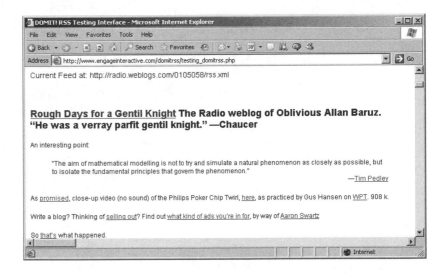

## Other PHP-based RSS converters

RSSProcessor is an RSS converter ($79.99) that you can find at www.scientio.com/rssprocessor.aspx (**Figure 9.30**).

**Figure 9.30**
Sciento includes a link to view a site that uses RSSProcessor.

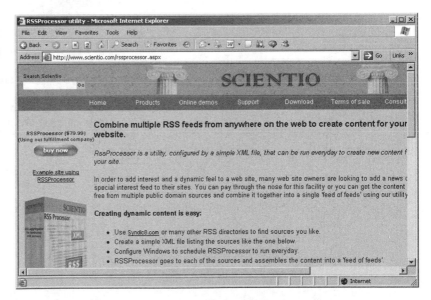

RSSProcessor also converts multiple RSS feeds into Web page content.

# Converting RSS to Applets with RSSViewerApplet

Here's a cool one—RSSViewerApplet (www.webreference.com/cgi-bin/xml/rssappletconfig.pl). This package displays RSS feeds in a Java applet in your Web page. Applets are bits of Java-powered code that work in browsers and display their results in a section of a Web page.

Select the RSS source you want to read from, choose and configure the colors you want for your feed, and click the Preview button (**Figure 9.31**). You'll see a preview of the applet, and a box containing the applet's code.

**Figure 9.31**

RSSViewerApplet lets you select colors for your feed.

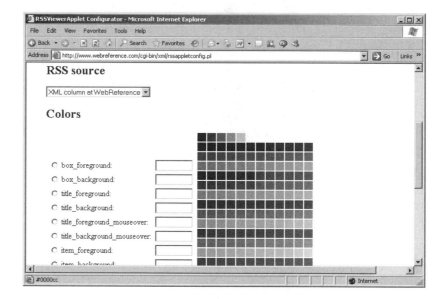

Just copy the applet code and place it in a Web page of your own, like this:

```
<html>
  <head>
    <title>Using RSSViewerApplet</title>
  </head>
```

```
<body>
  <h1>Using RSSViewerApplet</h1>
  <APPLET code=com.exploringxml.rss.applet.RSSViewerApplet.class
  archive=http://www.webreference.com/xml/rssApplet.jar
  codebase=http://www.webreference.com/ width=300 height=300>
    <PARAM name=src
      value=http://www.webreference.com/webreference.rdf>
    <PARAM name=title.font.family value=sansserif>
    <PARAM name=title.font.size value=10>
    <PARAM name=title.font.style value=bold>
    <PARAM name=item.font.family value=sansserif>
    <PARAM name=item.font.size value=10>
    <PARAM name=item.font.style value=bold>
  </APPLET>
</body>
</html>
```

The applet displays the WebReference news (www.webreference.com)
RSS feed (**Figure 9.32**).

**Figure 9.32**

RSSViewerApplet is at
work displaying a news
feed.

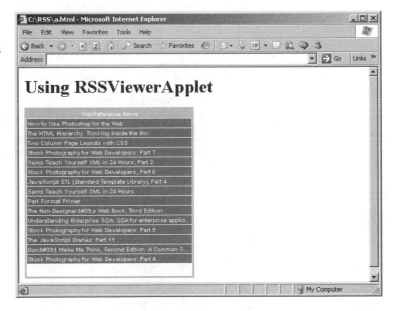

# Handling RSS With Perl Scripts

Besides PHP, there are other server-side languages available, such as Perl. You can find more information about Perl at www.cpan.org.

If you're more familiar with Perl than PHP, take a look at RSS Fetcher, which is a Perl script that lets you convert RSS feeds and display their headlines in Web pages. Actually, the RSS content is stored in text files that you can include in Web pages using floating frames or server side includes (SSI).

You can pick up RSS Fetcher at http://cgi.resourceindex.com/detail/ 05142.html (**Figure 9.33**).

**Figure 9.33**

RSS Fetcher uses Perl scripts.

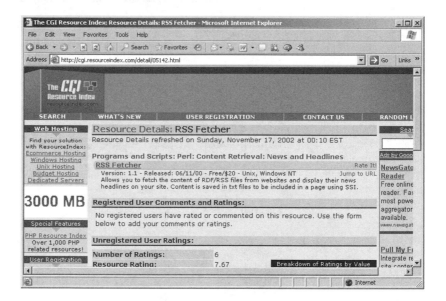

Another Perl script is rss2rss (www.aaronland.info/perl/rss/rss2rss). This one takes a group of RSS feeds and combines them into a single RSS feed.

Although most server-side RSS-to-HTML applications are written in PHP, you can find software available in just about every server-side language, from Perl to .NET. Just use a Web search engine like Google to locate what you're looking for—it's out there.

# 10

# Doing It Right: RSS Best Practices

It's morning and you're checking your email, just as you did in Chapter 1. Your in-box is still packed with email and spam, but now you don't worry about it so much, because you use an RSS reader to track your news. In fact, you've started your own RSS feed.

And now you're getting email from the readers of your feed. You're sure this is going to be good. But as you peruse your email, you see an unhappy story—most of your readers can't read your feed!

Uh-oh. Did you validate your feed before publishing it? That's number one in this chapter's list of best practices. To get the most out of publishing your own RSS feeds, you should follow the best practices described in this chapter—these are the most effective ways to create and publish your feeds. This chapter is geared toward making a feed that readers can read—and want to read.

# Validate Your Feed

The most basic of the best practices is to make sure you validate your feed before publishing it, using a feed validator like the one at www.feedvalidator.org (**Figure 10.1**).

**Figure 10.1**

Use a feed validator before publishing your feed.

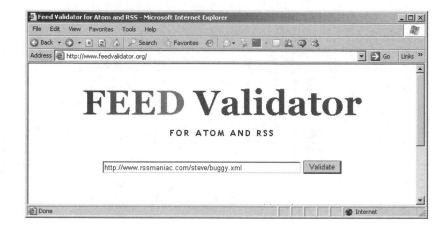

Yes, validating your feed is a pain. But if you want to publish a smooth feed that readers can count on, this step is essential. People can't read an invalid feed. Even if you use an RSS feed-creation editor, you should still validate your feeds—at least until you're certain that your editor is producing flawless RSS as it should.

Spotting validation problems isn't easy if you're trying to do it by eye. Can you spot the validation error in this otherwise flawless RSS document?

```
<?xml version="1.0"?>
<!DOCTYPE rss SYSTEM
   "http://my.netscape.com/publish/formats/rss-0.91.dtd">
<rss version="0.91">
  <channel>
    <copyright>Copyright 2005.</copyright>
    <pubDate>Wed, 14 Dec 2005 07:00:00 GMT</pubDate>
    <lastBuildDate>Mon, 12 Dec 2005 07:00:00 GMT</lastBuildDate>
    <docs>http://www.rssmaniac.com/steve/info.html</docs>
```

```
<description>This feed contains news from Steve!</description>
<link>http://www.rssmaniac.com/steve</link>
<title>Steve's News!</title>
<language>en-us</language>
<image>
  <title>Steve's News</title>
  <url>http://www.rssmaniac.com/steve/Image.jpg</url>
  <link>http://www.rssmaniac.com/steve</link>
  <description>Steve's News</description>
  <width>144</width>
  <height>36</height>
</image>
<managingEditor>steve@rssmaniac.com (Steve)</managingEditor>
<webMaster>steve@rssmaniac.com (Steve)</webMaster>
<skipHours>
  <hour>8</hour>
  <hour>9</hour>
  <hour>10</hour>
</skipHours>
<skipDays>
  <day>Sunday</day>
</skipDays>
<item>
  <title>Steve shovels the snow</title>
  <description>It snowed once again.
    Time to shovel!>
  </discription>
  <link>http://www.rssmaniac.com/steve</link>
</item>
<textinput>
  <title>Search for other items</title>
  <description>What do you want to find?</description>
  <name>search</name>
  <link>http://www.rssmaniac.com/find.php</link>
</textinput>
</channel>
</rss>
```

An RSS validator can immediately pick out the problem for you. In this case it'll tell you that the item's closing `</description>` tag has been misspelled as `</discription>` (**Figure 10.2**).

To validate your RSS feed after it's online, just pass your feed's URL to a feed validator.

**Figure 10.2**

The RSS feed validator finds a problem.

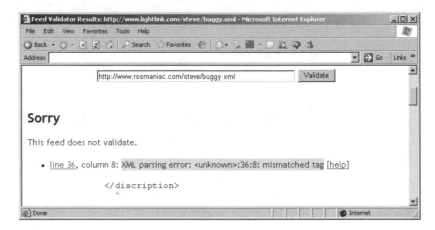

## Use the Right Encoding

Don't forget that RSS feeds are XML documents. Among other things, this means that if you use characters in your RSS feeds that are not in the default character set, which is UTF-8 (see http://www.utf-8.com), you have to use a different encoding. If, for example, you wanted to write your RSS feed in a language with another character set, such as Japanese, you would have to use the appropriate encoding. You specify the XML encoding in the XML declaration of the RSS feed:

```
<?xml version="1.0" encoding="UTF-8" ?>
<!DOCTYPE rss SYSTEM
  "http://my.netscape.com/publish/formats/rss-0.91.dtd">
<rss version="0.91">
        .
        .
        .
</rss>
```

For the legal encodings you can use with RSS, see Table 4.1 in Chapter 4, "Creating RSS Feeds from Scratch."

# Avoid Using the Same Title Twice

How can RSS readers tell if they've already read an item from your feed? Various readers check in different ways, but one way is by examining the titles of your items when they check your feed. If you re-use the same title for different items in your feed, that could be a problem—some RSS readers might not know the second use of the same title is a new item.

You can also update the `<pubDate>` element to indicate the date of different RSS items—most RSS readers will use that information if you supply it.

```
<item>
 <title>Steve shovels the snow</title>
 <author>steve@rssmaniac.com</author>
 <description><![CDATA[It snowed once again.
  Time to shovel!]]></description>
 <pubDate>Thu, 08 Dec 2005 08:39:51 -0500</pubDate>
 <link>http://www.rssmaniac.com/steve</link>
</item>

       .

       .

       .
```

You can also use the `<guid>` element to make each RSS item unique (as discussed in Chapter 4). GUID stands for globally unique identifier, and it is often a unique URL that points to the page for a specific item.

```
<item>
 <title>Steve shovels the snow</title>
 <author>steve@rssmaniac.com</author>
 <description><![CDATA[It snowed once again.
  Time to shovel!]]></description>
 <pubDate>Thu, 08 Dec 2005 08:39:51 -0500</pubDate>
 <link>http://www.rssmaniac.com/steve</link>
```

*(code continues on next page)*

```
<guid>http://www.rssmaniac.com/48393.html</guid>
</item>
      .
      .
      .
```

Note that not all RSS readers will make use of the <guid> element.

# Avoid Overwhelming Servers

Another thing to consider when you start a new RSS feed is the number of possible readers. Having thousands of people checking your Web site hourly for updates could be a problem if your Web server limits your bandwidth or, worse, charges you for bandwidth over a certain amount per day. You might end up with substantial costs, or some readers might not be able to get your feed.

On the other hand, RSS is XML, which means it's text. That's good because text is relatively small, so it won't take too much bandwidth to send. Still, there are a number of things you can do to avoid taking too much bandwidth to support your feed:

- Don't put an item's entire text into your feed if you have pages and pages of text for an item. Just put the first few paragraphs into the RSS item and add a link to the full story on your Web site.

- Don't include images in your items. You can add HTML to your RSS items to download images.

- Check out a caching service like www.rsscache.com. Caching can help you reduce your bandwidth needs. A caching service stores your feed, and you get a URL to use for your feed. Your readers use that URL to check if there's anything new, and the caching service sends out items only if there's something new to send.

If you're working with readers you know, you can ask them to change the frequency with which their RSS reader programs check for updates. For example, SharpReader lets you set the time between updates in the Options dialog (**Figure 10.3**).

**Figure 10.3**
SharpReader lets you set the time interval between checking a feed for updates.

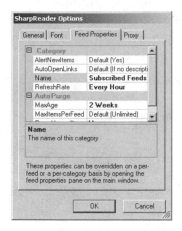

# Brand Your Feed

One of the best ways to keep readers coming back to your feed is to make it recognizable by *branding* it, much as you would for a product you want to sell. One of the main ways of branding your feed is to make the name of your feed stand out by giving it an image (**Figure 10.4**).

**Figure 10.4**
Use an image for your feed that readers will come to recognize.

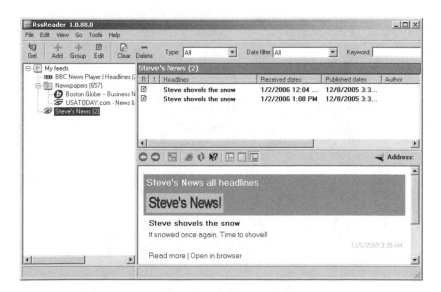

Adding an image to your feed is simple with the `<image>` element—just make sure the image you want to use has a URL (that is, it's online):

```
<?xml version="1.0"?>
<!DOCTYPE rss SYSTEM
  "http://my.netscape.com/publish/formats/rss-0.91.dtd">
<rss version="0.91">
  <channel>
    <copyright>Copyright 2005.</copyright>
    <pubDate>Wed, 14 Dec 2005 07:00:00 GMT</pubDate>
    <lastBuildDate>Mon, 12 Dec 2005 07:00:00 GMT</lastBuildDate>
    <docs>http://www.rssmaniac.com/steve/info.html</docs>
    <description>This feed contains news from Steve!</description>
    <link>http://www.rssmaniac.com/steve</link>
    <title>Steve's News!</title>
    <language>en-us</language>
    <image>
      <title>Steve's News</title>
      <url>http://www.rssmaniac.com/steve/Image.jpg</url>
      <link>http://www.rssmaniac.com/steve</link>
      <description>Steve's News</description>
      <width>144</width>
      <height>36</height>
    </image>
    <managingEditor>steve@rssmaniac.com (Steve)</managingEditor>
    <webMaster>steve@rssmaniac.com (Steve)</webMaster>
    <skipHours>
      <hour>8</hour>
      <hour>9</hour>
      <hour>10</hour>
    </skipHours>
    <skipDays>
      <day>Sunday</day>
    </skipDays>
    <item>
      <title>Steve shovels the snow</title>
      <description>It snowed once again.
        Time to shovel!>
```

```
      </description>
      <link>http://www.rssmaniac.com/steve</link>
    </item>
    <textinput>
      <title>Search for other items</title>
      <description>What do you want to find?</description>
      <name>search</name>
      <link>http://www.rssmaniac.com/find.php</link>
    </textinput>
  </channel>
</rss>
```

You can also use the <title> and <description> elements for the channel to carry branding information, especially if you have a trademark you can use in those elements.

# Avoid Including Only Titles

In the early days of RSS, feeds often included items that contained just titles and a link to the full story:

```
<?xml version="1.0"?>
<!DOCTYPE rss SYSTEM
    "http://my.netscape.com/publish/formats/rss-0.91.dtd">
<rss version="0.91">
  <channel>

        .

        .

        .

    <skipDays>
      <day>Sunday</day>
    </skipDays>
    <item>
      <title>Steve shovels the snow</title>
      <link>http://www.rssmaniac.com/steve</link>
    </item>
```

*(code continues on next page)*

```
    <textinput>
      <title>Search for other items</title>
      <description>What do you want to find?</description>
      <name>search</name>
      <link>http://www.rssmaniac.com/find.php</link>
    </textinput>
  </channel>
</rss>
```

These days, however, RSS items need more than titles. Items should always have a description.

# Avoid Long Titles and Descriptions

If someone subscribes to many feeds, they're often scanning up and down long lists of item titles, so it's best to keep titles brief. In fact, brevity goes not just for individual item titles, but for channel titles as well.

For example, take a look at the following RSS document, in which the item has a long title:

```
<?xml version="1.0" encoding="ISO-8859-1"?>
<rss version="2.0">
  <channel>

          .
          .
          .

    <image>
     <title>Steve's News</title>
     <url>http://www.rssmaniac.com/steve/Image.jpg</url>
     <link>http://www.rssmaniac.com/steve</link>
     <description>Steve's News</description>
     <width>144</width>
     <height>36</height>
    </image>
      <item>
```

```
<title>Steve shovels the snow, which might now be turning to
rain, and who knows what's next.</title>
<description><![CDATA[It snowed once again. Time
to shovel!]]></description>
<pubDate>Thu, 08 Dec 2005 08:39:51 -0500</pubDate>
<link>http://www.rssmaniac.com/steve</link>
</item>

       .

       .

       .

   </channel>
  </rss>
```

That long title might not be apparent when you're writing your feed. However, when you're viewing the RSS feed, it's much more of a problem—take a look at the item's title in the title list (**Figure 10.5**).

**Figure 10.5**

Try to keep your feed's titles short.

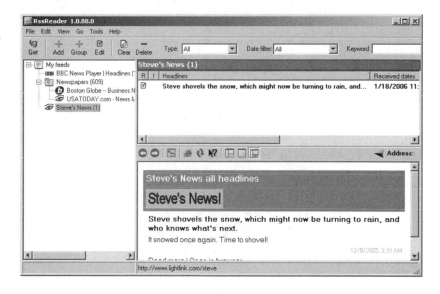

You should also keep descriptions from getting too long. Most of your readers want just enough information to get the gist of the article; if they want more information, they'll click the link.

How short is short enough? That's up to you, although you might find some recommendations online. For example, Paul Miller of UKOLN (www.ariadne.ac.uk/issue35/miller/) offers these guidelines: "Restrict RSS feeds intended for embedding in external Web sites, portals, etc. to not more than six `<item>`s, each with `<description>`s of up to 50 words in length." And he says this about channel titles and descriptions: "Restrict `<channel>` titles to less than six words, descriptions to less than 15 words, and images to less than 90 pixels along the longest side."

# Refine the Content

The best practice for creating RSS feeds is to make the content of your feed useful and interesting. Ask yourself, would you want to subscribe to this feed if you weren't creating it?

**People will be reading your feed outside the context of your Web site, so each item, theoretically, should stand on its own to some extent.**

## Make it accurate

Having read RSS feeds for a long time, I know that often, RSS publishers' standards of truth and fact-checking are low. That's one of the main criticisms of the blogging world: While trying to make a point, people sometimes forget about the truth and simply make up statistics and "facts." I've seen opinions in the mainstream press turn from being wildly supportive of blogs to turning away from them on this point alone. I hope the same thing doesn't happen when it comes to RSS feeds.

As you can imagine, if you publish things without checking the facts or providing references, it'll be hard for readers to take you seriously after a while.

## Make it useful

Using Web site statistics, you can determine which of your items people find the most useful. If you want to target what readers like to see, watch the statistics that give you the number of hits for particular RSS items on Web pages.

If something you've written about elicits an avalanche of positive interest, you know you're on the right track.

## Make it interesting

If you want to attract and keep readers, you've got to make your feeds interesting. Too many bloggers feel the need to write something every day, whether or not the content is interesting. So sometimes you end up with blog entries (which go out in RSS feeds) like, "Can't think of anything to say today. Nothing going on. *Borrrrring*."

And they're right, that's boring. As a publisher who wants to catch readers' interest, you have to look at your feeds from the readers' perspective. If what you have to publish is interesting to them, they'll keep coming back.

# Use Good Writing Practices

Many people who have little experience writing for publication end up writing hard-to-understand posts, and because they end up with few readers, there are few people to correct them or offer suggestions for improvement.

The writing style is up to you, of course—it's your RSS feed, after all, and no one can create a voice for it but you. Still, here are some writing tips that every creator of RSS should consider.

## Decide on your main point

Before you start writing, choose the point you want to make and stick to it. Many online authors start with one topic and then wander to others, and that's particularly hard on the readers of your feed. RSS items are, theoretically anyway, intended to be short articles focused on a single topic.

## Be context-independent

Many bloggers and RSS authors assume in their writing that they share a context with their readers, forgetting to explain themselves along the way, and thus lose their audience. Assuming context is one of the things that professional authors are very careful to avoid, and the principle applies to writing for RSS as well.

## Keep your audience in mind

As you write, it's a good idea to keep your audience in mind. Some authors picture someone they know well and write to that person as a representative of the audience. Doing this makes it easy to keep the tone of your feed aligned with your audience.

## Start with an overview

RSS items shouldn't be long enough to need an overview, but the article an item is linked to on your Web site might be. If you have a longer article, it might be a good idea to start with an overview. Because the reader can't take in your article at a glance, it might be helpful to provide a brief summary.

## Select your format carefully

Most blogs and RSS feeds are just straight text, and that can be fine if it suits your purpose. But bear in mind that you can choose from a number of formatting options for RSS items, such as the following:

- Frequently asked question (FAQ) lists

- Polls

- Questions and answers

- Case histories

- Lists of links

For that matter, you can always add links that point to diagrams or graphs to enliven the articles.

## Be concise

Because there's so much on the Internet, people don't have much patience for long passages. For this reason, some authors recommend that you write only 50 percent of what you'd normally write on a particular topic.

## Break up long passages

Long, continuous text passages, like the two-page paragraph, went out of style with the Victorian novel. If your text is getting long, use headlines and headings to break it up into readable chunks (something like the text in this book).

## Get feedback

Some RSS authors write as if they operate in a vacuum, and as a result their content and style become increasingly idiosyncratic and self-indulgent as time goes on. They never look for feedback on what they write or how they write it. When you start publishing RSS feeds that you plan to stick with, it can be invaluable to get some feedback. Criticism is hard to swallow, but in the long run it can be helpful. You can even get your feed edited if you wish.

# Devote Attention to Your Feed

People often start their RSS feed with big ideas and high hopes, but the one thing many of them don't understand is that to build an RSS feed with a loyal following, they have to devote attention to it regularly.

Is your idea for a feed energizing and sustaining enough to make your feed last a long time? As you get into RSS, you'll see hundreds of feeds that started well, even with multiple updates each day, but then petered out.

If you want your feed to be successful, you have to choose a lasting idea and keep at it. If you want to write a Web page, that's one thing— but a blog or RSS feed needs to keep going. A Web page is a one-shot deal: You write it, you post it. Not so with an RSS feed.

RSS readers are merciless on this point—they just keep checking your feed, usually every hour, waiting for something new. Successful feeds endure. In fact, the structure of RSS readers brings the feeds that are frequently updated to the reader's notice more often than those that are not. This in itself is one of the things that makes those feeds more successful. Thus you can think of your feed as competing with other feeds for readers' attention, and those that get more frequently updated catch their attention more often.

# Make Links Point to Items

If you've been clicking the links in the RSS items that appear in your reader, you know that sometimes the link takes you not to the full item's text, but to a page full of items, and you have to search for the desired item by title.

That's not good RSS. The best way to host the full text of RSS items on your Web site is to set aside one page for each item:

```
<html>
  <head>
    <title>
      Steve's news
    </title>
  </head>

  <body>
    <h1>Steve's News</h1>
    <h2>It's Snowing.</h2>
    It's snowing again.
    <br>
    Will it never stop?
    <br>
```

```
      People are trying to drive through this mess, and nothing
      doing.
      <br>
      Oh well, time to shovel again.
    </body>
  </html>
```

You can, however, group the full text of several RSS items into a single Web page if you provide a link to the specific location of an item's text in that page. You can do that with the HTML <a> element.

Here's how it works. You set the location of a link target with the <a> element, setting the name attribute to the name of the target.

```
<html>
  <head>
    <title>
      Steve's news
    </title>
  </head>

  <body>
    <h1>Steve's News</h1>
    <a name="welcome">
    <h2>Welcome to Steve's news</h2>
    You'll find all kinds of news from Steve here.
    <br>
    Stay tuned.
    <a name="snow">
    <h2>It's Snowing.</h2>
    It's snowing again.
    <br>
    Will it never stop?
    <br>
    People are trying to drive through this mess, and nothing
    doing.
    <br>
    Oh well, time to shovel again.
  </body>
</html>
```

Now you can make the browser jump to a specific link target by including the target's name in the link after a pound (#) sign.

```xml
<?xml version="1.0" encoding="ISO-8859-1"?>
<rss version="2.0">
  <channel>

       .

       .

       .

    <item>
      <title>Steve shovels the snow, which might now be turning to
      rain, and who knows what's next.</title>
      <description><![CDATA[It snowed once again. Time
      to shovel!]]></description>
      <pubDate>Thu, 08 Dec 2005 08:39:51 -0500</pubDate>
      <link>http://www.rssmaniac.com/steve/news.html#snow</link>
    </item>
    <textinput>
      <title>Do a Search</title>
      <description>What do you want to find?</description>
      <name>search</name>
      <link>http://www.rssmaniac.com/find.cgi</link>
    </textinput>
  </channel>
</rss>
```

The link http://www.rssmaniac.com/steve/news.html#snow points to the "snow" link target in the page http://www.rssmaniac.com/steve/news.html, so when the user clicks that link, his or her browser navigates to that location in the Web page. Thus the reader doesn't have to navigate through the whole page to find the correct article. Very nice.

**Another good idea is to use** *permalinks*, **which permanently point to the location they're supposed to. Too many URLs on the Web are broken, or become broken shortly after being published.**

# Use CDATA Around HTML in &lt;description&gt; Elements

Take a look at this feed, in which the &lt;description&gt; elements for both the channel and the RSS item include HTML.

```
<?xml version="1.0" encoding="ISO-8859-1"?>
<rss version="2.0">
 <channel>
  <generator>NewzAlert Composer v1.70.6, Copyright (c) 2004-2005
  Castle Software Ltd, http://www.NewzAlert.com</generator>
  <lastBuildDate>Thu, 08 Dec 2005 14:01:27 -0500</lastBuildDate>
  <pubDate>Thu, 08 Dec 2005 14:01:34 -0500</pubDate>
  <title>Steve's News</title>
  <description>This feed contains <b>news
   from Steve</b>!</description>
  <link>http://www.rssmaniac.com.com/steve</link>
  <language>en-us</language>
  <copyright>(c) 2006</copyright>
  <managingEditor>Steve@rssmaniac.com</managingEditor>
  <image>
   <title>Steve's News</title>
   <url>http://www.rssmaniac.com/steve/Image.jpg</url>
   <link>http://www.rssmaniac.com/steve</link>
   <description>Steve's News</description>
   <width>144</width>
   <height>36</height>
  </image>
   <item>
    <title>Steve shovels the snow</title>
    <description>It snowed once again.
     <br>Time to shovel!</description>
    <pubDate>Thu, 08 Dec 2005 08:39:51 -0500</pubDate>
    <link>http://www.rssmaniac.com/steve</link>
   </item>
   <textinput>
```

*(code continues on next page)*

```
            <title>Do a Search</title>
            <description>What do you want to find?</description>
            <name>search</name>
            <link>http://www.rssmaniac.com/find.cgi</link>
        </textinput>
    </channel>
</rss>
```

When you include HTML in your RSS feed's `<description>` element this way, you take the risk that the result will not be bona fide XML, as in this example. (This is true for any HTML you use in the `<title>` element—but you should avoid using HTML in the `<description>` element.)

Creating malformed RSS files is a big problem, because some RSS readers might not be able to read your feed, and you might not even know there's a problem unless you test all the RSS readers available.

One solution is to enclose the description text in an XML CDATA section. While XML documents are usually parsed thoroughly, XML parsers skip the text in CDATA sections. In other words, you can put any non-XML–conforming text inside a CDATA section, and the parser won't choke. Your RSS will be valid.

To create a CDATA section, you enclose the sensitive text in CDATA markup, which starts with `<![CDATA[` and ends with `]]>`. Some RSS creator programs, like NewzAlert Composer, routinely place all text in the `<description>` elements inside CDATA sections. Here's how that works with NewzAlert Composer, where all the sensitive text, including the HTML in that text, is stored inside CDATA sections:

```
<?xml version="1.0" encoding="ISO-8859-1"?>
<rss version="2.0">
 <channel>
  <generator>NewzAlert Composer v1.70.6, Copyright (c) 2004-2005
  Castle Software Ltd, http://www.NewzAlert.com</generator>
  <lastBuildDate>Thu, 08 Dec 2005 14:01:27 -0500</lastBuildDate>
  <pubDate>Thu, 08 Dec 2005 14:01:34 -0500</pubDate>
  <title>Steve's News</title>
```

```
<description><![CDATA[This feed contains <b>news
 from Steve</b>!]]></description>
<link>http://www.rssmaniac.com.com/steve</link>
<language>en-us</language>
<copyright>(c) 2006</copyright>
<managingEditor>Steve@rssmaniac.com</managingEditor>
<image>
 <title>Steve's News</title>
 <url>http://www.rssmaniac.com/steve/Image.jpg</url>
 <link>http://www.rssmaniac.com/steve</link>
 <description>Steve's News</description>
 <width>144</width>
 <height>36</height>
</image>
  <item>
   <title>Steve shovels the snow</title>
   <description><![CDATA[It snowed once again.
     <br>Time to shovel!]]></description>
   <pubDate>Thu, 08 Dec 2005 08:39:51 -0500</pubDate>
   <link>http://www.rssmaniac.com/steve</link>
  </item>
  <textinput>
    <title>Do a Search</title>
    <description>What do you want to find?</description>
    <name>search</name>
    <link>http://www.rssmaniac.com/find.cgi</link>
  </textinput>
 </channel>
</rss>
```

This raises another issue, however: Are there RSS readers that will choke on CDATA sections? That's possible, but after using about two dozen RSS readers, I haven't found any.

**Having trouble with HTML in `<description>` elements? Solution: Don't use HTML in descriptions at all. Plenty of RSS readers either have trouble with HTML or strip it out. Save the fireworks for the article associated with the RSS item on your Web site.**

# Stay Current on Formats

Can you tell what's wrong with this RSS document?

```
<?xml version="1.0"?>
<!DOCTYPE rss SYSTEM
   "http://my.netscape.com/publish/formats/rss-0.91.dtd">
<rss version="0.91">
  <channel>
    <copyright>Copyright 2005.</copyright>
    <pubDate>Wed, 14 Dec 2005 07:00:00 GMT</pubDate>
    <lastBuildDate>Mon, 12 Dec 2005 07:00:00 GMT</lastBuildDate>
    <docs>http://www.rssmaniac.com/steve/info.html</docs>
    <description>This feed contains news from Steve!</description>
    <link>http://www.rssmaniac.com/steve</link>
    <title>Steve's News!</title>
    <language>en-us</language>
    <image>
      <title>Steve's News</title>
      <url>http://www.rssmaniac.com/steve/Image.jpg</url>
      <link>http://www.rssmaniac.com/steve</link>
      <description>Steve's News</description>
      <width>144</width>
      <height>36</height>
    </image>
    <managingEditor>steve@rssmaniac.com (Steve)</managingEditor>
    <webMaster>steve@rssmaniac.com (Steve)</webMaster>
    <skipHours>
      <hour>8</hour>
      <hour>9</hour>
      <hour>10</hour>
    </skipHours>
    <skipDays>
      <day>Sunday</day>
    </skipDays>
    <item>
      <title>Steve shovels the snow</title>
```

```
      <description>It snowed once again.
        Time to shovel!>
      </description>
      <link>http://www.rssmaniac.com/steve</link>
      <enclosure url="http://www.rssmaniac.com/steve/shoveling.mp3"
        length="4823902" type="audio/mpeg" />
    </item>
    <textinput>
      <title>Search for other items</title>
      <description>What do you want to find?</description>
      <name>search</name>
      <link>http://www.rssmaniac.com/find.php</link>
    </textinput>
  </channel>
</rss>
```

The answer is that it's an RSS 0.91 document that contains an `<enclosure>` element, and RSS 0.91 doesn't support enclosures. This document won't validate.

The way to avoid problems like this is to know what your version of RSS or Atom can or can't do—and again, validate your feeds before publishing them. Another way is to use the most recent version, such as RSS 2.0, so that you don't end up using elements the language doesn't support.

# Limit the Number of Items in Your Feed

As you know, in the early days of RSS, feeds were restricted to 15 items maximum. In RSS 2.0 that restriction was removed: You can have unlimited items in a feed.

But that doesn't mean it's a good idea to put unlimited items into an RSS feed. Keep in mind that your readers are using RSS to handle information flow. If they start up their RSS reader in the morning and see "Nate's Hamster Feed: 2 new items, Suzie's Menu of the Day feed: 3

new items, Steve's Woodcraft Feed: 1,869 new items," which one do you think is in danger of being dropped?

While it's true that some RSS readers let people filter the news by displaying only RSS items with specific keywords in their titles, who wants to deal with a feed that gives you 1,869 new items each day? The best practice is to limit the items in your feed each day to a manageable number.

# Design Your Titles and Descriptions Carefully

Sure, titles are there to get attention and to summarize channels and items, but there's another consideration: Titles should be comprehensible out of context.

For example, the title "Not Again!!!" might grab attention, but who knows what it means? A busy person scanning RSS feeds might not want to take the time to find out. Ideally, RSS titles for both channels and items should make sense even when read out of context.

The title "New Announcement," for example, might not be as widely clicked as a title like "New Super Savers to Hawaii."

The same goes for descriptions. It always pays to write descriptions that provide some context. You don't want your readers to feel clueless as to what was intended. A little context goes a long way.

For example, define acronyms and don't refer to "this site," since your content may be aggregated and displayed on other sites.

# Avoid Using HTML in Titles

RSS readers consider titles data, and they're not supposed to contain display elements like HTML. The display of this data is up to the RSS reader. If you put markup in a title, even HTML or a CDATA section, you could end up making the title impossible for some RSS readers to display.

If you're going to use HTML, use it in descriptions only.

# Get Permission

Remember that a lot of the material and images on the Internet is copyrighted, so don't grab content and republish it without permission. At best, it's rude, and at worst, it could get you into trouble. If there's any question, be sure to ask first.

# Include Contact Info

Some of the RSS documentation is pretty unclear so even if your feed validates, some of your readers may still run into problems. For that reason it's helpful to include email contact information in your feed. This way your readers can alert you to potential problems. They can also stay in contact with you, which is great: Feedback can help you hone your feed to your readers' interests.

In RSS 0.91, 0.92, and 2.0, you use the `<webMaster>` and `<managingEditor>` elements to store email addresses of your Web site's Webmaster and your feed's managing editor.

In RSS 1.0, you use the `<dc:creator>` and `<dc:publisher>` tags.

There's another option for including information about your feed, if none of the established RSS elements seem right: an XML comment. Because RSS feeds are XML documents, you can use XML comments legally. However, there's some question as to whether or not that's considered good RSS practice—RSS readers that aren't expecting XML comments might not know what to do with them.

XML comments contain text that comments on the XML document. Just like comments in HTML, XML comments start with `<!--` and end with `-->`. The following example shows how to add a comment to an RSS document that wouldn't otherwise fit into an established RSS element.

```
<?xml version="1.0"?>
<!DOCTYPE rss SYSTEM
  "http://my.netscape.com/publish/formats/rss-0.91.dtd">
```

*(code continues on next page)*

```
<rss version="0.91">
  <channel>
    <copyright>Copyright 2005.</copyright>
    <pubDate>Wed, 14 Dec 2005 07:00:00 GMT</pubDate>
    <lastBuildDate>Mon, 12 Dec 2005 07:00:00 GMT</lastBuildDate>
    <docs>http://www.rssmaniac.com/steve/info.html</docs>
    <description>This feed contains news from Steve!</description>
    <link>http://www.rssmaniac.com/steve</link>
    <title>Steve's News!</title>
    <language>en-us</language>
    <image>
      <title>Steve's News</title>
      <url>http://www.rssmaniac.com/steve/Image.jpg</url>
      <link>http://www.rssmaniac.com/steve</link>
      <description>Steve's News</description>
      <width>144</width>
      <height>36</height>
    </image>
    <managingEditor>steve@rssmaniac.com (Steve)</managingEditor>
    <webMaster>steve@rssmaniac.com (Steve)</webMaster>
    <!-- Created using the RSS Maniac template. www.rssmaniac.com
    -->
    <skipHours>
      <hour>8</hour>
      <hour>9</hour>
      <hour>10</hour>
    </skipHours>
    <skipDays>
      <day>Sunday</day>
    </skipDays>
    <item>
      <title>Steve shovels the snow</title>
      <description>It snowed once again.
        Time to shovel!>
      </description>
      <link>http://www.rssmaniac.com/steve</link>
    </item>
    <textinput>
```

```
        <title>Search for other items</title>
        <description>What do you want to find?</description>
        <name>search</name>
        <link>http://www.rssmaniac.com/find.php</link>
      </textinput>
    </channel>
  </rss>
```

So including information about your feed by using XML comments is an option. But because people would have to read your RSS document directly to see those comments—and since those comments might cause problems in some RSS readers—it's still best to put contact and other information in the usual RSS elements if you can.

And that's it! You've finished the book, and you're now an honest-to-goodness RSS expert. Best of luck on creating your new feed, and may you find many dedicated and loyal readers.

# Index